My Airship Flights 1915–1930

MY AIRSHIP FLIGHTS 1915-1930

By

Captain George Meager, A.F.C.

WILLIAM KIMBER
22A QUEEN ANNE'S GATE, S.W.1

First published in 1970 by
WILLIAM KIMBER AND CO. LTD
22a Queen Anne's Gate, London S.W.1

Standard Book Number
SBN 7183 0331 8

Printed in Great Britain by
W & J Mackay & Co Ltd, Chatham, Kent

Contents

Illustrations

Line Illustrations

Foreword

I have compiled *My Airship Flights* from flying logs and diaries written at the time, supplemented occasionally by memories.

I dedicate the book to my loving and lovely daughters, Felicity and Faith, with whose encouragement I originally started it. I should like it also to be a memorial to General Edward Maitland, CMG DSO AFC; Squadron-Leader Frederick Michael Rope, RAF; Major George Scott, CBE, AFC; Wing-Commander Reginald Colmore, OBE, RAF; and Flight-Sub-Lieutenant E. G. O. Jackson, RNAS all of whom sacrificed their lives in the cause of airships. And I must record my gratitude to the crews of the Airships *SR.1*, *R.100* and *R.101*. Last, but not by any means least, I would like to name Flight-Lieutenant John Barron, RCN; Lord Ventry—without whom I should not have written it; Wing-Commander Ralph Sleigh Booth, AFC, and Bar, RAF—the finest 'Rigid' Captain we ever had; and Sir Barnes Neville Wallis, CBE, FRS—the Chief Designer of *R.100*.

GEORGE F. MEAGER

The Old Harroway
Penton Mewsey
Andover

Introduction

With the exception of my experience flying our only semi-rigid airship *SR.1* towards the end of the war in 1918, all my flying had been in small 'Non-Rigid' airships; after the war, in 1919, I also did some half dozen flights in rigids. The 'Non-Rigid' airship consists of an envelope of stream-lined shape from which a car is slung by wire suspensions. In some cases these are external as in the SS (Sea-Scout) and Parseval; in others, for example the Astra-Torres tri-lobe they are internal.

The envelope contains the gas—hydrogen in Britain—and is usually made of fabric, treated to increase its gas-holding properties. Inside the envelope along the base are one or more fabric air compartments called ballonets. These are for maintaining pressure in the envelope, which otherwise keeps its shape by the excess pressure of gas over the ambient air, this being of the order of 25–30 mm of water pressure. If you valve off gas to any great extent, the envelope would start to collapse; pumping air into the ballonets restores the situation.

In the SS ships steering was by means of a foot-bar connected to a rudder flap pivoted at the trailing edge of the vertical stabilising fin and, of course, operated by the pilot. In all larger ships, the steering was carried out by a separate coxswain using a wheel control.

For elevator control, the pilot operated a wheel which actuated a flap pivoted at the trailing edge of each horizontal stabilising fin. Above the size of a Coastal or C-star ship, this was often done by a second pilot or cox'n, though the chief pilot usually took over for take-off and landing.

Suspension of the car varied with type: all those of SS type—including the 'Zeros'—were slung to the envelope by Eta patches* with three wire bridles culminating in one at the fuselage—five suspensions each side plus two rolling guys to the king-post about midway along the fuselage. The Parseval car was slung to an elliptical patch around the base of the envelope whence fabric bands were run fanwise over the top of the

* The Eta patch was so named as it was designed for suspending the car of HM Army Airship *Eta*. (When the Admiralty took over the airships in 1914 this ship was given the Number 20 on the naval list of airships.)

The patch was made up of several layers of fabric stuck and machined together into the shape of a large palm with stumps of fingers. At the 'wrist' end a tubular D-shaped ring was incorporated, through which the suspension wire was threaded, formed into a loop, seized and sweated. See diagram on page 12.

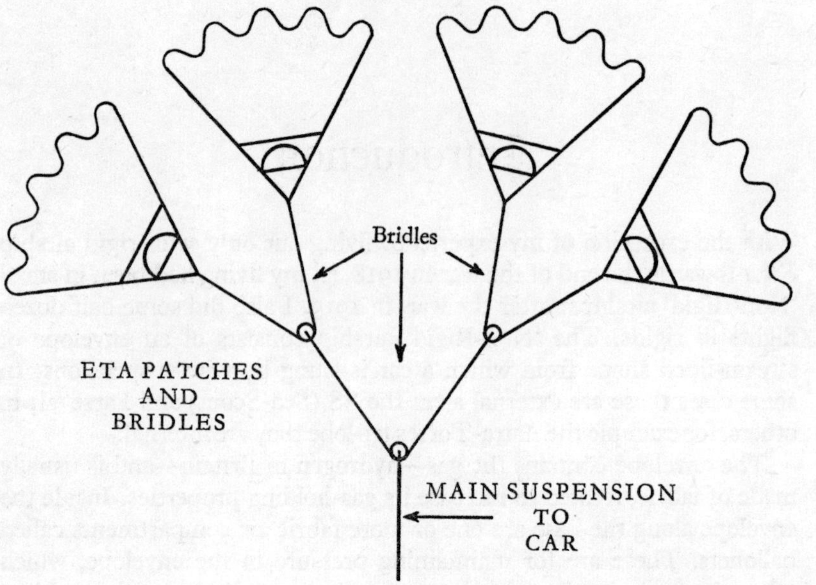

envelope thus distributing the load. The Coastal, C-star and North Sea cars were slung close up to the envelope by short strops to points on a jack-stay inside the base of the envelope which formed the apex of the triangle of globes forming the tri-lobe. From these points the load was distributed by fanning out cords to the top ridges of the trefoil and by fabric curtains between ridges.

The original SS ships—those with Maurice Farman (see drawing on page 13) or British Experimental fuselages or cars—had accommodation for two only—Pilot and the Wireless Telegraph Operator (I have spelt the latter out in full as quite recently I was asked what were the duties of a 'Watch Tower Officer'). This meant that the pilot had to work all the controls of the ship himself: the steering; elevating; engine (by lever controlled Bowden wire); gas and air valves; crab-pot controls for ballonets; fuel and ballast. In addition he had to keep constant vigil to see that the pressure in the envelope was kept between certain minimum and maximum pressures (20–30 mm) in order to maintain shape, and so controllability; keep an eye on his fuel consumption and engine oil pressure, pumping both at regular intervals; maintain course, height and airspeed; know his whereabouts from ground and map or, if out of sight of land, by Dead Reckoning, keep the ship in trim—that is in level flight and not too light or heavy; and last but not least, scan the sea for mines and submarines. Thus the pilot was pretty fully occupied and could not relax for a moment during the whole duration of flight.

GENERAL ARRANGEMENT OF SS AIRSHIP
MAURICE FARMAN TYPE CAR

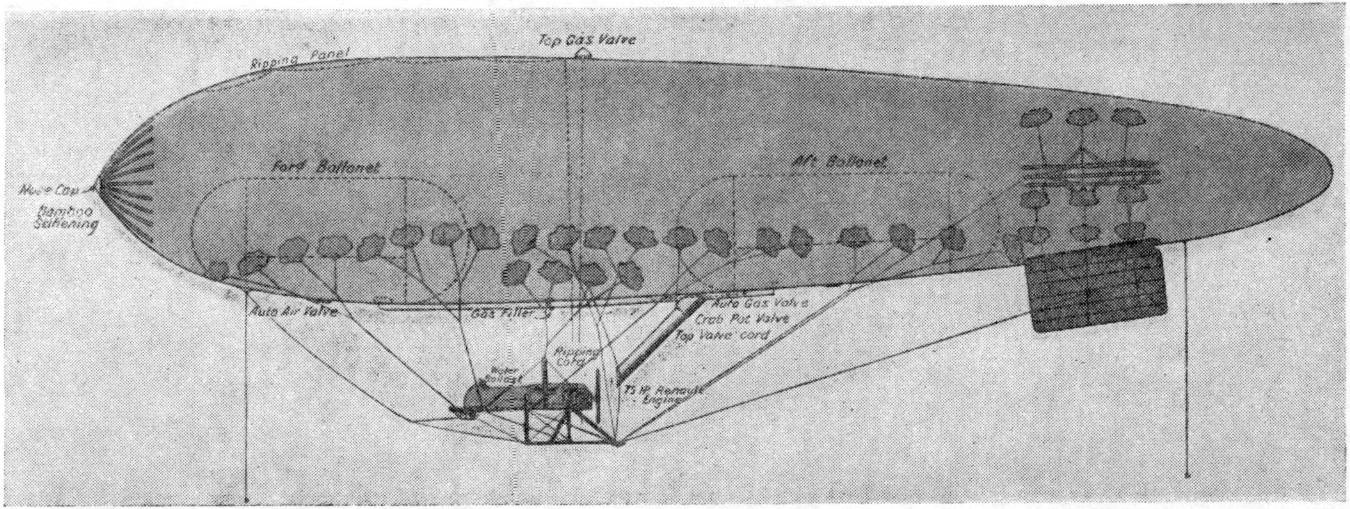

DIMENSIONS

Overall length (Envelope)	143 ft $3\frac{1}{2}$ in.
Overall height (top of Envelope to Skids)	43 ft 0 in.
Maximum diameter (Envelope)	27 ft 9 in.

VOLUME OF ENVELOPE 60,000 CU. FT. BALLONETS 6,000 CU. FT. EACH

As time progressed, certain of the B.E.2c fuselages had a third seat cut behind the pilot's seat. I remember, however, instructing a pupil perched up behind me in a seat lashed to the top of the fuselage; he must have been cold as he was in the full blast from the propeller.

All our 'Non-Rigids' had open cock-pits except those of the North Sea type. The three British-built Parsevals, Numbers Five, Six and Seven, were built with enclosed cars.

As the ships increased in size so did the flying crew, thus relieving the pilot of certain of his responsibilities. In Coastals and C-stars for example, four and later five were carried—a steering cox'n, a 2nd pilot, observer or navigator, and a gunlayer, in addition to the W/TOp and Pilot.

In the larger 'Non-Rigids' the Pilot often acted like the captain of a sea-ship; he merely gave orders for members of the crew to carry out. He usually took the elevator control himself, however, at take-off and landing.

Pressure was maintained by blowing air into one or both the ballonets; small variations would be corrected by slight adjustments in height. If pressure was allowed to fall below a certain value (5 mm) the nose would be in danger of being blown in, and the ship would become unmanageable. It might be that the loss of gas was such that the envelope sagged in the middle, bow and stern going up, or if the ship got out of level, the gas might rush to the higher end. This was known as 'surging'.

The method of taking a small ship into the air was to ballast up a little light, start up the engine and give the signal to 'let go', by raising both hands above the head. The handling party would then release the ship which would rise of its own accord. When a few feet above the ground, the engine would be opened up and the ship taken up to the height required on its elevators, pressure being released as requisite through the air valve forward—so as to keep the bow up until flying height was reached.

Taking off a 'Semi-Rigid', or large 'Non-Rigid', it was usual to ballast up much lighter than for a small ship. The engines were started up on the ground and run slow, in neutral or with pitch feathered. After 'let go' the ship was allowed to rise to 50 or 100 feet before the engines were run up.

The 'Rigid' airship differed in one important respect—its outer cover could not lose shape, as did the 'Non' and 'Semi-Rigids': the 'Non-Rigid' was really a powered balloon and the 'Semi' could only boast a form of keel which stiffened the underside of the envelope.

The 'Rigid' airship of whatever type consists fundamentally of a rigid framework, approximately circular in section, of transverse frames joined together by longitudinal girders. Both transverse and longitudinals are usually triangular in section. In between the transverse frames lie the gas-bags shaped like enormous fabric cheeses on end, and constrained by netting which transmits the lift of the gas—hydrogen or helium—to the main joints. The gas bags of both *R.100* and *R.101* were of one-ply cotton fabric lined inside with gold-beater's skin;* those of our earlier 'Rigids' were of two-ply rubberised cotton. Our largest bag in *R.100* had a capacity of 552,000 cubic feet, whilst three others were over 500,000 cubic feet. In all we had 15 gas-bags in *R.100*, numbered from the bow.

As regards piloting the three distinct types of airship—I may say I have piloted all three, though I was never captain of a rigid and piloted it merely as Officer-of-the-Watch—I would say that the 'Non-Rigid' undoubtedly required more unremitting attention to detail than the larger 'Semi-Rigid' and 'Rigid'. Comparing the 'Non-Rigid' with the larger ships is like comparing a sailing boat or motor boat with the *Queen Mary*. The smaller 'Non-Rigid' is much more handy and quick to answer controls; I used to say I could do anything with my 'Zero' except loop and roll her—a bit of an exaggeration no doubt, but it is an indication of how handy they were. They could turn almost in their own length, whereas with a 'Rigid', and to a lesser extent the 'Semi-Rigid,' a much larger area would be required, to say nothing of the time. During flight in a 'Non-Rigid' there was the ever present concern regarding one's gas pressure. This was entirely absent in the 'Rigid', and to a much less extent in the 'Semi-Rigid'. These two latter types were really very similar except that the rigid portion of the 'Semi-Rigid' was at the base of the envelope. On the other hand there was the ballonet which rendered the 'Semi-Rigid' analogous to the 'Non-Rigid' though not nearly as handy, and it was likened again to the 'Rigid' in having a compartmented gas container though not separate gas-bags.

They were all three, however, large or small, rigid, semi- or non-rigid, all subject to the law of displacement which Archimedes discovered when he noticed the difference in the high water mark as he jumped out of his bath shouting '*Eureka!*' Likewise they are all three, no matter what their size, subject to the wind to exactly the same extent when flying in the atmosphere. I have always found it very difficult to dispel the idea that the bigger the airship, the greater she is affected by the wind during flight. This only holds good when held on the ground, and even then need be of little consequence if kept head to wind.

Similarly a small free balloon would be taken by the wind exactly the same distance and direction as a large one—no more, no less—by the same wind in a given time. In the same way a large rigid or any other airship or aeroplane in free flight in similar conditions would be acted

* Gold-beater's skin is the inner lining or membrane of a cow's stomach. It is used by goldsmiths for beating out sheets of pure gold into gold-leaf.

upon to the same extent in the same time. The engined aircraft, of course, has its power and steerability to enable it to move at an angle to, or against, the wind. The main difference would lie in the rate of manoeuvrability due to the greater turning circle of the larger aircraft, but the point I am trying to make is that the amount of drift would be the same in all cases given the same conditions of wind and time, in free flight.

Another question I have been asked frequently is: 'Weren't you scared stiff at the thought of those thousands of cubic feet of highly inflammable gas above you all the time you were flying?' The thought of the potential danger never entered my head, nor, I think, that of any other of our airship pilots or crews. If it had, I doubt if any of us would have ventured to fly. Of course in the back of our minds we were aware of its presence and took all precautions against risk of fire. Does anyone nowadays think of the potential danger from fire of the petrol in the tank of their motor car—one does not, of course, light a match to see if there is any in the tank!

In the course of the narrative I have referred to a Schutte-Lanz airship: in outward appearance it looked similar to those of Zeppelin type, being covered in aluminium doped fabric. The girder work, however, was made of very strong laminated ply wood, made up into triangular girders. The form of the ship was similar to that of the Zeppelins. I do not know how many of this type the Germans possessed. One, L.21 (Works Number S-L11), was brought down over Cuffley, Hertfordshire, on 3rd September 1916.

As I have described later in the book, we, ourselves, possessed two airships of the Schutte-Lanz type *R.31* and *R.32*; they were built by Messrs Short Brothers* from plans and drawings smuggled out of Germany during the war. They were not completed until after the war ended, coming out in 1919. I flew three times in *R.32* in 1919—once under Major Elmsley and twice under Captain I. C. Little who two years later was lost with *R.38* in the Humber.

The only difference I could see between the Schutte-Lanz and the Zeppelin type was that the wooden ships were much more flexible or whippy in turns. They were also much faster, achieving a top speed of 71 mph as against the 55 mph of our 'R.23' Class, and the 60 mph of the *R.33* and *R.34* which were our most recent airships at that time, 1919. The difference in speed may have been due to better stream-line shape, or more probably to the fact that *R.31* and *R.32* had five 250 hp Rolls-Royce engines against *R.33*'s five Sunbeam 'Maori' engines of similar power—two in the after car in tandem driving one propeller.

* The last of the Short Brothers, Hugh Oswald Short, died in December 1969, aged 86.

GENERAL ARRANGEMENT OF COASTAL AIRSHIP

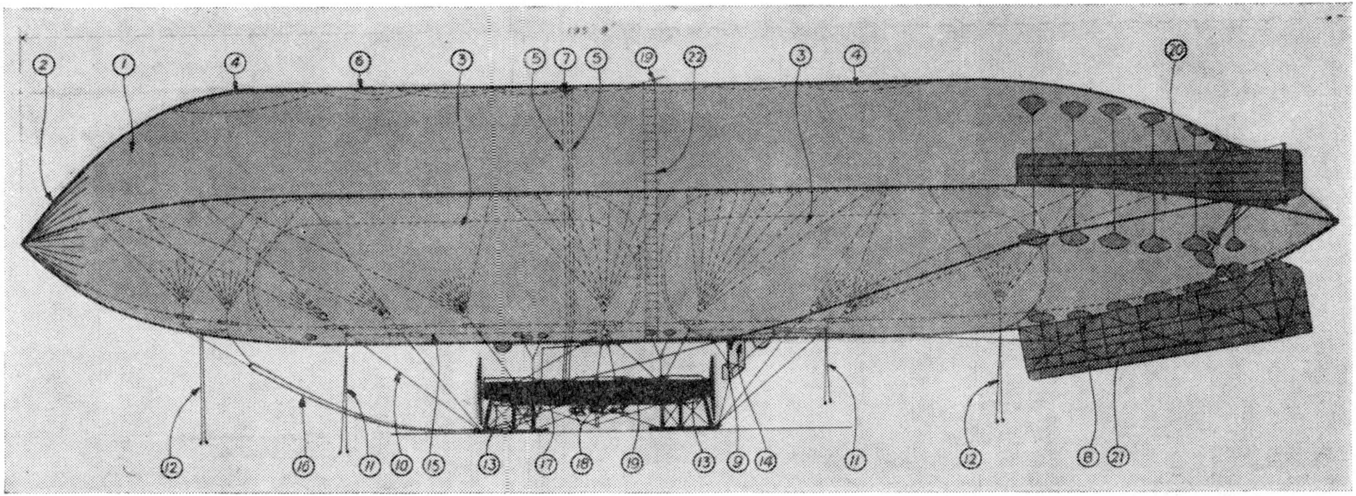

PARTICULARS

Capacity of Envelope	170,000 cu. ft
Capacity of Ballonets	51,000 cu. ft
Overall Length of Envelope	193 ft 9 in.
Overall Height (Ground to top of Envelope)	52 ft 1 in.
Overall Width	39 ft 6 in.
Maximum Speed	52 m.p.h.
Engines (h.p. and number of)	2 150 h.p. Sunbeam
Armament	2 Lewis Guns, 4 100 lb bombs
Crew	4 or 5

DESCRIPTION

1 Envelope
2 Nose Stiffeners
3 Ballonets
4 Ripping Panel
5 Ripping Cord
6 Top Gas Valve
7 Top Gas Valve Cord
8 Bottom Gas Valve
9 Auto Air Valve
10 Suspension
11 Midship Handling Guys
12 Handling Guys
13 Engine
14 Blower Pipe
15 Jockstay
16 Trail and Grapnel Rope
17 Cord
18 Bombs
19 Lewis Gun
20 Horizontal and Elevator Planes
21 Vertical and Rudder Plane
22 Gun Shaft

The reason an airship will rise is because the gas in its envelope or gas-bags weighs less than the air it displaces. This is known as the principle of Archimedes which he formulated over two hundred years BC.

In England we used hydrogen—weighing 5 lbs/1000 cu. ft—as our lifting agent for airships, and coal-gas—37½ lbs/1000—for our free balloons. In America helium—10 lbs/1000—was and is used for their airships. Air weighs 75 lbs/1000 cubic feet, so 1000 cubic feet of hydrogen will lift 70 pounds approximately. A 100,000 cu. ft would lift about 3 tons and a million would lift about 30 tons.

The main source of helium is in the United States, but export thence was prohibited, hence none of our airships, nor the German ones, either during or since the war of 1914–18 were filled with anything but hydrogen.

CHAPTER ONE

Commissioned into the R.N.A.S.

In the autumn of 1915 I was an able seaman, RNVR, in the Anti-Aircraft Corps; my station on most nights was the searchlight battery on top of the Great Western Railway goods yard in South Lambeth, but on the night of the 8th September I happened to be off duty and had actually gone to bed in the house in Bury Street, Chelsea, where I was living at that time. Suddenly, a series of terrific booms drove all ideas of sleep from me. Whether the noise came from our own anti-aircraft guns or was caused by the explosion of bombs didn't matter—either way it meant there was an air raid on. Slipping on my clothes I went out into the street; towards the City I could see tiny points of light high up in the sky, no doubt shells bursting.

I set off on my bicycle Citywards and followed a fire engine through Hyde Park Corner, along Piccadilly and up Shaftesbury Avenue, where I lost it. I had no further need of it as a guide, for a lurid glare in the sky told me in which direction the damage was being done.

I soon came upon a blaze in East Street, which was about the furthest west the raiders had reached. The flames were leaping and licking round the wooden supports and crossbeams of a house which was already a good way towards being gutted. It was from here that I saw a casualty being carried out—the only one I saw that night.

Continuing a little further I came into Lamb's Conduit Street, in Holborn, and at the junction of this street with Theobald's Road was a sight indeed: the ground floor of these premises was a mass of flames which roared and crackled and seemed to be very little affected by the volumes of water poured on them by the firemen. The fire would apparently be got under for a moment, only to burst forth again the next instant as fierce as ever. The roadway along Lamb's Conduit Street was littered with broken glass; as the crowd was getting thick and I did not wish to get a puncture, I picked my way over the broken glass and went in the direction of another big glow more in the heart of the City. At Holborn Viaduct I got my eyes full of charred paper and as I went down Newgate Street red-hot ashes were falling all over the place. At the junction of Newgate Street and Cheapside I came upon an unforgettable scene: the sky was one red glow as myriads of red-hot fragments were continually being flung high into the air from burning buildings like a fantastic firework display. The actual scene of the fire was in Wood Street, one of the worst possible quarters, being in the danger zone where extra premiums were charged for fire insurance. It was scarcely two hundred yards from St Paul's, the dome of which was lit up by the glare of the fire. I could get no further than Falcon Street, where I was told that the premises on fire were a silk warehouse belonging to Messrs Rylands. The air was filled with burning ashes which were flying about for more than a hundred yards around the building; clouds of smoke were rolling upwards, and the flames were dancing about like a legion of red devils.

A terrific crowd of people had gathered and this was augmented as the theatres emptied. People came streaming up—in taxis, private cars, traps, bikes and on foot; many clinging on to the backs of taxis and cars. About midnight a party of soldiers arrived, so I made my way off.

When I again reached Chelsea amazing stories were being bandied about—Piccadilly was in flames; London Bridge had been blown up and a Zeppelin brought down at Hampstead—all boloney! I believe it was a fact, though, that Farringdon Street Station and Liverpool Street had caught it as the Great Eastern traffic to London could get no further in than Bethnal Green for some time after.

The best story about the raid was told me by a policeman who said he saw it happen as he was regulating the crowd watching the raid from the top of Parliament Hill. The crowd was keenly interested in an anti-aircraft gun near by, which was engaging the raider. One big navvy in particular got very excited as the shells burst near their objective. When one burst underneath the stern of the Zeppelin he forgot himself completely and, just as an onlooker at a boxing match unconsciously works his fists in unison with the boxers, he swung his arm backwards across his chest—and knocked a little man standing beside him head over heels down the hill, as he shouted 'That's it! Give the buggers another like that!'

I suppose that this was really my first introduction to airships . . .

I served nearly a year in the Anti-Aircraft Corps as an able seaman and then in October 1915 I was given a commission as a probationary flight sub-lieutenant, RN, and appointed to HMS *President*. My commission in the Royal Naval Air Service was gazetted and published in *The Times* before I was actually notified; you can imagine my surprise when Kitto, one of my searchlight crew, suddenly swung me round and kicked my backside, saying: 'I've always wanted to kick the arse of a commissioned officer—and now I've done it!'

I was told to report to Wormwood Scrubbs Airship Station for a course in free ballooning. There was a shed on the Airship Station with one small airship in it, but the actual balloon ascents took place from the polo ground at Hurlingham. The shed was famous because it had been built to house the original French-built Clement-Bayard airship bought by the *Daily Mail* and presented to the Government.

On the 13th November 1915 I had my first trip in a free balloon with F/Lt D. W. A. Barton as instructor. He was the son of Dr Barton of Beckenham, Kent, who had built an airship some years before the war, though whether it ever flew I do not know. On our flight we reached a height of 6,450 feet. The experience was quite the reverse of what I had imagined, there being no sensation at all except when the balloon was descending rather rapidly—when one's ears get stuffed up by the change in pressure.

At the end of the flight we had some fun bumping along the ground with the trail rope out. For this the balloon is 'ballasted up'* in equilibrium or slightly heavy, so that as it tends to fall, the weight of the rope on the ground is taken off the balloon, which rises until the weight of the rope once again counteracts the lift and brings the balloon gently down (I don't know that I would like to try this nowadays with all the high-tension wires stretched over the country!). We eventually landed at the village of Sidley, near Bexhill. Not all my flights were uneventful. During a subsequent flight with F/Lt Vickers, a baker's boy on a bicycle was so intent watching us that he fell off his bike and his bread was all spilled across the road—which was fortunately dry!

After further instructional flights with Lts Kent, Barton and Pollock, I was taken up by Lt F. A. Baldwin, RNVR, to do my passing-out flight. From the ground the weather appeared dull and cloudy, but we soon got above the clouds and out into brilliant sunshine with blue sky above and the clouds below looking like hummocky snow. We alighted near Pangbourne, Berkshire, where we dropped a RFC pupil who was training for the Army Kite Balloon Section. We then continued our flight, trailing over the Berkshire Downs, and finally landed at Broom Manor, near Swindon, where we were entertained to tea by Major and Mrs Keelock.

On the 25th November 1915 I was sent up to do my solo balloon flight. I remember passing over Crowborough Beacon in Sussex, having to throw out some ballast to do so. As I was heading directly for the coast I thought I had better make a landing if I wished to avoid being blown over the Channel. I valved a little gas and came down quite

* To the layman the phrase would be better translated as 'balancing'—it does not mean simply *increasing* the ballast, but adjusting the ratio of lift to weight.

gently, without having to rip,* at Mill Farm, Hellingly, near Eastbourne, where I was right royally welcomed and entertained to tea by the farmer, Mr Howard, and his pretty sisters and cousin Sue. He helped me deflate the balloon and pack it in the basket and then drove me to the station in a horse-drawn farm wagon. We very nearly missed the last train to London; luckily, we saw it before it entered the station, Mr Howard whipped up his horse and we got to the station before the train started. We then had great difficulty in getting the basket with the balloon in it through the doors of the luggage van. The guard wanted to leave it behind, but with the help of Mr Howard we managed to force it through the doorway.

On the 18th December I was given my first flight in a small airship, *SS.36*, a Maurice Farman car slung under an envelope of 70,000 cubic feet capacity; there was an 80 hp Renault engine fitted at the rear of the car, which was therefore a 'pusher' type. The Maurice Farman cars, and the B.E.2cs in which I flew later, were actually aeroplane fuselages minus their wings and not specifically designed as airship cars; as aeroplanes they were not very roomy two-seaters, but as airships they could have an extra seat fitted. The first airship to have a specially designed car was *SS.Zero*—this, as the two types mentioned above, was still open—in an emergency it could be operated as a boat—and was rather more comfortable. *SS*, by the way, stands for 'Sea Scout'. The pilot was the same officer who had taken me up for my first balloon trip—F/Lt Barton. He was, later, to be my CO on an Astra-Torres tri-lobed 'Coastal' airship *C.27* at Pulham St Mary-the-Virgin in Norfolk. We only flew round the Scrubbs for a few minutes, but it was very pleasant in the still of the evening, there being no rolling or pitching.

During the first week of the new year, 1916, I was posted to HMS *Victory*, Portsmouth, for a course at the Navigation School. We lived in the school, which was in the Dockyard, and were very comfortable, each having a cabin; the food, too, was wonderful, with lashings of it, though you had to be careful not to put your knife and fork down before you had finished—your plate was instantly whisked away by a Marine steward.

We had no flying during the navigation course, though we had been promised a flip in a seaplane at Calshot and were twice taken there by picket boat for this purpose. On the way back from one of these abortive journeys we passed a seaplane upside down near Calshot Spit, the floats only above water, with the pilot sitting on one of them, seemingly none the worse for the experience, waiting to be towed in.

* This means letting out all the gas instantaneously by pulling a special line which tears out a strip from the top and side of the balloon. This is to be avoided, because it means machining and resticking the opening together before the balloon can be reinflated.

Following the navigation course, we did a short course in engineering in HMS *Fisgard*, which consisted of four old ironclads moored out in the harbour. We still lived in the Navigation School and were taken to *Fisgard* by steam launch.

After completing the engineering course we were posted to HMS *Excellent* at Whale Island for a gunnery course. *Excellent* is not a ship at all, being an artificial island in the northern part of the harbour, reached by a causeway. The discipline here was, and is, terrific, everything being done at the double, but the Mess was very comfortable. All we subs were in the Junior Officers' Mess called the 'Gun-Room'. Our instructors were mostly senior NCOs. I remember one expression repeatedly used by a CPO instructor was 'You'll find it in your famplet.'

Whilst at 'Whaley' I got quite pally with a young observer-sub-lieutenant named Romilly Swanston; some twelve years later I was to marry his cousin, though I only discovered the relationship long afterwards.

On completion of my courses at 'Pompey' I was posted back to Scrubbs to await allocation to my flying station. During my absence a new CO had been appointed in the person of Lieutenant-Colonel Waterlow, Royal Engineers; he was one of the Army officers in the RFC who had been transferred to the RNAS when the Admiralty took over all airships and airship personnel. He was great on theory and gave us daily lectures with frequent exams; he was unfortunately later killed in an accident at Cranwell when he was taken up hanging on to one of the handling guys of an airship during a sudden up-current and dropped off before the ship could be brought to earth again.

Within a week of returning to Scrubbs I was appointed to Llangefni Airship Station, Anglesey. In the train on my way there I sat down to lunch at the same table as a young officer in a Canadian Scottish regiment, the 48th Infantry, whose face was vaguely familar to me. After a little conversation it suddenly came back to me that he was the youngest son of the former manager of the insurance company in Pall Mall where I had started out in life. The young man was dumbfounded when I asked him if his name was Maxwell Scott and I told him that his father had taken a great deal of trouble to get me my commission in the RNAS.

When the train stopped at a small place called Gaerwen near the village with the long name shortened to Llanfair P.G.,* I was surprised to hear someone calling for me to get out, and there was Freddy Best,

* The maid at 'The Bull' in Llangefni was a native of Llanfair P.G. and gave me the full name, which I have never forgotten: LLANFAIR PWLLGWYNGYLL GOGERYCH WYRNDROBWLL LLANTYSILIO GOGOGOCH, meaning the church of St Mary in a hollow of wych hazel near a whirlpool and church of St Tysilio.

who had been with me at Wormwood Scrubbs and 'Pompey', with a tender—a motor car-cum-light truck, which was really the ancestor of the modern pick-up—to take me to the airship station. On arrival there I was welcomed by the CO, F/Lt G. H. Scott (later, as Major Scott, he was killed in the *R.101* disaster at Beauvais). As there was no accommodation for me at the air station he suggested I stayed at the 'Bull Hotel' in Llangefni—as he did himself; this I did, and stayed there practically all the time I was at Anglesey. A tender called for us each morning and took us back in the evening.

At the Airship Station I was under instruction for airship flying with F/Sub-Lt E. F. Turner, who was an enormous, very cheerful young naval officer nicknamed 'Tubby'. Most of my instructional flights were in *SS.22* (a B.E.2c car slung under a 70,000 cubic foot envelope). I also did some flying with Sub-Lt Scroggs in *SS.24*, and some with F/Sub-Lt Kilburn in *SS.18*, both with B.E.2c cars.

After thirteen instructional flights of from five to thirty minutes totalling 3 hours 4 minutes, I was sent up in *SS.24* to do my first solo on 10th May 1916: this lasted thirteen minutes, being followed immediately by another of half an hour. A week later I embarked in *SS.22* on my first anti-submarine patrol carrying CPO Gwilt as a passenger and AM Bingham as W/T op. We flew over Amlwch and out to sea, where I had a wonderful sight of a full-rigged sailing-ship with all sails set. I came down low and found she was the barque *Hedvic* flying the Norwegian flag. I regretted I had no camera, as she was a magnificent picture and one not likely to be repeated, for there are few full-rigged sailing-ships left. After patrolling the traffic lane to Liverpool for some time I turned in and made for Llandudno, off which I sighted *SS.24* with Scroggs as pilot. After circling Great Orme's Head, a forbidding-looking promontory, I received a message recalling me, so I immediately set course for the Station, passing over Puffin Island, and landed after four hours' flying.

The ordinary job of piloting consisted firstly of maintaining height, course, gas pressure, engine speed, and equilibrium. Then one had to gauge the speed and direction of the wind; this information had to be combined with the ship's own airspeed to calculate one's course and speed over the ground. From all this one could plot one's own position. In addition, the pilot had to pump petrol every half-hour from the main to the gravity tank; the half-hour frequency for the petrol was a safety margin, as the gravity tank held eight gallons, and cruising speed consumption ran at about four gallons an hour. In the same way, every two hours the oil had to be pumped up as well. We had no means of measuring the amount of oil in the sump, so our rather crude way of gauging it was to do some short pitching evolutions; a bluish-white smoke from the exhaust indicated plenty of oil. To complicate matters, each ship had a different system of cocks and taps, but this was simplified later with the advent of the 'Zero'-type ships, with their specially designed airship cars.

In the B.E.2c-type car—which was a tractor—the cockpit was open and the pilot and crew sat in the full blast of the propeller slipstream, with only a small triplex-glass windshield of about 8 by 5 inches fitted on the top front edge of the cockpit.

The instruments were fitted on a dashboard inside the cockpit, and consisted of rev counter; manometer—or gas pressure gauge; aneroid—or altimeter; airspeed indicator; and statascope—the rise and fall indicator. A liquid-filled magnetic compass of the Creagh-Osborne type was sited in front of the pilot at eye-level. The dial was arranged vertically and was calibrated in five-degree sections—it was not exactly a precision instrument! In later ships this was replaced by the 5/17 type, also vertical reading, but calibrated to the nearest two degrees.

We airship pilots had one advantage over aeroplane pilots in that the airship did not bank when turning, so our compasses were not subject to the effect of the vertical component of the earth's magnetism when turning—equally, as our turns were relatively slow, the swirl effect on the liquid was negligible.

Two days after my first patrol I did another fairly long flight, leaving the ground at 5.55 am in *SS.24*. I went in a southerly direction this time, passing over Llandwyn lighthouse, crossing Carnarvon Bay to Tremadoc Bay, past Penrhos, Criccieth and Porth Madoc; then I thought I would investigate the lie of the land, so I went up the Ffestiniog Valley, following the single line of the Ffestiniog Railway on which we saw the funny old steam train puffing away. There appeared to be no opening through the mountains, so when King, my wireless operator signalled that the wireless aerial weight had carried away, I thought it time to turn about; I was not at all sorry to be over the sea again, as the atmosphere in the valley between the mountains was decidedly bumpy. I cut across the peninsula over Criccieth and between Mynydd Craig Goch (2,000 feet) and Penny-Gaer (1,700 feet), where it was even bumpier than up the Ffestiniog Valley. I crossed Carnarvon Bay off Maen Dulyn and the west end of Menai Straits, and landed at 10.05 am. In the afternoon I took the same ship up again to familiarise myself with the country around the station.

Next day a submarine was reported in the Irish Sea. Our ships were out all day in relays. Soon after 5 pm I took *SS.22* up and went out west from Holyhead. It soon became very hazy and at 6.45 pm, being out of sight of land, I turned about and was off the South Stack light at 7.15, made for home and landed an hour later.

On 21st May 1916 the first Daylight Saving Bill came into force—we lost an hour's sleep, but gained more daylight for landing later in the evening. From my diary I see that I also made out my income-tax return; I discovered that I was in receipt of the princely sum of £282 per annum—which includes flying pay of eight shillings per day!

For a week I only did a few short flights, but on 27th May I took *SS.22* on patrol with AM Hallam as W/T op. We crossed Carnarvon Bay to Bardsey Island and thence out over the Irish Sea on the mail route. It became very misty, so I turned for base, flying through a rainstorm on the way back, and landed after four and a half hours' flying.

On 28th May I took up *SS.24* for three and a half hours with AM King as W/T op. We went over the Skerries and out to sea, where we passed near three Norwegian steamers: *Orn II*, *Bombay*, and *Svend Foyn I*, en route for Liverpool, and also a small fleet of fishing-vessels. We returned over Lynus Point and Amlwch, where it was very bumpy, and were back over the aerodrome by 2 pm, but had to cruise around whilst a landing-party was being mustered. As I came up to the landing-party, I was caught in a strong up-current which shot me up some 300 feet. I went round again and brought the ship down to within 20 feet of the ground. As there was a low hillock surmounted with trees between me and the landing-party, I was out of their sight and they thought I had force-landed. They came running towards me, but before they reached me I steered round the trees and dropped my trail rope right amongst the party. It was lucky I was so low, as the trail rope hung up about 30 feet down.

I was enjoying a quiet evening at 'The Bull' on the 5th June when Charlie Swayne, the First Lieutenant, arrived and told me I was to report next day at Cranwell for my graduation exam. I caught the midnight train from Holyhead and gave them all a surprise at home in London by turning up in time for breakfast. I caught the afternoon train for Sleaford, where I was met by a station car and taken out to Cranwell. I duly took my exam, but came an awful cropper in navigation. Commodore Payne gave me a proper dressing down and told me to come back in a month's time to have another go.

The Training College, Cranwell, was still under construction at that time, though it already had a hundred large wooden huts for airmen and fifty for officers; the cabin I was put into had no lights. The place was stiff with 'gold lace', there being a commodore; a fleet paymaster; a fleet surgeon; two commanders and many others, but very few airship people.

Soon after my return to Anglesey I took up Chichele Plowden's ship *SS.18* with AM Bingham as W/T op. I took her over Holyhead and soon lost sight of land. The wind increased to about 20 knots from the north-east and I received a recall signal from the station. I plugged away and began to wonder if I should ever see land again. Then for some reason the ship became very nose heavy and I had to fly with my elevators hard up to maintain height. I very nearly missed Holyhead in the haze, but fortunately for me my W/T op. spotted it dimly in the mist and we battled our way in over the North Stack lighthouse at the north tip of Holyhead Island. Over land, the air was very bumpy and the wind increased. I received a W/T message: 'Can you make the station?'—to which I replied 'Yes.' I was making good only about 10 knots and arrived over the Station at about 3 pm. Over the landing-ground the wind was all over the place. When I had managed to get near the landing-party a side gust caught me and blew me broadside on past it. I put my nose down and the wind on it blew me backwards over the landing-party, who hung on to my handling guys and pulled me down. The SNO at Holyhead, who was on the landing-ground, came over with Charlie Swayne and congratulated me on my handling of the ship in such conditions. This turned out to be my last flight from Anglesey and it was incidentally my longest flight to date—5 hours 5 minutes.

On 17th June 1916 our former First Lieutenant, Eustace Moyes, came for the week-end. In the evening we had a whale of a party. It all started by someone producing a woollen scarf about two yards long which was quickly turned into a tug-of-war rope with Scott, Scroggs, Kilburn and myself at one end pulling Underhill—'Mr WU', Moyes—'Useless Eustace', Charlie Swayne and Chichele Plowden at the other. We were much the heavier and stronger team and in no time had pulled them through the Mess door and out on to the veranda. They then tried to keep us out by shutting the door and pushing against it, but we heaved them back into the Mess Room and there formed a rugger scrum with someone's service cap as a ball. Then various couples broke off and had scraps and wrestling matches with each other. It was during this scrap that I remember getting Swayne by the waist and hurling him across the room. The surprised look on his face as he went sailing across the room was very funny. We then piled all the furniture in the middle of the room with the large fire extinguisher on top of it all—this, of course, got knocked down and set going—it bespattered us all; once started there was no stopping it until someone threw it out on to the veranda.

'Scottie', our CO, looked a woebegone sight sitting on the floor with his hair all streaming and his coat soaked with extinguisher liquid. We were all turning in when we heard the sounds of another fracas. Mr WU blew out 'Lofty' Kilburn's lamp—there was then no electric light on the station and Kilburn dashed into WU's cabin and tore all the bedclothes off the bed and dumped them out of the back door of the hut. Mr WU was in an awful 'blight' and nearly speechless with rage; all he could say was 'My God, Kilburn'—which he repeated about fifty times before eventually gathering up his bedclothes. He was carting them back to his cabin when we heard the sound of money rattling along the passage. Swayne came out of his cabin to find out what all the row was about; Mr WU, still livid, blared off at him, 'I've lost all my money and I'm bloody well going to find it, so you can b-well pack up and go to bed', which he duly did, with Kilburn popping his head out of his door and shouting, 'Keep quiet, little man!' Underhill, when he later retired from the RAF, became a clergyman.

Next day when we cleaned up the mess we found very little damage done; an armchair was minus a couple of legs and a panel of the Mess door was cracked where a chair had been thrown at it, but the Mess oil lamp was intact and no windows were broken. A black key was missing from the piano, knocked off when Swayne had tried to play the piano with a walking-stick.

Two days later I left Anglesey for Kingsnorth Airship Station, where I was to undergo a course in navigation.

The navigation course was preceded by a course in seamanship. This consisted mainly in learning how to make various knots and splices in steel wire and hemp rope, a knowledge of which has been very useful to me throughout my life.

Shortly before my arrival at Kingsnorth a 'Coastal' ship, *C.8*, had crashed into the sea and two CPOs of her crew had been drowned. My first job after arrival was the unhappy one of making an inventory of their effects. I had several flights 'round the gas works'* in *SS.14* with F/Sub-Lt S. E. Taylor, and in *SS.31*—known as the Flying Bedstead—with F/Sub-Lt T. B. Williams, but was properly thrilled when F/Lt Ian McDonald offered me a flight as observer in *C.1*. This was our first tri-lobe ship and based on the French Astra-Torres type; she still had her original yellow undoped envelope. The flight did not last long, as an oil pipe burst—the auxiliary blower broke down and likewise one of the engines. 'Coastals' had two Sunbeam engines of 150 hp each, one in the front and the other at the rear of a fairly long box-shaped car (in other words, one pusher and one tractor).

On 22nd July I took F/Sub-Lt Lacy in *SS.31* over the 3rd Battle Squadron at Sheerness, among the warships being the *Dreadnought* and the *Hibernia*.

In the meantime the navigation course was under way, being taken by a commander naval instructor in the billiards room of the Ward Room —the Senior Officers' Mess. The weather was swelteringly hot and it needed an immense effort to keep awake during the hot afternoons. I used to sit next a F/Sub-Lt named Brook who regularly dropped off to sleep. This by itself would not have mattered much, but he would snore

* Airship jargon for 'round the block'.

in spite of reapeated nudgings on my part; the old NI went droning on, seeming not to notice, or, if he did, quite unconcerned.

We juniors lived in the Gun Room and were occasionally honoured by a visit from 'Jimmy-the-One'—the First Lieutenant—when there were high revels, usually a rugger scrum in the Mess. I remember one case in particular when Jimmy-the-One was as tight as a lord and fighting everyone. He must have been a good boxer in his younger days, for he put Barr and Randall-Stevens out for the count, and was himself escorted back to the Ward Room absolutely paralytic. Altogether, we managed to enjoy our courses!

One night we had a water and Pyrene fight in the Gun Room after dinner, during which I was thoroughly soaked by Lacy emptying a fire bucket of water over me; that same night—31st July 1916—there was a Zeppelin raid over Thames mouth. Jackson was Duty Officer and just at the end of the fight was sent for by Number One. He reported in his pyjamas, absolutely soaked to the skin as a result of the fight. During the night he was continually being rung up on the telephone, which made him wild.

At about 2 am tinkle-tinkle goes the bell again; 'Jackie' grabs the receiver and yells down it: 'What the bloody hell do you want now?'—only to find that his caller is no less a person than the C-in-C at the Nore!

This was reported to our CO, Commander Dane, who gave Jackie a proper telling off.

After several short flights in the SS ships and another in *C.1*, I was taken up as observer by F/Lt Wheelwright in *C.17*. We flew over the Thames to Southend. The sun was shining brightly, so I told Johnny Wheelwright that I was going up on top of the ship for a bit 'OK', he said, so I went up the gun tube through the centre of the ship, clambered out of it on to the top lobe of the envelope, lay down and basked in the sun for half an hour. When I returned to the control car Wheelwright greeted me with, 'Hallo, Meag; I thought you must have slid off the top.'

This was my last flight from Kingsnorth, for three days later I was posted back to Scrubbs to take my graduation exam once more. On my arrival, however, the CO—Lieutenant-Colonel Tim Waterlow—roped me in for his course in aerostatics, so this postponed my exam until the middle of September.

On the night of the 2nd/3rd September I was Night Duty Officer. While doing the rounds I went into the wireless hut, where I was given a pair of earphones; suddenly, the operator exclaimed 'Hello, here's a Zeppelin!' I could hear it buzzing away in code. I listened to four Zepps exchanging signals with Heligoland; they had a very high clear note to their signals, the unmistakable Telefunken note.

At 10.55 pm the official air raid alarm was given, followed by an order from the Admiralty: 'Take air raid action.' I asked the Duty Officer at HQ if the landing lights were to be laid out on the Scrubbs; he said he would go and inquire of the Wing Captain. A few minutes later he rang back to say the lights were to be placed in position on the Scrubbs. I had them placed out there, but before lighting them up I rang the DO again to confirm that they were to be lighted. He replied: 'Yes, light up.' So I did. They made an awful glare in the dark of the night, and I would not have selected the Scrubbs as an ideal place for them. I believe questions were asked in Parliament as to why the Scrubbs was lighted up, for I was called upon to give a full report on the matter. The lights, of course, were not meant as a target indicator for the Zeppelins, but as an aid to any of our own aircraft which might be up.

At about 2 am that morning, the 3rd September, I heard the unmistakable sound of aero engines—a very deep drone. I went outside and saw the sky lit up by searchlights, with anti-aircraft guns banging away and shells bursting like so many stars high up in the sky. Presently I caught a momentary glimpse of a Zepp away in the distance to the north-east, but too indistinct for description. After a few minutes she again came into view with shells bursting all round her, some near and appearing to hit her, and others miles away. She was in sight for about a minute and then, just before she disappeared again, a shell seemed to burst absolutely on her. I was then called to the telephone and when I went outside again the whole landscape and sky was suffused with a brilliant red glow, and away to the north-east was a blazing mass of bright red light, dropping slowly earthwards. Every now and again the light would die down, only the next instant to flare up even more brilliantly than before. Gradually it became less and less until finally I could see merely a small glowing fragment falling rather like the stick of a burnt-out rocket. This occurred at 2.20 am on the 3rd September 1916.

The order 'Resume normal conditions' came at 4.15 am, and I turned in for a couple of hours.

The Zepp that had been brought down was the *L.21*. What remained of her—a great mass of twisted and tangled wire and bits of frame—was brought from Cuffley, Hertfordshire, to the Scrubbs on the following Thursday. I believe the ship was actually a Schutte-Lanz, a wood-framed ship and not a true Zeppelin, which has a metal frame, though there was not a great deal of difference in appearance, and all the raiders came under the generic term of 'Zeppelin'.

We were fully occupied from 13th to 15th September with the graduation exams, which consisted of papers in navigation, meteorology, armament, engineering and aerostatics, with practical tests in rigging, squad drill and signalling—pretty comprehensive. I obtained 830 marks out of 1,000, a very satisfactory result after my former débâcle at Cranwell.

I was instructed to report back to Anglesey, but this was almost immediately cancelled and I was appointed to Capel-le-Ferne Airship Station, which was perched on top of the cliffs about midway between Dover and Folkestone.

CHAPTER TWO

The Dover Patrol and Pulham

There were three sheds at Capel, two for SS ships and one for a 'Coastal'. One of the SS sheds had been erected too low to take the ships, so a channel was dug out along the centre-line and the car rested in this. I think 'Skipper' Cunningham must have been standing on the edge of this pit when in 1915, he flipped *SS.12's* envelope with his finger and echoed the sound he made by saying 'blimp!'—thus giving another word to the English language which amongst us pilots came to mean exclusively the SS airships. For some reason unknown to me, the American pilots called them 'Pony-Blimps'. It may have been to distinguish between the smaller and larger ships, as between a pony and a horse, for by the time the United States joined us we had many ships larger than the SS type.

A couple of days after my arrival at Capel I was put in command of *SS11*, which had a B.E.2c car. After a couple of short trial flights I took her on patrol to the Varne lightship and on to Cap Gris Nez. I returned to Capel, where I was greeted with the 'Negative' flag, so I went across to France and back again, but no 'Affirmative' flag, so I pushed off along the coast to Dungeness so as to learn the lie of the coast. Returned and landed after four and three-quarter hours.

Soon after I had landed some German seaplanes flew over Dover and were met by heavy fire, but all got away. During the night there was a Zepp raid over Kent.

For the next week I was up daily in *SS11* with AM Hitchcock as W/T op. We used to do three patrols of approximately two to three hours each, usually via the Varne light-vessel to Gris Nez or Boulogne. Nothing much of interest occurred on these flights except that on one flight we lost eight gallons of petrol through a leaking petrol pipe. On another we saw a large school of porpoises disporting themselves off Boulogne.

Early in October 1916 I was detailed to inflate and rig *SS4*, as her pilot, Charles Verner, had been posted to Kingsnorth. This was completed by the middle of the month, but owing to bad weather it was not until 2nd November that I took her out for three short trial flights. For the remainder of November I was patrolling the Channel and occasionally escorting troopships to France. I was told by some Army 'bods' later that

A Coastal landing at Pulham, 1917. The air-gunner is at his post on top

A Sea Scout with Maurice Farman car, Kingsnorth, 1916. Flight Sub-Lieutenant T. B. Williams in the pilot's seat

The Coastal *C.17* in trouble

Below: Lieutenant Wheelright, the pilot, is on the right, walking the ship back to the shed

Above: The pressure has fallen still lower, but we got her operational that night, all the same. February 191

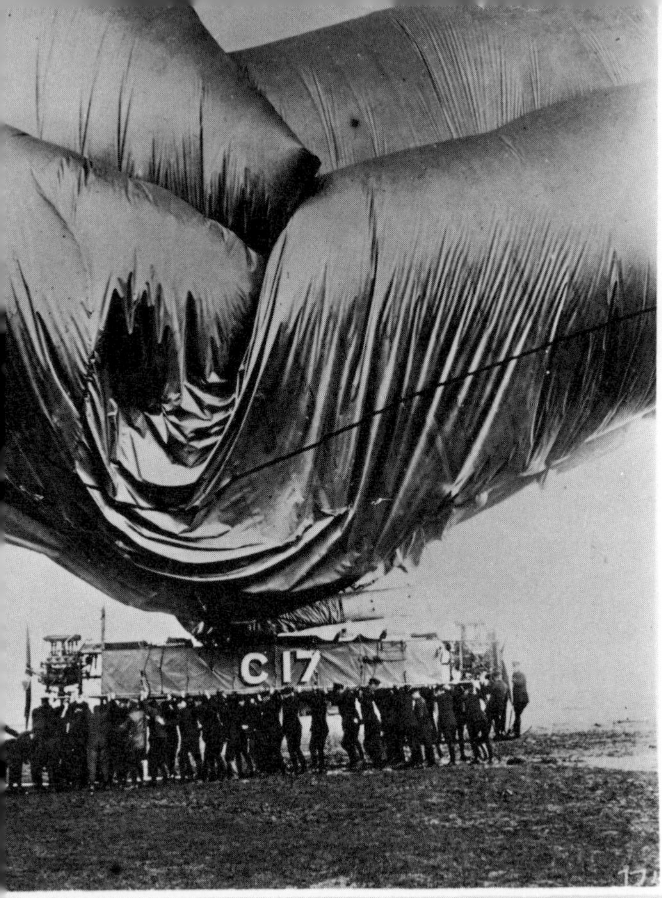

the troops only felt it was safe to go below if an airship was patrolling overhead. During many of these flights I was giving instruction in piloting to F/Lt Cleary, known in the service as 'The Count', and F/Sub-Lts Parry and Roach-Smith. We now had enough lift to carry two 65-pound and eight 20-pound bombs in addition to the extra person.

About this time we heard that one of the Anglesey ships had been lost with all hands; in fact, the loss of life was confined to one, the engineer, AM Young. The facts as related to me later by the pilot, F/Sub-Lt A. D. Thompson, were that he had run into a cow when landing on the aerodrome at Anglesey; the cow was killed and his undercarriage smashed. His W/T op jumped clear; and the ship, being lightened, shot up into the air and was blown out to sea. Eventually, she came down heavily on the water. The engineer was either thrown out or jumped off, and the ship, with only Thompson now on board, went up again, coming down with a crash on the water; the envelope and car broke in two, but Thompson managed to cling on to one of the planes, from which he was rescued by a coal tramp. The engineer, I am sorry to say, was never seen again. I was very glad that Thompson was saved, because he was the sole supporter of his widowed mother.

During the night of 26th/27th October we heard sounds of firing out at sea and next day we heard there had been a scrap in the Channel. There were rumours that the *Queen*, a Folkeston-Boulogne Cross-Channel boat, five trawlers and two of our destroyers had been sunk, whilst the Germans had lost two destroyers definitely sunk and two others in a sinking condition—quite a miniature battle.

During the remainder of November I did numerous flights of from three to six hour's duration, usually to the Varne light-vessel, Cap Gris Nez and the Colbart light-vessel off the French coast. On one occasion I paid a visit over the French airship station at Marquise. This was quite a small place with just one canvas shed. During December the engine of my ship became very unreliable, probably due to the cold, but on one occasion our Engineer Officer, F. M. Rope, found the petrol filter had got choked with mud. In mid-December our 'Skipper', Squadron Commander A. D. Cunningham, left us to become, later on, chief assistant to Air Commodore E. M. Maitland at Airship HQ at the Admiralty. I was very sorry to see him go, as he had always been very nice and considerate to me, but his successor, the Hon. Roger Coke, seemed to be a very nice chap. As it turned out I only outlasted Cunningham a week at Capel, for on the 21st December 1916 I received orders to report to Pulham Airship Station, Norfolk, for training as a 'Coastal' pilot. Although it was a step on the ladder, I did not feel too happy at my transfer, as I had got a good crew together and was settling down with my ship. Fortunately there were some of my former cronies there, with one of whom, 'Tiny' Mostyn, I travelled down. He also was a former Capel man, having been Armament Officer there, and he made me feel at home in the Mess at once. I also met old 'Jackie' again, of whom I was very fond. He was a rough diamond, but solid and genuine—an ex-Merchant Service officer. Dixon and Kilburn, other former Scrubbs and Anglesey boys, were also there so I did not fall among strangers. I don't think there was ever a happier crowd than at Pulham at this time.

On Christmas Day we had a great spread in the Mess presided over by the CO, Colonel E. M. Maitland, who was another of the Army officers transferred with the airships when the Admiralty took them over. He stood champagne all round and I had my first taste of it, though I cannot say I was much gone on it; although it had a nice, fresh, clean taste, I found it a bit sharp for my palate.

The following morning I went up as cox'n to Johnny Wheelwright in *C.17*, with Dixon as observer. I found the 'Coastal much more difficult to steer than an *SS*, as it used to get a terrific swing on one way if not checked early. However, I soon got the knack of it, and before I left I could steer one within five degrees either side of the required course and generally within a degree or so—at that time our compasses were still marked in divisions of five degrees. Our flight lasted four and a half hours, going out to sea over Lowestoft and in over Great Yarmouth. Next day we went out again; this time I was observer and part-time pilot; Farquhar was our engineer and the W/T op was Richards. Lieutenant Roberts, RNVR, an experimental officer, was cox'n. He was trying out a gadget he and Wheelwright had concocted for indicating to the cox'n the course to steer. This consisted of red and green lights. To indicate a turn to port the pilot shone the red light; for starboard the green one; when the ship was on the course required, the pilot shone both together. At that time we had no intercom and the roar of the engines in the open cockpit drowned one's voice—to indicate a change of course, the pilot had to jot down directions on a signal card and hand it over to the cox'n in front. This flight we went via Kessingland—five miles south of Lowestoft—to Smith's Knoll, Haisboro', Mundesley, in over Cromer, Aylsham and Norwich, and back to Pulham. Unfortunately it was too murky and misty to see much of Norwich. We were five and a half hours in the air. Our next flight in *C.17* was cut short by the wind getting up to gale force on reaching the coast.

After dinner on the last day of 1916 all the officers left in the Mess trooped off down to Harleston and serenaded the First Lieutenant then crossed his garden and did likewise to Dr and Mrs Maidment, whilst Number One and his wife were preparing a bowl of punch; back at Number One's, we were kept in fits of laughter by a most amusing little RNVR lieutenant named Sammy Atkins telling stories and doing conjuring tricks. Just before midnight Number One brought down his little boy aged about five, in his pyjamas, to propose the toast of the New Year. The punch was terrific and nearly knocked me over. We formed a ring with crossed hands and sang 'Auld Lang Syne', and returned to Pulham and bed having had a thoroughly good and amusing evening.

In January 1917 I was attached as Second Officer to F/Lt D. W. A. Barton on *C.27*. This was the last of the 'Coastals' and Barton had just flown it up from Kingsnorth. We did a short trial flight on the 5th January 1917, followed by two bomb-dropping practices over the Batchelor Mirror.

Barton was sent off on a course and F/Lt Godfrey took over the ship temporarily. We went on our first patrol together on the 22nd January. On reaching the coast at Lowestoft we headed into wind, slowed down and found it to be blowing from east by south at 18 knots. We then flew to some of the lightships marking the sandbanks off this coast. Each has a distinctive top mark for recognition by day as the names which used to be painted white on the sides of the red hulls had all been erased. The Cross Sands lightship had a black double triangle, apex to apex; Newarp had three black balls one at the top of each mast; Haisboro' a single black ball on the mast top. On Cromer beach there was a wrecked steamer in two pieces about a quarter of a mile apart and the Haisboro' Sands, which were showing above water, were thick with wrecks, with a perfect forest of masts sticking up all over the place.

On the return journey we lost our way after Norwich, so I worked out a course to steer, but after following it for about five minutes Godfrey saw a likely-looking road and followed that. The result was we found ourselves east of Bungay, or about ten miles east of Pulham, which shows how important it is to shape a course and stick to it! Next day we went out again, but did not get beyond Lowestoft as the wind was blowing about 40 knots.

Wheelwright and I did a couple of bomb-dropping runs in *C.17*, taking turns as pilot and cox'n. It was a difficult evolution, as we did it in blinding snow and could scarcely see the target. My hand became numb and frozen after I had raised my arm once to operate the valve; it was very painful as the circulation returned.

Godfrey and I did a six-hour patrol on 31st January 1917, this time to the southward to the Outer Gabbard, Harwich, Cork and Shipwash lightships. We sighted three British submarines and two minesweepers besides numerous ships following the War Channel. It was snowing heavily when we landed and we could scarcely see the ground. This was about the coldest flight I had so far experienced. The carburettors

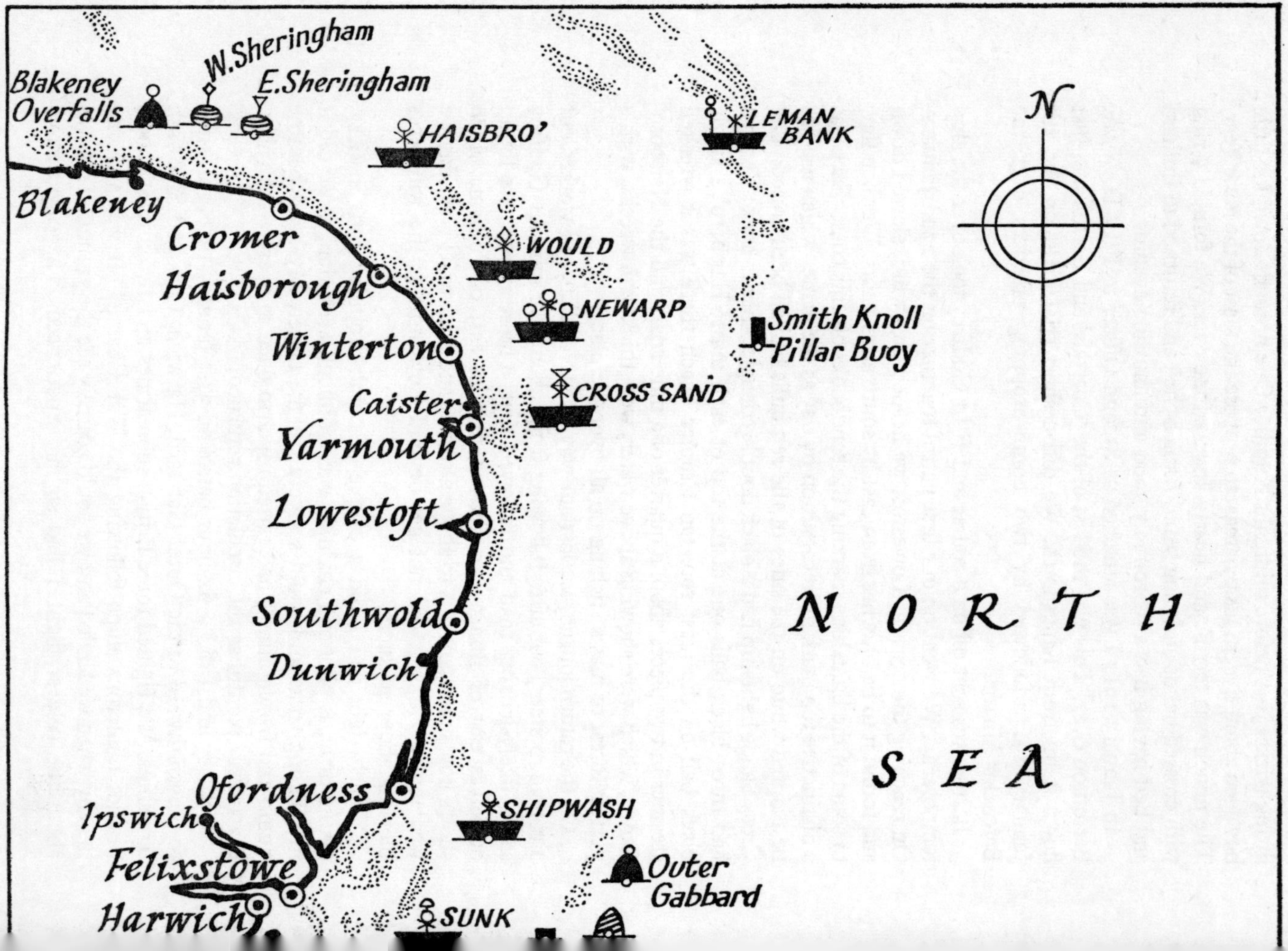

Blakeney Overfalls
W.Sheringham
E.Sheringham
HAISBRO'
LEMAN BANK
N
Blakeney
Cromer
WOULD
Haisborough
NEWARP
Smith Knoll Pillar Buoy
Winterton
CROSS SAND
Caister
Yarmouth
Lowestoft
NORTH
Southwold
Dunwich
SEA
Ofordness
SHIPWASH
Ipswich
Outer Gabbard
Felixstowe
Harwich
SUNK

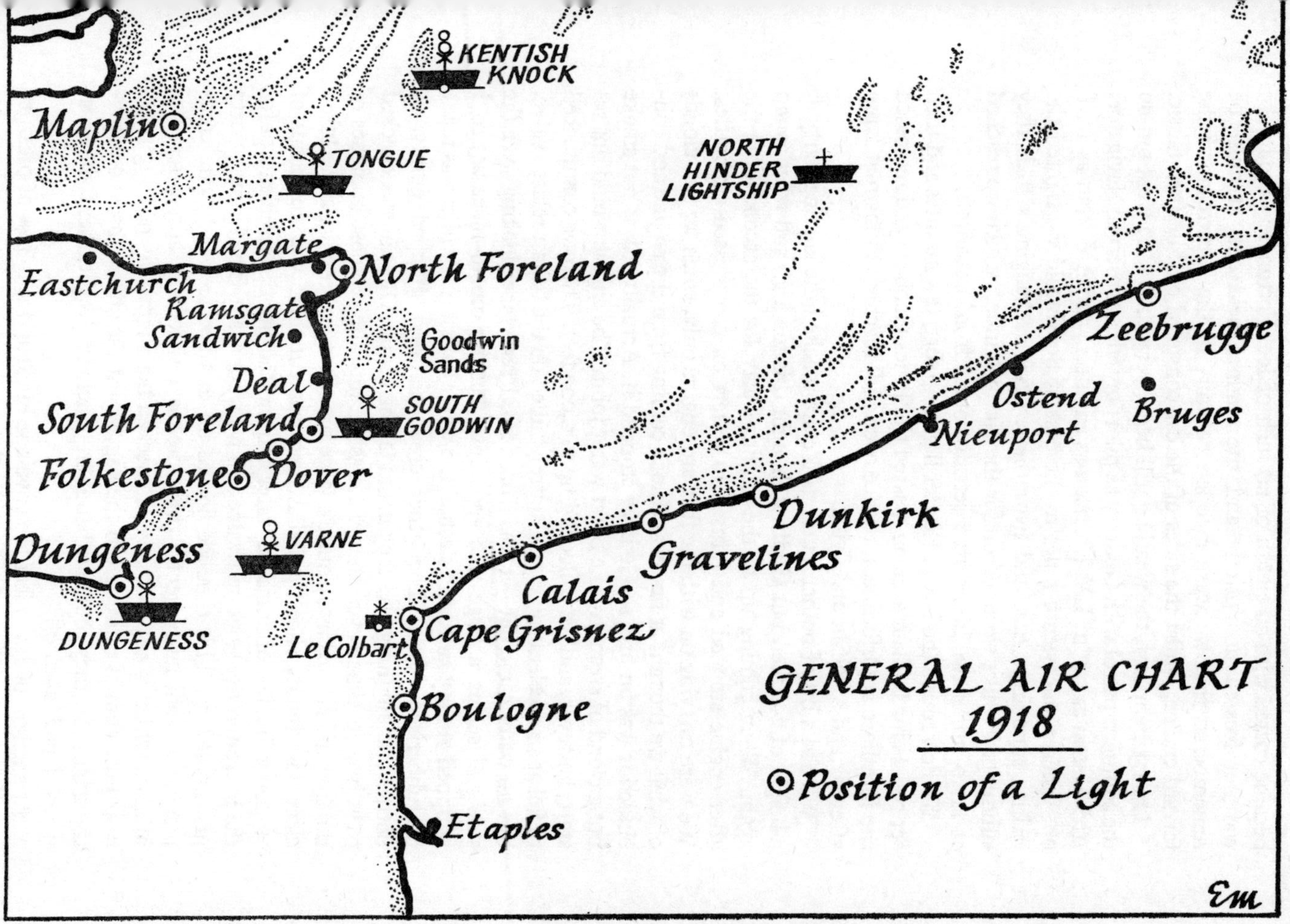

GENERAL AIR CHART
1918
Position of a Light
Maplin
KENTISH KNOCK
TONGUE
NORTH HINDER LIGHTSHIP
Margate
North Foreland
Eastchurch
Ramsgate
Sandwich
Goodwin Sands
Deal
SOUTH GOODWIN
South Foreland
Folkestone
Dover
Dungeness
VARNE
DUNGENESS
Le Colbart
Cape Grisnez
Calais
Gravelines
Dunkirk
Nieuport
Ostend
Bruges
Zeebrugge
Boulogne
Etaples
Em

became coated with an eighth of an inch of ice. Fortunately the intake was not frosted up entirely and the engines held out. It must be remembered that we were in open cockpits in the slipstream of the forrard engine, whilst the sides of the car consisted of thin linen fabric.

On 1st February, the weather still being very cold, *C.27* went out on the southern patrol with Godfrey as pilot; myself as observer Navigator; AM Martin as cox'n; LM Harrison as engineer; and AM Pratt as W/T op. When about twenty miles to the east of Southwold we sighted the British submarine *E.46* and two others. After exchanging signals they submerged whilst we stood on for the North Hinder, which we reached at 11.50, about two hours after setting course from Lowestoft.

We flew round the North Hinder lightship for a few minutes and then set course for Pulham at noon, passed the Inner Gabbard and recrossed the foreshore at Orfordness, thence overland, reaching Pulham at 2 pm after six and a half hours' flying.

We had a bit of bother landing. We approached the landing-party at a height of 200 feet, but Godfrey thought this too high and went round again. When coming up to the landing-party for the second time the after engine stopped and refused to restart on compressed-air bottles. We were carrying on with the forward engine only, when we saw clouds of what we thought at first was smoke coming from the engine and concluded it was on fire, so Godfrey stopped it. Actually it was not smoke but a cloud of steam from a burst water joint. The engine would not restart, however, and we ballooned up to 2,000 feet. Then we commenced to fall at an accelerating rate. Godfrey pulled on the ballast release valve, but no water came out—it was frozen up. I remember looking over the side and seeing a large tree apparently rushing up to meet us, so I whipped out my knife and slashed the water ballast bag which was made of rubberised fabric. The other crew members dumped empty air bottles and anything else they could lay hands on. Our fall was checked only just in time; even then we crashed into the topmost branches of the tree and carried away quite a large branch in our rigging as we lifted clear. Of course, once the ballast bag was cut there was no means of stopping the flow of unfrozen water and the bag emptied itself except for the ice round the sides and valve; up we went again. The landing-party just missed us. This time we floated up to 3,000 feet and again commenced to fall, fairly gently this time, as I timed her at 350 feet per minute, which is not excessive. I checked her slightly by heaving overboard the chunks of ice left in the bag, whilst the others threw out anything movable they could lay hands on—including my leather flying-coat which I had taken off.

At a height of 1,000 feet the envelope buckled due to loss of pressure and the car turned over on its side, due to the slackening of the central suspensions and the tautening of the fore and aft ones as the nose and tail went up. These latter were attached to the ends of the skids under the car. We all had to get out of our seats and sit on the rail round the bottom of the car normally used for handling. Thus we came gently to earth again, having drifted about a mile away from the landing-party.

Just as the ship hit the ground Godfrey gave the order to jump, but it struck me that if we all did so the ship would float away again with no one on board to bring her down, so I did not jump. It was perhaps as well, for Godfrey, in jumping, got hung up by his flying-coat in the undercarriage wires. The ship, lightened by most of her crew, started to rise, whilst Godfrey struggled to disentangle himself. I yelled out to him: 'Hang on!' and, grabbing hold of him by his leather coat collar, yanked him up on to the rail, by which time the landing-party had come up with us and got hold of our guy ropes and pulled us down. As old Robbie said to me after: 'You don't know your own strength.'

Many years afterwards Johnny Wheelwright recalled this happening when we met at a gathering of ex-airship people in about 1957—I had completely forgotten about it all. Wheelwright had been in charge of the landing-party which finally hauled us down and walked us the two and a half miles across snow-covered country back to the shed. In the actual landing, little or no damage was done, but in righting the car afterwards, the after skid and the fore prop were smashed.

Once in the shed we quickly put the envelope up to pressure. I went over the top to have a look at things and found only a small tear caused by the Lewis-gun mounting when the envelope buckled. I stuck on a patch which temporarily stopped further gas leakage until the cox'n and riggers could effect a permanent repair.

There were neither spare skids nor struts in store and the engineers also ran into a great deal of trouble: first the forward radiator leaked badly, then the after engine oil radiator sprung a leak. We borrowed an engine from *C.17* which was undergoing overhaul, but were held up for over a week awaiting the skids and struts. When they finally arrived on the 8th February the CO issued an order that the ship was to be ready for flight first thing the following morning.

We practically had to re-sling the car. I remember about midnight Jackson and Dixon paid us a visit to see how we were getting on. We were having great difficulty in joining up the bobstay or straining wire connecting the two skids. Jackie and Dickie showed me how to draw them together by a Spanish windlass using only a lead pencil. We worked all night and finished the rigging part at 4 am. The engineers then tried to start the engines. The after engine would only fire on four cylinders, and it was found necessary to replace a magneto. They completed their job by 7 am, when the ship was ready for flight. We did not go out on patrol, but carried out some parachute dropping and cinematograph experiments. A dummy was dropped from a height of only 200 feet. It seemed to me to hit the ground with a hell of a bump, but 'Tiny' Mostyn, the Parachute Officer, who was on board, and Colonel Maitland, who was watching from the ground, both said it was a very good descent. The 'chute opened fully about 75 feet from the ship and checked the fall at about 100 feet.

Next day, the 10th February, we resumed patrolling. At first it was fairly clear and we made Cross Sands lightship, but visibility deteriorated and by mid-morning we could not see the sea from 500 feet; ten minutes later we could not see it from 100 feet, so we made for the coast, which we sighted at Horsey Gap and Haisboro' lighthouse. We followed the coast to Lowestoft and returned to Pulham, landing in a snowstorm at 2.10 after five and a half hours flying.

On 12th February we left the ground again for patrol, but again there was thick fog over the sea, which was invisible from 500 feet so we returned, having flown only an hour and forty minutes.

Next day Colonel Maitland went up in *C.17* to try an experimental live drop from 1,000 feet, from which he landed quite safely. We in *C.27* took photographs and cinema shots of the drop. For the photograph we carried PO Manistre, and for the movie PO Barrett.

On 14th February we carried out a fairly long patrol of eight hours—Lowestoft, Cross Sands, Smith's Knoll and North Hinder lightship, near which we sighted a submarine which promptly gave the recognition signal. Then we turned in to Harwich, Shipwash and back to Pulham via Aldeburgh. We had magneto trouble on the way back, but by running the engine slowly it lasted out.

Our next flight, on 16th February, we went northward from Lowestoft via Cross Sands lightship and Smith's Knoll. When about seventeen miles north-east of Cromer we came upon a recent wreck marked with a green buoy. We reached Skegness at 12.50; thence to Sheringham and overland past Norwich to Pulham. Soon after crossing the foreshore we had to stop the after engine, as the propeller had sheared all its bolts. We proceeded on our forward engine only and landed at 4.25 pm after a flight of eight hours all but five minutes.

Whilst a new prop was being fitted in *C.27*, I went out as cox'n to Wheelwright in *C.17*. We made for Cromer in thick fog, but found it clear over the sea and patrolled over the Wash. Very soon the forward engine stopped, but started almost at once. However, after ten minutes of uneven running it was stopped again, as the engineer, LM King, found it was loose on its bedplate; we turned about and made for home on the after engine only. Over the land the fog was still very thick, but we made Norwich all right and cruised over the city to pick up our bearings, flying fairly low to do so, as the fog was so thick. I remember Wheelwright yelling out to me: 'Mind you don't hit the Cathedral'—Norwich Cathedral has a very tall spire.

The previous night there had been a Zeppelin raid over the city, I think some of the inhabitants thought we were another Zepp paying them a visit, for we distinctly heard the sharp crack of two rifle shots. Owing to the fog we did not see many people, but those we did see seemed very scared, as directly they saw us they scurried indoors.

From Norwich we set off on a south-west by south course for Pulham, picked up the main line to London, but lost it almost immediately, so thick and low was the fog, and though we were flying at no more than 100 feet we saw only occasional glimpses of the ground. We sighted a single-line railway which we concluded was the Waveney Valley line which runs between Diss and Lowestoft, and as it runs through the Pulhams we turned to follow it. Almost immediately our only running engine stopped short. We ballooned about for a short time, rising to 1,000 feet and drifting slowly north-east. We restarted the engine on the compressed-air bottle and came down very low to locate our whereabouts, but had some difficulty in keeping up the pressure in the envelope, which began to sag so that the ship became unsteerable and we were completely lost.

Eventually the fog thinned a bit and we found ourselves over a double-line railway which we commenced to follow until the engine packed up once more. We ballooned about again for a short space. Wheelwright and King managed to restart the engine on our last air bottle and very soon we found ourselves over a magnificent mansion and park with a Hampton Court-like maze and large circular flower gardens laid out in a beautiful scroll pattern. We could not locate it on the map, not having the faintest idea whereabouts to look, so decided the safest thing was to make for the coast from where it was not difficult to work back and pinpoint the beautiful mansion as Somerleyton Park, which is quite near the sea. Lowestoft was like reaching home again, and we followed our usual route to Pulham along the Waveney Valley. We reached Harleston, about three miles from Pulham, when the after engine started running unevenly and the water in the radiator boiled away like a kettle. King the engineer was busy climbing along the handling rail, transferring water from the front radiator by means of a thermos flask. By this means he managed to keep the engine going until we finally landed after eight hours' very trying flying, mostly in thick fog, with one and a half hours of it as a free balloon and another five hours with only one engine—and that not too reliable.* Wheelwright

* The crew on this flight were: *Pilot:* F/Lt J. Wheelwright. *Cox'n:* F/Sub-Lt G. F. Meager. *Observer:* LM Cox. *Engineer:* LM King. *W/T Op:* AM Macario.

was awarded the DSC for bringing his ship back safely and I was Mentioned in Despatches.

On 22nd February 1917 I went up with Godfrey in *C.27* to do my 'Coastal' passing-out test combined with some runs over the mirror for bomb-dropping practice. I was coming up to land when Godfrey told me to open up the after engine; as a result I overshot the landing party and nearly hit a crane—needless to say, I was not passed out.

Next day I was up again with Godfrey, Martin, Harrison and Pratt in *C.27* for patrol, but we got no further than Beccles when our after rolling guy carried away into the prop and smashed it. The after engine was stopped and we returned to base.

On 28th February I went up as cox'n of *C.17* with Wheelwright. From Lowestoft we patrolled to about forty miles north-east of Cromer, sighting *C.26* at Smith's Knoll. We sighted hundreds of red rings floating about. They were probably markers for a trawl net. When about thirty miles east of Lowestoft we sighted submarine *V.8* and four destroyers. We proceeded south-eastwards and passed Black Cat Buoy and very soon reached the Shipwash lightship, about ten miles east of Orfordness. Near here we came upon a British submarine escorted by seven trawlers. As the wind was increasing from the westward, off shore, Wheelwright decided to make for home. We crossed the foreshore at Thorpe, two miles north of Aldeburgh, and landed at 5 pm, having completed seven hours ten minutes' flying.

Barton had returned by now and taken over his ship; I went up as cox'n to him on 1st March with Godfrey as observer. We had reached Cross Sands lightship when the magneto coupling on the after engine sheared. We made for home on the forward engine only. Next day when leaving the ground in thick fog we nearly hit the 'Rigid' shed which was under construction. The fog was shallow, but we did not see the ground until we reached Lowestoft. About five miles out we sighted a wreck. As fog was lifting over the land, Barton decided to take advantage of this and make for home.

It was still misty when we went up in *C.27* on 3rd March, but the wind at 500 feet was very light being only 7 mph from the south-east. We patrolled for twenty-five miles east of Lowestoft, where we found it was raining; when about twenty miles east of Southwold we sighted a loose mine floating about, so we had some Lewis gun and rifle practice at it and finally sank it. We made for Shipwash lightship to inspect four ships in the War Channel, but before we reached them the magneto coupling on our after engine sheared so we turned for home on our forward engine only and landed safely after six hours in the air.

On 5th March a number of us from Pulham attended the funeral of two young pilots of Yarmouth Seaplane Station who had crashed; one of them had a hand in bringing down a Zeppelin off Yarmouth. The cortège was a tremendous length, all naval and trawler men. I remember once as it was passing a lengthy hoarding alongside the road practically the whole procession broke ranks to pump ship. The actual funeral was at Caister, to the north of the town, and as the seaplane base is at the southern end we had to slow-march over two miles. Altogether it was a bit of a strain.

In the evening there was a terrific wake at the 'Royal Hotel' on the front. The barmaid at the 'Royal' was a young, extraordinarily attractive and pretty girl named Mildred. In our party we had two or three officers from the Air Construction Corps stationed on the far side of the aerodrome at Pulham Market—as Pulham St Margaret's was colloquially known. We had the greatest difficulty in getting Haslett and Miroy to quit the festivities; Barton and I wished to get away early, as we were due to fly first thing next morning. We would just succeed in getting them to the entrance, when two RNAS officers, Campbell and McNab, would collar them for 'just one more'. This happened about five times. We eventually got them out the front door when pretty little Mildred ran round the corner; as she turned, her dress flew up and showed her undies. Haslett cried out, 'That's done it', broke away from us and headed straight back after her into the smoking-room, and back to the crowd of RNAS and Army officers in there, followed, of course, by his pal Miroy. It was another hour before we could get them out again. When we did finally get them to our tender, the beastly thing would not start it was so cold: we had no self-starters in those days. Poor Miroy turned and turned the starting-handle until he made himself sick, after which he got into the back of the car saying, 'You can consider me dead'.

At midnight Barton went into the 'Royal' and got the crowd to come out and give us a push. They eventually got her to go and immediately everyone who could jumped on board; the load was too much and she stopped and refused to restart in spite of our getting the Coast Defence people to give us a tow along the front. It was no go, however, and at 1.30 am we gave it up and turned in at the 'Royal' for the night. Next morning a very nice flight lieutenant named Thompson showed us over the Seaplane Base, where amongst the machines we were shown a huge seaplane which carried a 15-inch torpedo.

A few days later we flew over to Yarmouth to give our friends of the wake a chuck-up. They all came out and waved to us whilst we went down very low and nearly carried away the flagstaff on the beach. We then patrolled eastward for some twenty-five miles, then north-west to Haisboro' lighthouse and out to our familiar line of light-vessels—Haisboro', Would, Newarp and Cross Sands. We sighted a loose mine and tried to sink it, but although we holed it we did not succeed in this.

We reported its approximate position for destroyers or trawlers to finish the job.

After this flight I was passed out by F/Lt Barton as a fully fledged 'Coastal' pilot, much to my satisfaction.*

When we left the ground on 13th March the visibility was no more than twenty yards, but clear at 800 feet. As we could not see the ground we proceeded by dead reckoning out to sea over Yarmouth, which we still could not see. At 11.08 we received a wireless fix which put us over Cross Sands at 10.54 am. Almost immediately the after engine threw in its hand, so we turned in for the coast, which we sighted at Minsmere Level—between Southwold and Aldeburgh. We proceeded up the coast to Lowestoft, where we had a good view of a cruiser leaving the harbour. With us on this flight as observer was F/Lt R. V. Goddard. He was back from France, where he and Chambers had been flying a black-painted SS—*SS.40*—on night reconnaissance for the Army. It was painted black so as to be less visible at night. This enterprise had now been closed down and the pilots returned to England for 'Coastal' training. I acted as cox'n for this trip and found the job of steering very difficult, as we were practically entirely in fog with nothing to steer on except the compass, and as we had only the forrard engine from Cross Sands, it would have been a difficult job at the best of times.

We intended going northward on the 22nd March, but we ran into a heavy snowstorm when over Long Stratton; fortunately we came out into clearer weather after passing through the squall and it was beautifully clear over Norwich. We took some excellent photographs of both cathedrals. We were proceeding northward to patrol over the Wash, but before reaching the coast our pressure gauges began to read inaccurately. Then the forward engine began to play up and started missing badly, so Barton very wisely decided to turn about and return to base, which we did, the engine missing all the way with the usual magneto trouble; there must have been something radically wrong with their design or fitting.

On 24th March, when we were patrolling to the east of Lowestoft, Barton stopped the forward engine with the idea of conserving petrol. An hour later he restarted it all right on the air bottle, but immediately clouds of steam blew out of the radiator; as we were 3,000 feet up the water must have become frozen. It was perhaps unwise to have stopped the engine; anyway, there it was, we could not keep the engine going with the radiator frozen up, so it was stopped and we made for home on the after engine. Before we reached land it started running unevenly, as if there were water in the carburettor, but by nursing it carefully it lasted

* The crew on this seven-and-a-half-hour flight consisted of: *Pilot:* F/Sub-Lt G. F. Meager. *Observer:* F/Lt D. W. A. Barton. *Cox'n:* AM Martin. *Engineer:* AM Whyte. *W/T Op:* AM Richards.

out until we were actually coming up to the landing-party. Then it stopped. However, the first turn of the air bottle restarted it and we made our landing without further trouble.

On 25th March, when about ten miles north-east of Lowestoft, we received 'Return at once, weather deteriorating' from Pulham. We turned for home straight away. Off Yarmouth we sighted one of our early seaplane carriers, but I did not note her name. As the weather remained fine after we reached Pulham, we improved the shining hour by carrying out bombing practice over the mirror before landing at 11.05. We went up again almost immediately to drop a parachute with a dummy and a live 65-pound bomb at a target. Our bombing practice had not done us much good, for the bomb fell 15 yards short and 30 yards to the right of the target!

We had not been in the air five minutes on the 27th March when the after engine started spluttering, so we landed at once. The trouble was put right in twenty minutes and off we went again. Over Lowestoft harbour we acted as 'target' for testing the sights and range-finder of *HMS Glow-worm*, after which we proceeded on patrol with a nice westerly breeze behind us. Very soon, however, we ran into a heavy snowstorm, but our speed should have prevented any settling on us. However, Barton went up the gun tube to make sure whilst I took over the controls. While on top he had some Lewis gun practice with the gun on the Scarf ring fitted there.

It was still snowing when we reached Haisboro' light-vessel at 11.04 and sighted our sister ship *C.17* a mile to the north, whilst below us were our submarines *D.1*, *D.4* and *D.6* and their escort. We proceeded southward to Cross Sands lightship, where we received a message from Pulham: 'Advise return.' We turned in towards land and recrossed the foreshore at Kessingland and landed after eight and a half hours flight.

Again we had snow soon after taking off on 31st March with myself as sole pilot of *C.27*. We had reached Bungay when the water pump started leaking badly, so I decided to return. It was still snowing when I got back to Pulham, so I ballasted up light; even then, when I slowed down on approaching the landing party, snow settled on the elevator fins and brought the tail down—the rudder plane grazed the ground, luckily without damaging it. Memo for future: when landing in snow, ballast up *very* light and make a high approach!

On 4th April 1917, Jackson took me up in *SS.28*—a Maurice Farman pusher—to do her trials. She was for some reason almost unsteerable, and to keep some steerage way on her Jackie landed somewhat fast. The small landing-party managed to hang on to the trail rope, but some of them were being dragged along on their backs whilst the remainder were running their hardest to avoid a similar fate. When the ship finally was stopped Jackie wanted to know 'Why the bloody hell didn't the landing-party run ahead with the trail rope to bring the ship head to wind?'—which was a bit steep considering they had had all they could do to prevent themselves being dragged over the ground on their backs.

After some alterations to the rudder he took her up again in the afternoon with Barton and myself as observers. We had not been up five minutes when the vertical stabilising-fin started performing all kinds of weird evolutions—flapping about sideways, or pressing the skid up into the envelope. Obviously the riggers had not tautened up the fin suspensions after making the alterations. When we mentioned to Jackie how the fin was behaving he thought we were pulling his leg and trying to put the wind up him.

The following day I went up as cox'n to Victor Goddard in *C.17*. We patrolled the War Channel* off Yarmouth to the northward. Over Newarp light-vessel we sighted *No. 4*, a Parseval purchased from the Germans before the war. She was a very good shape, rather like a shark with a pointed tail. Originally, to trim her fore and aft, she had a mechanical means for shifting the position of the car along the centre-line, but this was not a success and at the time we saw her she had elevators and fins like our own ships. At that time she was our largest airship, being about 300,000 cubic feet capacity. She had been flown down from Howden to Pulham by F/Lt Moyes on 24th March 1917. When Moyes was First Lieutenant at Anglesey I did not know he was a pilot, as he never flew while I was there. I remember he made a bit of a mess of landing; after several attempts he finally hit a tree and smashed one of his props. But this is getting away from our patrol in *C.17*.

During our return to Pulham it became frightfully bumpy over land and poor old 'Goddles' must have had great difficulty in controlling the ship; I know I had an awful job trying to keep a straight course, as she was bumping about like nothing on earth. However, we eventually got her home in the dark, safe and sound after nine and a quarter hours.

I did not go up in *C.27* on her next trip and was not sorry, as apparently Barton had an awful gruelling. After she left, the wind increased and blew nearly a gale. We on the ground began to fear she would not get back. Fortunately her engines held out, but she was umped and bumped about so much that poor Barton became sick and hit the deck with his front skid when landing. Beyond displacing a strut and snapping a bracing-wire no damage was done.

Goddard in *C.17* also had a bad time, as he had an inexperienced cox'n who kept getting off the wind in coming up to land. The landing-party finally got hold of the trail rope, but before they could run ahead with

* This was the swept channel used by our shipping, marked on both sides with lettered buoys; it was regularly cleared by minesweepers.

it and get the ship head to wind she was blown over until the envelope touched the ground. The fore skid and prop were smashed and the rudder plane buckled. Then she broke away from the landing-party and was being blown straight towards the shed. Fortunately she was light and lifted just over the top of it when Goddard got his after engine going, came round and landed safely after another terrific struggle, with the nose at times touching the ground or the ship careening over and brushing the deck with her side lobe. Phew!

A tragedy occurred at Pulham on 19th April 1917. We were just sitting down to lunch in the Mess when we heard a loud boom. Someone said laughingly: 'There goes the gas plant', little thinking that this was what had actually happened—the silicol plant had exploded. In about a minute poor little Milton, one of the Gas Officers, came staggering into the Mess with his hands to his head. I got him down to my cabin. His ears were full of caustic soda, which was sizzling away in an uncanny fashion. I cleared out as much as I could and took him to the Sick Bay and went, myself, to the gas plant. Nothing could be done there. Lieutenant Wildman and a rating had been blown through the side of the gas-house and were lying 10 and 20 feet respectively from the building; Wildman was dead and the rating badly burned, having been covered with caustic—he died later after the doctor had given him morphia. Lieutenants Bevington and Pollett and a civilian workman were also burned, the latter badly, but the others not so seriously, though Pollett was burned about the face. The injured men were rushed to the large Military Hospital in Norwich. Both Pollett and Wildman had only been with us a couple of days, having come here for instruction.

A lesson might be learned from the fact that the dead man's rubber boots were not in the least affected by the caustic, but the whole crux of the matter lay in the fact that there was no safety valve—such as a water seal around the base of the gas-holder—by which excess pressure could escape.

Between 13th and 20th April we did three relatively short flights, all being cut short by adverse weather conditions, but on 21st we surpassed our previous record, leaving Pulham at 6.50 am and landing at 4.30 pm —9 hours 40 minutes. We patrolled north-eastwards from Yarmouth into a wind of 10 knots with very good visibility, though the sky was overcast. We passed over our usual well-known sea marks—Cross Sands light-vessel and Smith's Knoll pillar buoy, and turned north-westwards, sighting *C.26* about ten miles away to the south-west; then in to the Wash, turning back eastwards off Wells-next-the-Sea, past Sheringham and out to Haisboro' lightship; here we turned south-west for home, crossing the foreshore once more at Mundesley on the north-east coast of Norfolk about eight miles south-east of Cromer. We passed over Norwich at

4 pm and landed at Pulham half an hour later, not being sorry to get the ship safely back into the shed, as the wind became strong and gusty before we landed. In fact, we were bumped about in somewhat similar fashion to *C.17*, while coming in to land and being hauled into the shed; at times the envelope was blown over sideways and brushed the ground with her side lobe—an uncanny feeling sitting in the car when this happened, as you felt you were being tipped out.

This was a disastrous week for Pulham, for when we returned that day we learned that *C.17* had not returned, the last wireless contact with her having been at 9.30 that morning. A trawler had reported 'a Zeppelin brought down in flames fifteen miles off the North Foreland', whilst the Admiralty reported an extract from the German wireless which stated: 'Off Nieuport an enemy airship was shot down into the sea by our airmen from a range of twenty metres in spite of intense counter-defence. In the gondola were eight men and two machine-guns. Berlin Wireless.' In fact, there were only five men on board.*

Thus dear old Jackie and 'Pay' Warlters went. It was a terrible blow to me, as Jackie was my best pal in the service, we having been together off and on since joining at Wormwood Scrubbs. He used to come into my cabin the last thing before going to bed, sit on the end of my bed, and we would air our moans to each other before turning in. Pay Warlters was also a great loss, being a very quiet, unassuming, cheerful chap, always willing to enter into anything that was going on. Goddard would normally have been in the crew—he was away on leave, so Warlters was only up on a 'joy-ride', not being a flying man.

This was not the end of our troubles, for two days later, on 23rd April 1917, we heard that *C.11* from Howden had crashed, fortunately without loss of life. She was flying in thick fog returning from patrol when a hill loomed up immediately ahead. Hogg-Turnour, who was piloting, yanked her up steeply, but the after skid hit the hill and tore off the after part of the car complete with engine and engineer. Thus lightened, the ship, with half a car and minus engine and engineer, shot up like a rocket to 3,000 feet. As the control wires and valve lines had been carried away when she hit, old Hogg could not valve any gas to bring her down or even into equilibrium, so he tried to start the rip panel to ease out a little gas. Unfortunately the pressure of gas at the top of the ship was such that once started there was no stopping it and the rip carried away entirely and split the envelope a further 8 feet beyond. Of course, the ship practically deflated in the air, dropped like a stone, hitting the ground an awful crack, and smashed the remains of the car to matchwood. The pilot, Hogg-Turnour, and the cox'n, whose name I have for-

* *Pilot:* F/Sub-Lt E. G. O. Jackson. *Observer:* Asst Paymaster R. Warlters. *Cox'n:* CPO Chivers. *Engineer:* LM Farquhar. *W.T.Op:* AM Monro.

7 making a force-
ling, February, 1917

: Flying the force-
ling pendant

tre: The handling
y have her under
trol. Her shed can be
away to the right

tom: Safely down
ready for the long
back to the shed

The author at Kingsnorth in 1916

A British SS B.E.2c ship at Grottaglie in Italy in 1917

gotten, each had both legs broken; and the wireless man had internal injuries. The engineer, who became a wing commander in World War II, came off lightest with a broken arm and shock. He and the after engine landed on Scarboro' racecourse about half a mile away from the other part of the ship. He ran to the nearest post office and sent a telegram to Howden: 'Landed safely with engine.' It was lucky they were not all killed. Thus ended a black week for airships.

Next day, 24th April, we were out again in *C.27*. Since the loss of *C.17* we now carried a gunner as a member of the crew. His flying station was with the Lewis gun on top of the ship, and must have been a cold and lonely job, as we rarely did less than seven hours now. We went straight out from Lowestoft for some thirty miles in beautiful weather with a light wind from north-north-west. In conditions like this you feel you are lord of all you survey. Two hours later we were at the south end of Broken Bank when we picked up a message from *C.26* that she was returning from patrol, as her after prop was broken.

At 11.30 am we were a mile south of Haisboro' light-vessel, making for Yarmouth; we reached there just as the seaplane boys were trooping into the 'Royal' for lunch, so we came down low and gave them a chuck-up, and set off for Cross Sands and Would light-vessels through patches of thick fog or low cloud. Then we turned in for the coast and crossed the foreshore at Haisboro'. We passed over Norwich in brilliant warm sunshine which heated up the gas and made us very light, so much so that the landing-party could not hold us after we dropped our trail rope, so we had to valve her down, which we accomplished successfully.

On 26th April 1917 we set off south-eastward and crossed the foreshore at Southwold. With a blue sky, light wind from north-north-west, and a visibility of about thirty miles, we made our usual track for Smith's Knoll pillar buoy, which lies thirty-two nautical miles north-east from Southwold. Thence we carried on northward until about fifty miles north-east of Cromer. The wind was backing all the time; at 11 am it was blowing 12 knots from due west and we altered course for the north coast of Norfolk, which we made at 1 pm near Haisboro'. Then south-east to Cross Sands and in to Yarmouth, where the wind had now backed to due south. We carried on southwards over the War Channel which hereabouts lies about two miles off the coast, turned in and recrossed the foreshore at Orfordness, reaching Pulham at 4.25 pm, having done nine and a quarter hours with seven up, plus two 100-pound bombs, 315 pounds water ballast and 180 gallons of petrol, of which we used 130 gallons.

Barton was not feeling well on 30th April, so I took the ship up myself; then over Lowestoft to our usual happy hunting-ground at Smith's Knoll and carried on up to the Leman Bank. About a mile from the south end of this I sighted a periscope moving through the water. It looked exactly like a black pencil being drawn through water. I had a little difficulty in getting the cox'n to alter course for it, as he could not spot it, by which time it had submerged and left no trace; although when it was above water it made a distinct V, the water was so choppy that no wake was left. As I was the only one aboard who had sighted the periscope, I began to doubt the evidence of my own eyes. However, when we returned reports had been received of submarines off Harwich proceeding north, so this was probably one of them. I sent a W/T report giving position as latitude 53°N Longtitude 2° 10′E which is about a mile from the light buoy at the southern end of Leman Bank. Liaison with the naval authorities was pretty bad, as it took three-quarters of an hour before the report got through to them.

I cruised about the area for a bit and then turned westward to Haisboro' and Would light-vessels, where we spoke to *C.19* from Howden and gave her the position where the periscope had been seen. Returned south to Yarmouth and in to Pulham, landing at 3 pm after seven and three-quarter hours.

Barton was better on 1st May, when we took *C.27* out to Smith's Knoll again. The forward engine was running badly, so Barton stopped it. Harrison, our engineer, found that one of the magneto drives had sheared and the other was half gone. We carried on with the after engine only. These mags were awful; the drives were continually shearing, due, no doubt, to vibration—they should have been robust enough to stand it as they were made up of half-inch-thick steel bars!

Off Lowestoft we sighted two submarines one of which submerged but came up almost immediately. We thought they were ours and asked for the recognition signal—which we received only after another twenty minutes' delay. We *should* have been notified when our subs were expected to be in a certain area, and they should have been instructed to give the recognition signal promptly. Delay could have led to tragedy, as we had orders to bomb any submarine not giving the signal—which they should have done by giving a double spurt of water like a whale. Their excuse for the delay was that, with periscope only above water, they could not see us, which was valid enough, except that when we first saw them their hulls were above water.

Off Aldeburgh we sighted a mass of floating wreckage, timber and barrels, obviously the flotsam from a ship very recently sunk. We heard later that the vessel had been the *Gena* of about 3,000 tons which had been sunk by a torpedo fired from a seaplane. Two had attacked her about two hours before we sighted the wreckage, and she had brought down one of them. The crew of the ship got ashore safely.

We continued southward to Shipwash lightship about ten miles east of Ordfordness; then out to the Outer Gabbard, off which we had a gust properly put up us when we sighted three large warships and eleven destroyers firing their guns! A seaplane came bearing down on us and Barton opened full out, thinking it was a German and we were for Jackie's fate; he told us to put on our life-saving waistcoats—they were not called Mae Wests then. We were much relieved when the seaplane was seen by her markings to be our own, as also were the ships which were from Harwich and carrying out firing practice.

On our way back we saw the remains of the torpedoed ship. It had been beached near Aldeburgh and seemed to have had the after part blown clean off.

Next day, 2nd May, we left Pulham at 6.50 a.m. Soon after leaving Lowestoft in a north-easterly direction we sighted a mass of glass globes upholding a net. In the net were three mines with which some trawlers were dealing. An hour later we sighted a wake on our starboard quarter with no vessel in sight. We made the requisite course for it, only to find it was made by a trawl net being drawn through the water.

We then set course northward and in half an hour reached our old friend Smith's Knoll pillar buoy; continuing northward we soon reached the light buoy at the south end of Leman Bank; then north-west until reaching a point about twenty miles south-east of Spurn Head, where we joined the War Channel and followed it to the Humber. This part of the War Channel was marked by a double line of green conical buoys about two miles apart, each pair having a similar letter different from the other pairs.

At 1.20 pm we were over the Inner Dowsing light-vessel, whose top mark was a smaller black ball superimposed over a larger one at the top of the mast. This lightship lies about sixteen miles north-east of Skegness. Fifteen minutes later we were over the north-east Docking light buoy, a spherical buoy with black and white horizontal stripes lying just off the south-east end of the Dudgeon shoal. We continued southward and were soon over the unmistakable Blakeney Overfalls to the north-west of Cromer. We followed the coast from Cromer to Yarmouth, where we turned in overland and made for Pulham via Norwich. We had been out for ten hours.

C.27 did not go out on 3rd May, as the forward engine was being changed. Colonel Maitland asked me to take him up in *SS.28* to view the newly painted 'Rigid' shed. We went up to 4,000 feet, from which height it was scarcely possible to distinguish the shed from the surrounding country so skilfully had the painting been done to join in with the roads and fields surrounding it. The design for this painting had been made by Johnny Wheelwright, who had been a professional artist before the war.

We had recently received information that German submarines were in the habit of surfacing just before dawn in order to recharge their batteries, so we started trying to get out over the sea early in the hope of catching them—without much success, I'm afraid, though we certainly kept them under water. One extract from the log of a captured German submarine came our way which, in translation, read: 'Sighted airship—submerged'—which is what we wanted to hear.

On 4th May 1917, with our new forward engine fitted, we left the ground at 4 am for its first trial. This was not very encouraging as, immediately after we left the ground it stopped, though it restarted at once on the compressed-air bottle.

We patrolled over our usual line of Lowestoft, Smith's Knoll, Yarmouth, Cross Sands—where we spoke *C.26*; Newarp and Haisboro' Sands—here we carried out some Lewis-gun practice at the wrecks on the sands.

We sighted the submarine *H.10* near Haisboro' lightship. She promptly gave the recognition signal, so our complaint about delay on a previous occasion had borne fruit. In to Yarmouth and home at noon.

On 5th May we left the ground at 4 am and proceeded out to sea from Lowestoft, but saw nothing until 8.15, when, north of Haisboro' light-vessel we sighted a floating mine which we sank with the Lewis gun. At 9 am we were over Broken Bank and altered course to the southward, reaching the pillar buoy at the southern end of Smith's Knoll at 10.10 am; turned westward and made Cockle lightship three miles south-east of Winterton; proceeded coastwise to Yarmouth, where we turned in for Pulham, which was reached at 11.45 am, landing a quarter of an hour later, a trip of exactly eight hours. At 2.50 the same day we went up again to carry out some parachute dropping of dummies for Rear-Admiral Everett and Commodores Ellison and Tyrrwhitt.

I was not sorry the weather was too bad for flying on the 6th May, Sunday, as we had averaged over seven hours a day during the previous week and were getting a bit browned off. I borrowed Barton's Douglas motor bike on which to go to Mass at Bungay—our nearest church and ten miles away. On the way back I ran into some loose gravel at the Rushall turning near the aerodrome. The bike skidded and I came down an awful cropper, landing on my nose and the side of my face. I was practically knocked out, as I remember getting up and falling down again, when along came the tender with the rest of the RCs, who quickly loaded up the bike and myself and took us on to the station. I must have displaced the septum in my nose, as for some forty years afterwards one nostril would be blocked up depending on which side I lay in bed. This was not cured until 1957, when I was hit plumb on the nose by a full toss when playing cricket, which spread the septum and completely blocked *both* nostrils, so that was that—I was sent into hospital, where they completely removed the septum. My nostrils were then as clear as they had been before I had the spill off Barton's motor cycle in 1917, some forty years earlier!

I must have looked a pretty sight after the spill, for my nose and the side of my face and head were all grazed, and I had two black eyes. However, I wouldn't go sick and we did another eight-hour flight on the 7th May, taking with us a Commander Brock who was the son of the firework king. He wished to test some special tinted glasses for use in goggles and binoculars which greatly intensified any colour with red in it. It was so cold during the night that we spent an hour and three-quarters trying to get the engines started; we did not get away until a quarter to six. We went our usual patrol via Lowestoft, Smith's Knoll, Would and Haisboro' light-vessel. When over the latter I began to feel the after effects of my spill, probably what is now called 'delayed shock', and felt fed up with flying. My face was sore and I had a splitting headache, so I asked Barton to make for home, which he did, as Brock had completed his tests. We completed our usual eight hours just the same. After lunch I went straight to bed and slept solidly for sixteen hours, at the end of which I felt as right as rain except for my two black eyes.

On 9th May we were again late in getting away. We went out to Smith's Knoll and in order to test the accuracy of the direction-finding system we asked for our position, and were given one seventeen miles away from where we were. Not very encouraging for accuracy.

When about forty-seven miles north-east of Lowestoft we sighted what appeared to be a periscope and prepared to bomb it, but our cox'n lost sight of it and we were too far away to drop our bombs at random. Soon after we altered course to south-west. On reaching the vicinity of Lowestoft we patrolled up the War Channel in Yarmouth Roads, recrossing the foreshore at Winterton, and landed at Pulham at 3 pm, having completed 8 hours 10 minutes.

I was feeling very cock-a-hoop these days, as I had my second ring and was now of the exalted rank of Flight Lieutenant, RN, dated back to 1st April 1917. (Ominous date! Exactly a year later, with the advent of the Royal Air Force, I was demoted.)

On 10th May we patrolled east from Lowestoft for some thirty miles and then turned back for Yarmouth; then to Cross Sands and out eastwards again for thirty miles; in to Winterton and out to Smith's Knoll, where one of the forward petrol pipes burst. The engineer took it off and bound it with sticky tape and replaced it. By this time we were back off Winterton, where we sighted submarine *H.1*, which promptly gave the recognition signal. We recrossed the foreshore at Winterton and had an uneventful journey back to Pulham. When landing, the trail rope carried away, but Barton made an excellent landing on our fore guys.

We did no flying on the 11th May, as the ground engineers decided to take out our after engine for overhaul, it having run 150 hours. It was a pity, as we lost a beautiful flying day. After lunch I took up *SS.28* to test her elevators. These were OK, but she still flew nose heavy.

The ground staff had not replaced our engine by the 12th, so I again took out *SS.28*, this time to get some photographs of the 'Rigid' shed. Our after engine having been replaced, we took the ship up for an hour's test on 13th May. We also did some runs over the mirror, but did not go on patrol. On the 14th, when over Carlton Coalville, a small village about three miles south-west of Lowestoft, we ran into a bank of fog which was wafted in from the sea and in which we could just see the ground at 400 feet. It remained thick in patches as we proceeded eastwards. When about twenty-five miles east of Lowestoft we sighted the new large Astra-Torres, *NS.1*. She is a similar type to the 'Coastal', but about twice the size, much more streamlined and a better shape. She was under the command of Lieutenant Commander Robinson. He apparently thought there was a danger of our colliding in one of the fog patches, for he signalled us by lamp 'Keep out of my way', though we were about a mile from him and steering a parallel course. Anyway, we turned about and set course for Yarmouth, over whose pier we headed into wind and slowed down to ascertain its strength. We came down a little too low, for our wireless weight caught in the pier and carried away. We soon rigged up another by lashing on the shaft of our starting-handle, and made for Smith's Knoll; reached the pillar buoy at 10.30 am and turned in for Winterton, off which our after engine stopped for no apparent reason, but restarted at once on the air bottle. We set off again to north-east and reached a distance of some forty miles east-north-east of Winterton, where we altered course westward and in an hour found ourselves over the grey conical buoy at Leman Bank after flying through thick banks of fog. In another hour we recrossed the foreshore at Mundesley on the north-east coast of Norfolk about seven miles south-east of Cromer. Over the land it was quite clear, but the fog appeared like a white wall of cotton wool along the coast and over the sea. We had a very bumpy journey back, but were safely in the hands of the landing-party at 4 pm.

On examining the forward engine after we landed, all the propeller bolts except two had sheared. We were lucky the prop had not flown off.

On 18th May I was busy finishing off the rigging of *SS.28*, so was not available for *C.27*. Barton took her up on his own, but the fog clamped down on him and by the time he reached Beccles he could not see 50 yards, so he decided to make a forced landing which he did at the Lovat's Scouts' camp near that town. He rang me up and asked me to take over some sand bags and air bottles. This I did and acted as cox'n for the return, still in thick fog. I managed to stick to the Waveney Valley line, which led us safely back to Pulham, where Barton made an excellent landing on the skids. Had he maintained height to drop the trail rope we should not have seen the landing-party at all, which gives some idea of the thickness of the fog.

We did not get off the ground until 9.30 am on the 19th May. We made our usual route to Smith's Knoll, where we saw an uncommon buoy, a small conical one with a diagonal blue and red flag attached at the top and a line of three black spheres floating from it on the water. I never found out what it meant! We then made our way to Cromer and out to Haisboro' light-vessel, followed the line of sands to the Would and in to the War Channel from Winterton to Yarmouth, and so back to Pulham, having put in only six and a quarter hours, using seventy gallons of petrol.

We went off at 7 am for our next flight, but had got only about two miles beyond Harleston—five miles from the aerodrome—when the cox'n reported the forward petrol tank leaking badly. One could see it spurting out in a jet where it had previously been mended. We turned about at once and were over the landing-ground in a few minutes; signalled by lamp 'Petrol tank leaking, desire to land immediately'; then had to fly round until the landing-party was mustered. We landed at 7.45 am, and found we had lost forty gallons of petrol in the short time we had been out. I was in sole charge on this flight, Barton being away.

Barton was still unavailable on the 25th May, so I took the ship up. We left at 6.50 am with ninety gallons of petrol in each tank. We had no sooner left the ground than the forward engine stopped, but restarted immediately. It was somewhat misty over the sea off Lowestoft, with visibility three to five miles, with a light wind behind us. Very soon we saw a beautiful sight—two Dutch sailing-vessels, *Spesmel* and *Zwerein*, under full sail.

When about thirty miles out I altered course to north-west and hit off Smith's Knoll centre buoy, a black can buoy with a black globe as top mark. I came in to Yarmouth, where I found the wind had increased and the visibility had improved to about ten miles. I followed the War Channel until off Winterton, when I set off eastward again, reaching the pillar buoy at the south end of Smith's Knoll at 11.05 am, where I set course 345°T., and made the light buoy at the south end of Well Bank an hour later. Harrison here took a petrol check and reported we had used eighteen gallons from the forward tank and thirty from the after one, leaving seventy-two and sixty gallons respectively.

At one o'clock a W/T message came from Pulham asking for our position; I replied in code: 'At 1 o'c. B.S.T. position over Haisboro' middle buoy.' We proceeded in over Cromer and then out to the Haisboro' and Would light-vessels. A little later we received 'Return to Pulham'—so we turned westward and recrossed the foreshore at Yarmouth, running the forward engine slowly, as it was behaving shakily. I finally landed at 5.50 pm, a duration of eleven hours and my longest flight up till now. Had I not been recalled I should have beaten the Pulham record of twelve hours by Dixon in *C.26*. Perhaps it was just as well, as after landing it was found that propeller bolts on the forward engine had sheared.

As it turned out, this was my last flight at Pulham until I returned there in *S-R.1* a few days before the war ended.

A new envelope arrived for *C.27* on 26th May 1917 to replace our present one, which was a bad shape and twisted. We deflated at once preparatory to rigging the new envelope. In the meantime, however, we had our first Station Sports Meeting, the highlight of which was a donkey chariot race.

I was a member of the Sports Committee and with others had been all round the neighbourhood trying to persuade the owners of donkey chaises to lend both their donkeys and chaises to us for a race. The owners were mostly old ladies, whose only mode of conveyance round the countryside and for shopping they were, so it is small wonder that most of them were very chary of lending, fearing that they might be ill-treated. I promised there would be no whips or sticks used and finally persuaded four old dears to lend us their mokes and vehicles. The animals were all in first-class condition, but the vehicles were the most ramshackle-looking conveyances imaginable.

At that time we had four ships in commission on the Station, so we numbered each chaise with a ship's number and rigged up four of the Committee in flying-clothes as 'pilots'. It is impossible to describe the scene when they lined up—everyone was shrieking with laughter; never in all my life have I seen such a funny turn-out. No sooner had we set them off than the captains of the four ships sprang on to the track and ran to the head of the donkey drawing their respective 'ship', and tried to help them along.

The oldest car, which must have come out of the ark, had the best donkey, and was proudly led home by the captain of *NS.1*, Lieutenant Commander Robinson, closely followed by Cole-Hamilton leading *No. 4* and Dixon with *C.26*; Godfrey with *C.27* brought up the rear, a poor last.

We commenced inflating our new envelope on 8th June, but could not complete it, as the gas-holder ran out of gas. I applied for week-end leave, which I was given, but, on arriving home, I found a telegram instructing me to report to the 'Cecil Hotel' in the Strand. This was the

RNAS Headquarters in London and known throughout the service as 'The Bolo'. I called on Commander Hunt, who was personnel chief, and he asked me if I would like to go to Italy as Second-in-Command to John Barron. The Admiralty had sold half a dozen SS ships to Italy and our job would be to rig and test them and instruct Italian officers in flying them. Of course, I accepted and was immediately packed off to the Crystal Palace to be inoculated. When I returned to Pulham, I requested an interview with Colonel Maitland and told him that I had accepted the Italian job—he knew all about it, of course, as he had recommended me for it and had initiated the telegram instructing me to call at the 'Cecil'.

After doing most of my packing I returned to London for my second inoculation and to be measured for my khaki drill uniform.*

On arrival at Liverpool Street, I found it had been subjected to a daylight air raid by fifteen aeroplanes. A train entering the station had been hit and all the glass in the station roof was gone. About 150 people were killed and 500 injured. This apparently was the first daylight raid on London, and all the raiders got away.

I met John Barron, whom I had liked so much at Anglesey. He was an officer in the Royal Canadian Navy and the son of a Canadian judge. We went down to Wormwood Scrubbs together, where the ships were being collected prior to dispatch to Italy by rail. He was going on ahead with the main body of our party consisting of twenty-three ratings, while I was to follow later with our Engineer Officer, Lieutenant Geoffrey Maund, RNVR, who was then at Scrubbs assisting with the overhaul of the engines before dispatch.

* I have recently (1965) presented the tunic of this uniform to the Royal Naval Museum at Greenwich, as they apparently wanted RN uniforms of the First World War.

CHAPTER THREE

Grottaglie Aeroscalo, Italy

According to Admiralty Orders for July 1917, I had been appointed to *HMS Queen* at Malta for service with *Queen II*, a subsidiary ship moored in the Mare Piccolo at Taranto, additional for service with the Italian Naval Airship Station at Grottaglie, a small village about six miles from Taranto on the road to Otranto.

I picked up Geoff Maund at the Scrubbs and we caught the 8.50 am train from Charing Cross to Folkestone; had a smooth crossing and spent the afternoon sight-seeing around Boulogne. We caught the night train for Paris, which was frightfully slow, crawling along at about ten miles an hour and stopping at every station. Arrived in Paris we called on the Italian naval attaché, Commander Leone, who invited us to lunch at the 'Ritz'. Then we caught the night train for Rome via Turin. After a good sleep on the train we passed through the most glorious scenery of mountains and lakes, the former wreathed in mist and the latter as blue as the sky above. We changed into an Italian train at Modane, near the frontier, and had a clean-up at a hotel in Turin before catching yet another night train for Rome, where we arrived early on the morning of the 28th July 1917.

We dumped our gear at the 'Continental Hotel' and, after nearly scalding myself by turning on the tap marked '*caldo*' because it looked like 'cold', we hired a horse-drawn carriage and signalled to the driver to drive us around the city. We spoke no Italian and he no English. Anyway, he took us a good round, to St Peters, the Janiculum Hill, the Pantheon, the Capitol, the Forum and the Coliseum, so I think we received good value for the eleven lire the old cabby charged us. We also stood him lunch at a café near St Peter's. I remember our amazement at the enormous helpings of spaghetti or macaroni served, and the dexterity with which the Italians manipulated their forks in eating it. In the evening we went to the Opera House and heard *Pagliacci* and *Cavalleria Rusticana*, in which the principals were magnificent, but the chorus rather poor.

Next morning I went to St Peter's and heard Mass sung by Cardinal Rampolla, who would have been Pope but for Austrian opposition. He had a beautifully strong voice, very clear, but I did not think much of the

Sistine choir. Their tone was harsh and loud, especially the boys, who shouted—not a patch on my old choir at the Brompton Oratory! In the afternoon we went to the Catacombs of St Callistus. At the entrance was a little Trappist monk who gave us a special welcome as we were British, saying he was the same, being a Maltese.

On 30th June Maund and I went to the Vatican for an audience of Pope Benedict XV, arranged for us by Father Denis Sheil of the Birmingham Oratory. We were conducted through various rooms, in one of which were Swiss Guards in their picturesque, variegated, slashed uniforms. In another were several scarlet-clothed footmen, one of whom led us into the antechamber where a gaudily dressed officer of the Papal Guard, with gold epaulettes and sash, was pacing back and forth before a dozen or so persons awaiting audience. We were then conducted into the Audience Room, in which was a dais with a plain red and gold throne.

The 'Maestro dell'ante-camera' came up and greeted us and told us what we had to do. He was an Irishman named O'Neill and told us how pleased he was to be able to speak English with someone. We were then conducted into yet another room with a throne, and lined up to await the entry of His Holiness, who was preceded by a bishop in purple; we all knelt down and the Pope passed along the line offering his hand and ring to be kissed, saying a few words to each. He was a short, thin man with a dark complexion; dressed completely in white, which stood out in strong contrast to the gaudy dress of the officials. When he came to me he asked me in French if we were Belgians; I replied, 'Non—Anglais—English.'

That evening we took the train for Taranto, arriving there at 10 am next morning. We had no idea where we were to go, so we called at Commodore Murray Sueter's office; he was out, so we went and made our number with *HMS Queen*, lying at anchor in the Mare Piccolo. Very soon a car arrived for us and took us to No. 6 Wing Base at Pizzone, a small village about two miles out of Taranto. Here we were glad to see John Barron, who introduced us to the CO, Commander Beuttler, RNVR, whom we found a really charming chap. He is the man who used to do the comic drawings for *The Bystander*.

We were to stay at Pizzone for the time being, as the quarters for the men were not ready at the *Aeroscalo*—the airship station. We went over there and found that our stores had arrived and we also had a pleasant surprise when we found that one of the officers stationed there was Vigliani, who had been at Kingsnorth when I was there.

We spent nearly three weeks at Pizzone with occasional visits to Grottaglie, where we were made very welcome in the Mess. John Barron was to live on the station, but as there was no accommodation there for Maund and myself, we had been given a nice little white stone bungalow on top of the hill above the village of Grottaglie. It was quite close to some cave dwellings cut in the chalk—hence the name of the village. Some of these are still occupied and the chimneys, with smoke emerging, can be seen sticking up through the top of the chalk. I am sorry now that we did not ask to see inside some of them.

As it was the hot time of the year, we started early and finished early, with a siesta between lunch and tea. The routine was:

First parade	5.30 am
Breakfast	8.00 am
Divisions	8.30 am
Dinner	11.00 am
Siesta	
Tea	3.00 pm
Second parade	3.30 pm
Supper	6.00 pm
Lights out	10.30 pm

A car fetched us in the morning in time for the first parade and took us home after dinner in the mess in the evening—we had all our meals in the Mess with the Italians. Most of the meat we ate was goat or kid flesh, and very good it was, too. None of us spoke Italian, but we got on pretty well with Vigliani, who spoke very good English, as our interpreter. Unfortunately he was soon posted away to the new SS Station being opened at Otranto. He later on became a member of the crew of the large 'Semi-Rigid' *A-1*, which was being constructed at Ciampino, near Rome. This left only the Second-in-Command, Mezzadra, with any English and that only a smattering—meal-times after Vigliani had left were great fun!

We got stuck into inflating the first ship straight away, but found it was a longer job than we had anticipated, as the gas plant could make only 15,000 cubic feet at a time; then the plant had to be cleared out for another charge. It took us all day to get the envelope up to shape, after which it did not take long to get the car rigged.

In the evenings we played tennis on a court laid out on the concrete outside the shed doors. None of us were any great shakes, but it was a scream to see some of the Italian Army officers attached to the station. They used to play in full uniform: hat, jacket, breeches and spurs! Needless to say, the tennis was not of a very high order.

John Barron and I were given a trip lasting about two hours in the Italian *M-6* of some 440,000 cubic feet capacity. We went out to sea for about ten miles from Taranto. The water was pellucidly clear, and the mine-fields showed up quite clearly in rows of pale green spots against the deep blue of the Mediterranean.

We were all being bitten to death by sand-flies and stung by mosquitoes—the itching was torture until we obtained some anti-mosquito ointment from the Sick Bay. Then Maund and I had an attack of dysentery. Maund was pretty bad and had to be taken to Pizzone to be attended to by our naval doctor, Surgeon Dyke. I got rid of most of mine during the night by vomiting and diarrhoea, and was left with occasional tummy pains and general weakness. However, I managed to do some of the trials of *SS.22*, the first ship we completed.

I spent all the week carrying out these trials; the flights were not of long duration and I took the opportunity of giving Geoff Maund and some of our NCOs and men a flip, which they much appreciated.

One night we had a terrific thunderstorm, with enormous flashes of forked lightning about every two seconds lighting up the whole sky—some were vertically zig-zag and some horizontal, a most impressive but fearsome sight. I was jolly glad to be safe on the deck. Another evening, Geoff Maund and I went with four Italian officers to the local theatre in Grottaglie. The main audience consisted of dirty-looking, unshaven and unkempt Italian infantrymen. We were the élite in a box! The orchestra was a scream, mostly brass, and exactly like the prewar itinerant German band with its *Oom-pom-pom*! *Oom-pom-pom*!—but out of tune and time. If the audience didn't like a turn, they were not backward in showing disapproval, blowing out 'raspberries', and shying coppers on to the stage.

During the latter half of August 1917 I was occupied in giving Italian officers instruction in piloting before handing over the ship to a pilot from the small Italian airship station on the coast at San Vito, about ten miles from Grottaglie. My instruction was mostly in dumb show, because I was not yet exactly conversant with the language! As another ship now arrived, we handed *SS.22* over to the Italians and they flew her to San Vito. At the end of the month. I was taken in the Italian *M.6* on a short patrol over the Mare Grande as far as the twin islands of Saints Peter and Paul.

There was great excitement on the station on Sunday, 2nd September. *SS.22* was adrift in the upper air. It seems that her engine stopped during flight and her pilot valved her down. When near the ground, the W/T op and the engineer jumped out and the ship, thus lightened, shot up to 3,000 feet with only the pilot aboard. She had then come down pretty heavily. The pilot said he was thrown out when she hit the deck, though I think he may have jumped out like the others. Anyway, the ship floated away up to about 10,000 feet and three Nieuports were sent up to try to bring her down with their machine-guns. This was accomplished successfully and the ship landed a few miles away little the worse for the experience beyond the envelope being riddled with holes. She was brought back by lorry to Grottaglie. I examined the car and engine immediately on her arrival and found the gravity tank empty—obviously the pilot had forgotten to pump up his petrol, thus causing the engine stoppage.

Unhappily a sad tragedy resulted, for on one occasion when the ship came down to earth an old man working in a field had hung on to the trail rope or one of the handling guys; he did not let go when the ship went up again until she had reached a height of about 50 feet from the ground and so he was, of course, killed.

Our riggers spent the whole of the following week repairing the envelope, which had over two hundred bullet-holes in it. Repair of those in the main envelope was plain sailing, but it was not so easy to locate those in the ballonets—which are in the base of the envelope. We eventually overcame the difficulty by letting down some hand torches through the top valve and then, crawling up into the ballonet, one could see the pinpoints of light shining through the bullet-holes. When the repairs were finished the envelope looked like an aluminium-coloured leopard, with all its little round patches. Even when doped over they still showed up.

Grottaglie village is pretty ancient, as there is a hospital there founded in 1474. The village children we saw were a pitiable-looking lot, being small, stunted, pale and anaemic, most of them with sore eyes and scabs on their faces. Women seemed to do all the work in the fields; the only men we saw were the old men sitting outside their front doors; the young ones were, of course, all away in the army.

Two Capronis landed on 27th September, *en route* for Albania. These were enormous machines, being about 90 feet wide. Imagine this great machine looping the loop, which one of them did at a height of about 3,000 feet before landing. It seemed to loop very slowly, making a comparatively small loop, and landed as slowly as an SS ship.

Although the car and engine of *SS.22* were undamaged, we were asked to rig one of the Italian cars to the repaired envelope; we therefore slung their car numbered *DE.4* to it.

An envelope for *SS.5* arrived at Grottaglie railway station on 17th September. Thinking to save time, Maund and I and some ratings went along in our Lancia tender and a trolley to collect it. Instead of saving time by taking a short cut across the fields, we lost it by becoming bogged, and had to get a heavy lorry from the *Aeroscalo* to pull us out. We thought we had missed our lunch, but it had been kept for us; moreover the CO, De Bei, sent us in a bottle of Tokay wine which we polished off with great gusto.

There was much excitement at the *Aeroscalo* one evening on account of an air-raid alarm. Brindisi was bombed and we could see many shells bursting in that direction. The enemy planes did not reach us, though they were reported over Francavilla a town about five miles away.

We had an extraordinary experience at lunch one day. Whilst eating and talking away merrily, there came a terrific bang and a bright flash from the electric light over our heads. There was a thunderstorm at the time, and a lightning flash must have struck the building and run down the electric wiring, shorting it, as there was a hole through the metal piping carrying the wires. Fortunately no one was struck, but it was an unnerving experience and a close shave for all present.

We had an enjoyable picnic early in October. John Barron and I, with Robinson, the engineer officer at Pizzone, and his friend Peck, an officer in the Rifle Brigade, and a dozen men of our port watch, borrowed the *Queen*'s picket boat and went in it through the canal joining the Mare Piccolo to the Mare Grande, and dropped anchor in a sandy bay on the eastern shore of the Mare Grande; we all had a swim and then waded ashore with our lunch of ham sandwiches made with lovely white bread which we had obtained from the *Queen*—it was a pleasant change from the dark brown Italian bread. We topped up with cheese, apples, peaches, grapes, figs and nuts in the eating line, and bottles of Pommard and Marsala for drinks. After this repast fit for a king, I finished a very amusing book by W. W. Jacobs and then enjoyed a siesta before we weighed anchor and returned.

On one of our visits to Pizzone, Squadron Commander Edmonds informed John Barron and myself that we had both been Mentioned in Despatches: I racked my brains trying to think what I had done to deserve it, but really I could think of nothing outstanding.

There was little work we could do for a time, as the shed space was fully occupied by Caproni aircraft and the Italian ships. Moreover, we were awaiting the arrival of our next ship to rig. John Barron thought it a good opportunity for seeing more of Italy and we managed to get in a good spell of sight-seeing.

When we returned we found we might have taken a longer holiday, as there was still no shed space available. However, ten days later the Italians, after some persuasion, rearranged the Samls and Capronis and we were able to inflate *SS.5* on 7th November 1917. Two days previously the Italian officer responsible for testing and taking over the ships from us took out *DE.4*—the one we had re-rigged on the repaired envelope—and unfortunately tore the envelope on the shed door as he was taking her out. A hole about 6 feet in length was torn in her and she quickly deflated, though we managed to save her planes from any worse damage than a tear in the fabric covering. The repair would entail two entirely new panels so this was indeed an unlucky envelope!

We completed rigging *SS.5* on 9th November, but it was not until the 14th that John Barron was able to take her out for her first trials. After a further week of bad weather I took her up for more trials and got her up to 7,300 feet at which height her ballonets were completely empty of air, the envelope being full of gas; because of this I could properly assess the correctness of her rigging, that is, whether she was down by the nose or tail when in equilibrium. Most of the ships rigged at Wormwood Scrubbs before being sent out to us we found to have been rigged down by the nose, and we had to alter the lengths of the suspension wires in order to correct this. It was pretty cold at the height I have mentioned, and the engine was missing from 5,000 feet upwards.

On 22nd November 1917 I took *SS.5* up for an hour to give instruction in piloting to an Italian WO named Mendozza. When ballasting up for landing, I found the ship to be very light so I pulled on the lower gas valve to level things up. On coming up to the landing-party, I was amazed to find the ship heavy, and it was only by opening up the engine to full throttle that I managed to clear the handling-rails which run out on to the landing-ground from inside the shed. I took the ship round again as she picked up height on her elevators, with the engine going full out, and had just got round the shed and was approaching the landing-party when I found I could not hold her up any longer. I had to land on some newly ploughed land under the lee of the shed. I hit the ground rather heavily; No. 2 suspension wire carried away, went into the propeller and smashed it. One of our riggers, 'Ginger' Mann, came running up and closed the gas valve, which had stuck open—the heart-shaped thimble holding the control wire had jammed in the fairlead and so prevented the valve closing. It was fortunate no greater damage was done, and we had the ship ready for flight the same evening.

During another flight next day we experienced numerous bumps in the region of a funny little village called Villa Castelli perched right on top of a hill about a thousand feet high. I would make good about 200 yards and then a gust would catch me on one side of the bow and blow me backwards, so finally I called it a day and went in to land. It was still gusty and bumpy, even on the ground, and just after the landing-party had got hold of the trail rope and were hauling the ship down, a side gust blew her off wind and bumped her down sideways on to one of the landing-wheels, bursting it; then another gust from the opposite direct tion dumped her on to the other wheel and burst that one also. I was more than glad when the ship was finally housed in the hangar safe and sound.

The acceptance flight for Tenente Ilari was a two-hour trip over the Gulf of Taranto. The engine was missing badly and we found on landing that the carburettor was nearly choked with ice; it was decided to fit a muffler over the air intake.

Both John Barron and I felt the cold very much. This was surprising, as John was a Canadian and used to very much colder weather in Canada, but it was a damp cold here which got right into your bones and we had no warm clothing—and only one blanket at night. I slipped

A North Sea Astra-Torres ship showing petrol tanks slung on the side of the ship

The Would Light Vessel in 1917, from the author's airship

Lowthorpe Mooring-out Station showing the narrow entrance to the clearing

Pulham air station in 1916 from *SS.28*

An SS. ship during inflation at Grottaglie

Lunch over the Mediterranean aboard the Italian *M–1* from Ciampino. The author is seated, left, with the Commander, Major Leone. August 1918

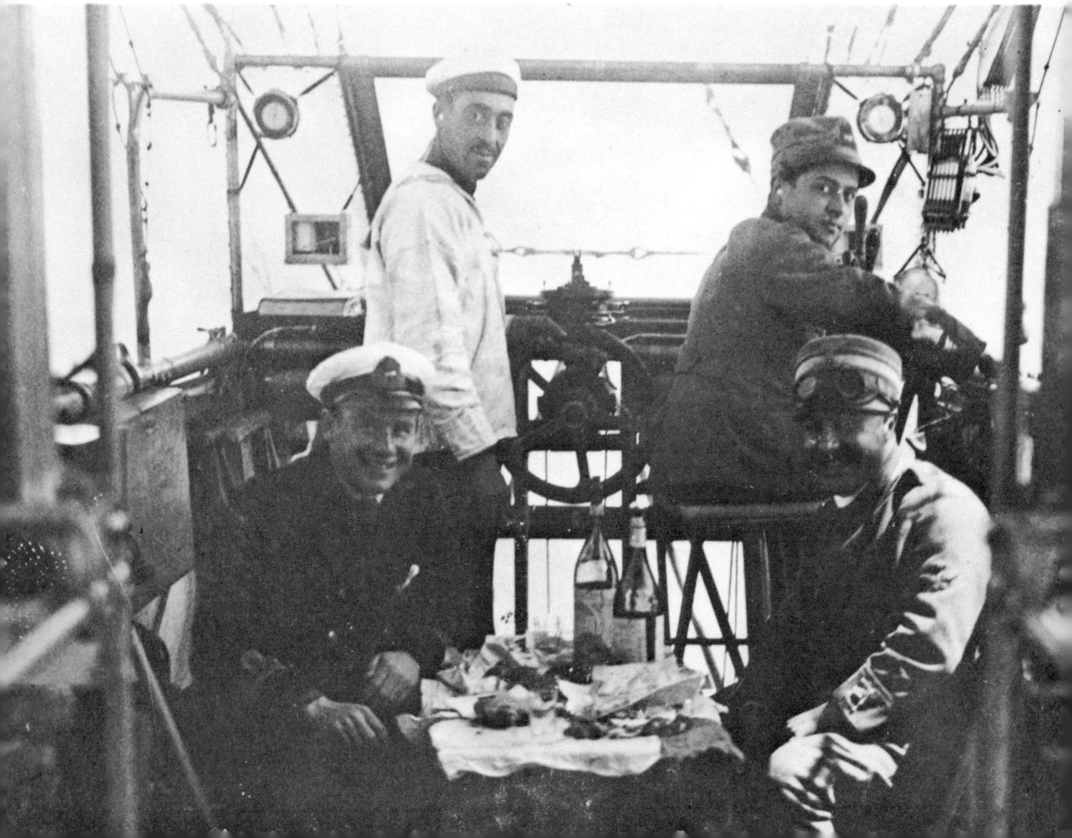

newspapers between my sheet and blanket, which conserved the heat. Apparently such cold weather in this area is unusual and there were no fireplaces in the bungalow or in the Mess. On 5th December 1917 an almost unknown event occurred in the district—a heavy fall of snow. We woke up to find the ground white with it, and during the day had some more. It was bitterly cold in the shed with only our tropical uniform.

We saw some glorious sunsets from the hill above Grottaglie where our bungalow lay. The sun setting behind the mountains of Calabria, some fifty miles away, threw the peaks into silhouette until they looked no more than ten miles away. The sky was magnificent, changing from a bright red to a dull copper, then through various shades of green until only the sombre grey of the clouds tinged with red was left. I wish I had had a colour cine-camera, but I don't think they were invented then!

We read in a small paragraph in an Italian paper that a British airship had been brought down by a German seaplane in the southern part of the North Sea on 11th December. This turned out to be dear old Dixon in my former ship, *C.27*. It was lost with all five hands; next day Kilburn spent the whole day in *C.26* searching for any remains or survivors. He ran out of petrol before he got back to Pulham and was blown as a free balloon across the North Sea to Holland, where he landed and was interned. With him on this flight was Chichele Plowden, another old Anglesey boy.

On Christmas Day 1917 the *Aeroscalo* at Grottaglie was honoured by a visit from a nephew of the King of Italy—Prince Aimone di Savoia—who was being trained as a seaplane pilot at the Italian station at Pizzone. He was a quiet, unassuming type, of about twenty years of age, standing about six-foot-two and had a good strong handshake. After a cinema show he came to the Mess for dinner, which dragged on until 10.30 pm. As I had been up since 5.30 am for the inflation and slinging of the car of *SS.11*, I was feeling properly tired and was not sorry when the Capitano di Corvetto accompanying the Prince sent for the car to take them back to Pizzone.

John Barron went on a visit, with Squadron Commander Lucas of our Airship HQ in London, to Ferrara—an Italian operational station near Venice; when he got back he carried out the trials of *SS.11* on 31st December 1917. I did some further trials in her on 1st January 1918, and was then asked to go up with an Italian officer for acceptance trials. I was given to understand that he was a fully qualified SS pilot, but it did not take me long to twig that this was his first flight in an SS, or probably in any other airship, as he took absolutely no notice of his gas pressure, whilst taking the ship up at an incredibly steep angle to 4,000 feet, where the engine started missing, probably due to ice in the carburettor. He shook me good and proper, and I had my work cut out trying to keep the pressure within bounds. Finally, coming in to land, he kept his engine going full tilt, and I had to close his throttle for him. Even then we landed too fast and dragged the landing-party over the ground a bit. They were very good, however, and did not let go—and no one was hurt, for which I was very thankful.

We had rigged a second envelope to *SS.6*, as the original one had had some acid spilled on it, causing holes. Soon after completing the rigging of the second envelope I was woken up at 2 am by our chief rigger, PO Clarke, who reported that *SS.6* was down on the deck. I quickly threw on some clothes and hurried to the shed to find that his report was only too true—the tail was sagging on to the floor of the shed. To prevent damage to her planes, I told Clarke to unship them and while this was being done, I organised the insertion of eighty-one tubes of hydrogen into the envelope—which brought her back to shape and pressure. We had to do all this in pitch dark, as there were no lights in the shed.

Apparently what had happened was that the Italian gas guard had allowed the pressure to fall very low; this altered the shape of the ship and caused a pull on the top gas valve and so the envelope had begun to deflate of its own accord. This had started at 12.30 am, but the gas guard had not called PO Clarke until 1.30, by which time the after part of the envelope was down on the deck. Clarke promptly closed the valve by the tricing-line and called me. Little damage was done beyond a plane skid being broken and the rudder kingpost bent, whilst a small hole was made in the envelope when taking down the planes in the dark. The gas guard must either have fallen asleep or did not know his job.

I took up *SS.6* for further trials on 6th January. With me were our Stores Officer, WO Hardy, and PO Whyte, an engineer. Amongst other things I tested the 'crab-pots'. These are reversible fabric valves for blowing air into the ballonets so as to maintain pressure without altering height; there is one for each ballonet. They are situated in the air duct which runs along the bottom of the envelope and are connected to the blower tube or scoop up which the air is blown by the speed of the ship through the air or by the blast from the propeller. The crab-pots are opened and closed by means of wires operated by the pilot. The ship was then tested by the acceptance officer and, this completed, she was duly accepted and orders were given to deflate and pack her up for transport to her station.

We could now see the end of our mission approaching, as we had only two more ships to complete.

Although *SS.4* and *SS.11* had been taken over by the Italians, it was left to us to deflate, unrig and pack them up for dispatch. So it was not until the 9th January 1918 that we were clear to start the inflation of *SS.4*—this had been another of my old ships at Capel in 1916.

We completed her on 12th January and I took her up for first trials and to carry out a bomb-dropping experiment for information relative to a proposed invention by Commodore Murray Sueter.* His idea was to drop two torpedoes simultaneously down chutes set at an angle on either side of the fuselage. The torpedoes were joined by wire underneath. A mechanism was incorporated in them by which, after being dropped a-straddle an object in the water and immersed, they were turned inwards towards the object. Our part in the experiment was to ascertain how far apart the torpedoes would fall when dropped from heights of 500 and 1,000 feet, the angle of the chute being the same for each height. We did not use torpedoes, of course, but large stones. The respective distances apart were 53 and 107 feet measured on the ground.

Acceptance trials were flown on 14th January and we had unrigged, deflated and packed up *SS.4* for transport by the 16th. We commenced inflating our last ship, *SS.10*, next day.

On the 16th January the CO of *M.6*—Commander De Bei—offered John Barron and myself a patrol trip in her. As soon as we were out over the Mare Grande and into the Gulf of Taranto, De Bei asked me to take over the elevators. We flew east past Cape Santa Maria di Leuca at the southern tip of the heel of Italy, out into the Straits of Otranto, sighting Fano and Corfu islands; then turned north for Otranto, off which there was great activity of motor launches, drifters and seaplanes. There were fourteen people on board for this flight of six hours. We heard later that one of our No. 6 Wing Short seaplanes had bombed a submarine that morning.

SS.10 was completed on 19th January and John Barron took her up for first trials on the 21st. Afterwards I took our Assistant Paymaster back to Pizzone in her, landing in a field opposite the Officers' Mess. I was welcomed by Commandante Valli, the CO of the Italian seaplane station there, and by Commander Beuttler, the British CO, whom I picked up and took back to lunch at the *Aeroscalo*, first flying over Taranto, our Seaplane Erection Base at North Shore and the British army camp at Cimino above the north side of the Mare Piccolo. Further trials were carried out on 22nd and 24th January, on which date she was accepted and taken over by the Italians.

On 22nd January a submarine was reported off Gallipoli, a small town

* Murray Sueter was one of the prime movers in the invention and construction of the original tank, in company with Tennyson d'Eyncourt and, I believe, Fred Boothby, later on to be my CO at Pulham, where we had one of the original tanks towards the end of the war. Boothby's idea was to use tanks to haul airships in and out of the sheds.

on the coast near the southern inside heel of Italy, and De Bei offered me another trip in *M.6* to try to locate it. We left the ground at 11.20 am with thirteen on board, armed with bombs and a 37 mm cannon. Except for numerous English motor-boats, we saw nothing, but had a very pleasant flight over the Mare Grande and Gulf of Taranto, during which I took the controls for an hour.

I spent the 23rd checking over stores and spares with Ilari. This was a long tedious job, as Ilari insisted on counting every bolt and nut, and I had the job of translating the names of the various items. John Barron was busy in Taranto making arrangements for our journey home. In the evening John and I went for a walk up the hill to 'Old Grottaglie', a collection of cave dwellings cut in the chalk hillside, and still inhabited. We made our way back across country along the line of an aqueduct being laid in a ditch, and saved the life of a sheep which we discovered on its back in the ditch and unable to get out.

When I was over at Pizzone on 21st January, Commandante Valli had offered me a flight in a seaplane, so, as we had little more to do, I went over there on the 28th and was welcomed by Prince Aimone, who fitted me out with flying-helmet and jacket. I was then taken up in an Italian FBA, a small flying-boat—I believe the initials stood for Franco-British-American. It glided over the water very smoothly, and I was unaware when we left the water. What struck me most in the flying of this machine was the extreme delicacy of the controls, as the pilot never seemed to move either elevator or rudder more than about half an inch. Apart from moving faster, there is little difference from airship flying, though in first planing down to make a landing you get a pleasant tingling feeling in your tummy. Skimming over the water after alighting was like riding in a splendidly sprung car running along a road that undulates at regular intervals. This was my first trip in a plane of any kind and I thoroughly enjoyed the experience.

In the afternoon De Bei offered me another patrol trip in *M.6*, which, of course, I accepted. As soon as we cleared Taranto into the Mare Grande I was put on the elevator controls, where I remained until the end of the trip, including the landing, and was congratulated on my handling of the ship by her Captain. Fifteen persons were on board for this trip.

The chief of the Italian Airship Section, Cap. di V. Denti, came to dinncr that night at the *Aeroscalo* and personally thanked John Barron for our work and told him that he had recommended us both for the decoration of *Cavaliere dell'Ordine della Corona d'Italia*—Knight of the Order of the Crown of Italy. John was going home ahead of the main party and I went to see him off at Taranto; also at the station were some of the officers from Pizzone and the CO and other officers of the *Aero-*

scalo, an indication of how well liked and respected John was by both British and Italians.

I felt like a fish out of water without old John, who was one of the finest men I have ever met—absolutely straight, infinitely kind and always ready to go out of his way to do one a good turn. He was wonderful with the men, and the Italians loved him, though he never learned a word of Italian the whole time we were there. His one attempt at Italian was '*noce crackio*'—*schiaccianoce* or nut-crackers!

The morning of 29th January I spent in the shed superintending the final packing up of *SS.10* and our own gear, which we completed just as '*Mensa*' sounded for lunch.

Although pleased that we had completed our job and were going home, I felt a regret that it would be the last time I would sit down to lunch with the very friendly Italian officers in the Mess, both naval and military. The Italian airship people are mostly naval, whilst the various auxiliaries such as the fighter defence squadron pilots and anti-aircraft defence officers are Army. They had all been most kind and hospitable to us; their affectionate name for me was '*il Piccolo Giorgio*' because I am only 5 foot 4½ inches in height. They gave us a great send off when we finally left.

The rest of our party and myself were to join a military train from Cimino Camp on the north side of Mare Piccolo; on the way there I looked in at No. 6 Wing Base at Pizzone to say good-bye to Commander Beuttler, Ferris Scott, Lister and the other officers who had always treated us as members of their Mess. Assistant Paymaster Curd took me by car to Cimino. Our men with the baggage were already there. There was no first-class accommodation on the train, so I had to make do with a second-class carriage without seat cushions and with one of the windows without glass. I managed to scrounge some seat cushions, with one of which I blocked up the paneless window, and I made myself fairly snug and warm with a blanket, my 'lamby suit' or duffel jacket, overcoat, and finally my dressing-gown. I had the whole compartment to myself, as the broken window and lack of cushions had put others off. There was, of course, no heating or lighting on the train, and it was very difficult to get any water either for washing or drinking. Anyway, it was a great deal better than the *Hommes 40*; *Chevaux 8* of the French trains of the period.

CHAPTER FOUR

Return to England

We finally left Cimino at 7.30 pm on 29th January 1918 to commence our seemingly interminable journey up the east coast of Italy, right across the country to the Riviera, and across France to Cherbourg. We reached Bari at 6 am next morning and were there issued with our day's rations, consisting of half a loaf of bread, a one-pound tin of corned beef and a half-pound tin of jam between five—not a very fattening prospect. I also managed to cajole from the engine-driver enough hot water for a wash and shave, after which I felt fine.

Being a military train, the personnel on board were mostly soldiers going on leave, but there was also a sprinkling of naval personnel, including our little party, all under the charge of Lieutenant House, RN, who occasionally came down and had a chat. It turned out that he had been a shipmate of 'Skipper' Cunningham, my former CO at Capel. There was a colonel in overall charge of the train, but he kept very much to himself. A very nice RAMC captain named McKie used to spend quite a time in my compartment, and we usually shared our meals; he told me he was on his way home from Egypt *en route* for South Africa, where he had landed a job as a professor at the University in Cape Town.

Soon after Ancona we left the coast and proceeded cross-country, stopping for three hours at Faenza, where I had time to look around the town and have dinner at the 'Hotel Corona'. The weather was still bitterly cold. At Voghera we stopped long enough to get a good lunch in the town—roast beef, chipped potatoes and peas were a very pleasant change from the bully beef and bread we had been living on. Snow was still on the ground when I turned in just before we turned along the Riviera coast near Genoa.

We reached Albenga in the early hours of the morning of 2nd February, and there we stayed for a solid thirteen hours whilst the debris from an accident a little further along the line was cleared away. We pulled up right beside the sea, some way out of the town, and I was greatly tempted to have a swim, as the weather now was in direct contrast to what it had been twenty-four hours before, warm and sunny with not a cloud in the sky. Unfortunately we had no idea when the train would go on, so I merely lay out in the sun and enjoyed a good long sunbathe on the lovely soft sand.

I was amazed at the facility with which the Tommies got a fire going beside the train whenever we stopped for more than half an hour; one could see fires burning merrily all along beside the train, with mess tins, buckets or anything that would hold water being heated up for a drop of tea or coffee.

Probably owing to the uncertainty as to how long we should be delayed, the old Colonel did not issue any rations. As he walked along beside the train he was greeted with a concerted cry from the tommies: 'We want our "four-lettering" rations!'

We reached Ventimiglia by the evening of the 3rd February. There were no customs formalities and we did not have to change trains. At Marseilles I had a spot of bother with some French soldiers who tried to gate-crash into my compartment. At Saincaize, about ten miles south of Nevers, the train was stopped for the issue of rations, as the Colonel probably thought he ran no risk of running out seeing we were half-way across France. At Cherbourg on the 8th February we boarded the transport at 8 pm. I managed to get a berth for five shillings and had a good night's rest. We landed at Southampton twelve hours later, but were kept hanging about until 11.30, when we were told there would be a special train from the Central Station at ten minutes past twelve. I had a bit of bother with the Naval Transport Officer, who refused me transport for the broken prop I had brought all the way from Taranto. However, when his back was turned I got a couple of our men to hump it on to the lorry and off we all went to the Central Station, only to find that the prop was just 2 inches too long to go in the guard's van. So I left instructions for it to be forwarded on, doubting if I should ever see it again. We eventually left at 3 pm—some organisation! After a cup of tea at Waterloo, I took the party down to the RNAS Depot at the Crystal Palace and then reported to the 'Hotel Cecil'. I was given ten days' leave, most of which I spent at Airship HQ clearing up matters relating to AEF No. 6. I was now appointed to Howden Airship Station, a large station in East Yorkshire between York and Hull, lying about forty miles from the sea—which would mean two long overland trips over the very hilly country of the Wolds.

I arrived at Howden the day they were giving the CO, Captain F. L. M. Boothby, RN, a going-away dinner. We had a rare old rough-house in the Mess afterwards, including cock-fighting and rugger scrums. I remember my steed in the cock-fighting was F/Lt Don, who later became the Captain of the King's Flight when it was first formed. They were certainly a jolly crowd, and I did not feel a stranger there, as I knew quite a number of the officers.

I had only been at Howden a day when a signal came for me to go to the Scrubbs to bring back one of the new 'Zero' SS ships which were replacing the B.E.2c and Maurice Farman ships.

The 'Zero' had been designed by my friend at Capel, Lieutenant F. M. Rope, and WO Righton, who were engineer officers there. The ship was a very trim neat little boat-shaped three-seater car slung under a 70,000 cubic feet aluminium doped envelope, and powered by a 75 hp Rolls-Royce 'Hawk' engine, water cooled and fitted at the rear end of the car. This was the best little airship engine ever built, only stopping when switched off or if the petrol supply failed—such a change from the Sunbeams in the 'Coastals'.

The ship I was to take to Howden was not ready and, as I had never flown a 'Zero' before, I was sent down to Polegate near Eastbourne for instruction and practice with them. I had two short flights in *SS Z.30* and one in *Z.8*, and found them delightful little ships to handle. They were much pleasanter for flying in, too, for although the cockpit was still an open one, it was a 'pusher' type aircraft and the crew did not sit in the slipstream from the prop as we did in the B.E.2c type.

I spent a week at Polegate and returned to Scrubbs just in time to witness the landing there of *NS.6* under the command of Ian Struthers —he had already sunk two submarines when stationed at Mullion, flying a 'Coastal'.

The NS—or 'North Sea' type—is a streamlined tri-lobe similar to the Astra-Torres type of 360,000 cubic feet capacity; numbers one to five were fitted with two Rolls-Royce engines of 250 hp each and numbers 6 to 16 had 260 hp Fiats set on gantries built out at the end of a walking-way from the control car. Between the engines was an enclosed cubby-hole for the engineers. The control car was also completely covered in and therefore relatively warm and comfortable, with plenty of room and a table for maps and navigation. The great advantage of this type of ship is that the rigging being mostly internal—that is, inside the envelope—the car can be slung much closer to the envelope. Also, as there are fewer external wires there is much less resistance and greater speeds are possible.

Second Officer to Struthers was 'Mr WU'—F/Lt W. Underhill—whom I have mentioned earlier when at Anglesey. I have always remembered two good pieces of advice he gave me—'When in charge, take charge' and 'Learn to tie a reef knot in the dark'.

The 'Zero' designated for me was *Z.32* and I took her up for her first trials on 12th March 1918, followed next day by W/T trials which I carried out over London. I took the opportunity of visiting many of my old haunts, such as the Oratory, my old school—Oratory Middle—and Clarence House, where my former employer the Duke of Connaught was still in residence. I had been Clerk to the Duke's Comptroller, Major Murray. The W/T trials were not a success, as we could not make contact with any station; moreover, I once again carried away my aerial weight, so returned to Scrubbs to have the set adjusted. This was done and I suggested to the CO, Squadron Commander G. C. Colmore, that it would save time if I did the wireless tests on my way up north. He agreed and I set off on my journey after lunch, intending to land at Pulham *en route*.

Arriving at Pulham just before dark felt like coming home. Who should be in charge of the landing-party but old Dick Wickham, a hard-shot if ever there was one. I remember him once, at Capel, back from week-end leave, staggering into the Mess with bloodshot eyes popping out of his head, saying, 'Give me a brandy quick, or I shall die.' I also met many former shipmates—Scottie, my former CO at Anglesey; 'Ginger' McConnell, a very clever Australian who had been at Pompey with me; Padre Jones, the Naval Instructor; our dear old PMO, Fleet-Surgeon Harris; and many others.

The weather broke that night and it was not until four days later that I got away for Howden. I set off a few minutes before 8 am, flying over familiar country to Norwich, Cromer, across the Wash and up the War Channel to the mouth of the Humber, where I turned in for Howden and landed at 12.30 on the 18th March, just in time for lunch.

On Saturday, 21st March 1918, I took *SS Z.32* on her first patrol, proceeding to Bridlington and north up to Whitby, where, at 2.25 pm, I received a wireless message that an enemy submarine was on the surface off Flamboro' Head, having shelled a vessel at 1.30. Just my luck to have missed it, as I had been off Flamboro' at 11.50 that morning. However, I immediately set off at full speed, reached Scarboro' at 3.15 and proceeded down the War Channel. I saw three large oil patches and a crowd of drifters five miles north of Flamboro' Head—these oil patches apparently marked where F/Lt Crouch in *C.4* from Howden had bombed and sunk the submarine a little earlier.

At this point I happened to glance sternwards and noticed that the radiator was boiling over—water pouring out of it. The engineer must have fallen asleep not to have noticed it. The draw-off tap had probably been shaken open by the vibration when I opened up the engine. The radiator was practically empty, but by using his cap and a chocolate box—he had no other receptacle—the engineer collected enough water from the ballast to fill up the radiator. After this I set course for Howden and had just rounded the head into Bridlington Bay when I saw a seaplane on the surface of the water. I went right down beside him, slowed down and carried on a snatchy, shouted conversation with the Pilot, F/Lt Peard. He asked me to send a message to his station, Killingholme, that his radiator had burst, but that he was going to try to return on the surface. We sent the message to Killingholme, but the W/T station at Howden also picked it up and caused our CO, Colonel Brabazon, some anxiety by giving him a garbled version, reporting that *my* radiator had burst and that *I* was going to land at Killingholme.

I soon recrossed the foreshore at Bridlington and reached Howden to see one of our new 'Rigids', *R.25*, emerging from the shed, so I had to wait until she got off the ground. I landed at 7.20 pm, having been in the air eight and a half hours.

Next day I did 9 hours 40 minutes over much the same ground, or rather sea—Bridlington—Whitby—Filey, off which I spoke *R.25* with lamp—Flamboro'—and out to sea north-eastwards. About ten miles north-east of Flamboro' I dropped a 230-pound bomb at a floating object from a thousand feet. I felt a considerable shock as the bomb exploded and was shot up some 200 feet. I covered about 320 miles on this flight.

On 23rd March I had another fairly long flight of nine and three-quarter hours. Up at 6.25 am, I reached the coast at Hornsea, where I found the wind was from west-south-west at 12 knots. I went out to sea for fifteen miles, then in to Filey, where I found the wind had decreased a little. Set course to make good 090°T, and at 10.30 reckoned I was some thirty miles east of Filey. I was somewhat shaken to receive a message that the wind had gone round to north-west, was increasing, and I was to return home. As I was well out of sight of land, I wondered how far I had been blown off course by the change of wind, but was soon somewhat reassured when I passed over one of the buoys marking the War Channel, and very soon recrossed the foreshore at Aldboro', which lies about midway between Flamboro' and Spurn Head.

Returning over the Wolds, I was properly 'umped and bumped and b—d' about, especially over a place called Burton Constable, where the ship became almost unmanageable, being bumped up and down, this way and that, like a thing possessed. However, once clear of the Wolds I came right down to within 50 feet of the ground and got along much better, finally landing at 4.10 pm.

On 24th March I made a course direct for Scarboro' as I wanted to have a look at a proposed mooring-out station at Kirkleatham, near Redcar, at the mouth of the Tees, and do a bit of patrolling on the way. I reached Scarboro' at 11 am and proceeded north-north-east for about twenty miles, then altered course to the west and reached Redcar at 1.50 pm. I located the RNAS Station at Redcar, but could see no sign of a mooring-out station, so I set course to make good due east. About twenty minutes later I sighted a destroyer to whom I made the recognition signal, but got no reply. I chased after her, but eventually I read *Marvel* on her stern and *G.28* on her bow, so I assumed she was British. It is not much use having a system of recognition signals, however, if they are not used. I stayed with her until about ten miles east of Hartlepool, but she was very fast and I had to open full out to do so.

We had excellent visibility all day and a light wind not exceeding 10 knots. In these conditions it was a pleasure to fly. I proceeded southward to Scarboro' and Flamboro', where I received 'Return to base'. I turned in over Hornsea Mere and landed at Howden at 7.20 pm. This was my last flight as a flight lieutenant RN. Henceforward I was to be Lieutenant (Honorary Captain) RAF, demoted without a court martial.

From 1st April 1918 we were no longer part of the Royal Navy; the RNAS had been swallowed by the Army side of the RFC, and then swallowed in turn by the new service, the RAF. We were given Army ranks and khaki or light blue uniform. There was much bitterness amongst the direct-entry personnel of the RNAS, who felt they had been let down by their higher-up representatives, who had agreed that direct-entry personnel should be reduced in rank, whilst the regular naval and volunteer reserve personnel should be granted their equivalent substantive army rank. Anyway, I now became a lieutenant (honorary captain) in the RAF, and as I was now junior to a former RNVR lieutenant (non-flying) I had to give up my cabin to him. However, I was as keen as ever on flying and I was allowed to wear out my naval uniform or at least go on wearing it until I could obtain one of the new RAF suits either of khaki or sky blue similar to French Army flyers. It's an ill wind that blows nobody good and we had just had a new Padre posted to us, a very decent sort and a good sport, Rev. Edwards by name, who later on became Chaplain-in-Chief to the RAF. He had been in the *Queen* at Taranto and had once come over to visit us at Grottaglie, so it was like meeting an old friend. He and I spent our spare time preparing the cricket pitch for the coming season.

The news from France was a bit depressing as the Boche were pushing for the coast near Abbeville, in what was to be their last offensive of the war. This, together with the pouring wet weather, made Easter a very dismal holiday.

On Easter Tuesday I took *Z.32* out again for patrol, but got no further than Grimsby, when I received the recall signal, as thunder was reported. I landed after three hours, making a glider landing on my skids.

I got into a spot of bother with the naval authorities during my next patrol on the 5th April. I had followed my usual route over the Wolds to Bridlington, then up north from Flamboro'; when about twenty-five miles out to sea I liberated a carrier pigeon and the bird got safely back to its loft at Howden. How do they do it? I then turned in to Whitby, where the ruins of the Abbey made a wonderful landmark on top of the cliff between the village and the sea. The trouble came when I sighted two submarines on the surface off Hartlepool. I came down low to have a good look at them, but they gave no recognition signal. A few days later I got a rocket and had to give my 'reasons in writing', as the Captain of Submarines had written to my CO complaining that I had flown at a dangerously low height over two of his submarines—'a highly dangerous performance'. Although certainly low, I was quite a distance away from the subs; I personally think they wanted to forestall my reporting them for not giving the recognition signal! I satisfied my CO with the explanation that I wished to get a close view for future guidance, and had kept a safe distance from them. Before landing from this flight of ten hours, I did some bomb-dropping practice, getting twice within 6 feet of the target.

On 8th April I was detailed to drop some pamphlets over Hull in aid of the VAD.* This I did and then proceeded south-east on patrol. We sighted *R.25* proceeding north and they flashed a message: 'Gun-fire at 9.52 S.E. of Spurn Point.' I saw nothing when I reached the Spurn lightship; proceeded to Flamboro' and on to Scarboro'. About fifteen miles north-east of Scarboro' I sighted a dresser floating; near by was a lifebuoy and two planks, which looked like some action hereabouts, though, of course, these things could have drifted with the tide.

Off Scarboro' I received 'Return to base', so proceeded down the War Channel and in over Bridlington, landing at 7.50 pm, being delayed thirty minutes while *C.4* landed.

My next flight was a short exhibition flight for the Army officer, General Gordon, who had been appointed head of the Group into which we had been incorporated. He had been coming up himself, but when we had a bit of trouble starting the engine in the shed he perhaps thought discretion the better part of valour and merely watched our cavorting about from the ground. One of his Staff, Major Michell, used to be on Commodore Sueter's Staff at Taranto and remembered me. After lunch I proceeded on patrol, but encountered thick fog over the sea. I persevered as far as Filey, but could not see the surface from 500 feet, so decided to return. Even over the land the ground was often invisible from the same height.

I was then sent down to Kingsnorth to do the trials of *SS Z.58* and fly her back to Howden. I did the trials on 20th April and flew the ship up to Howden on the 22nd, passing *en route* over Cambridge, Peterborough and Lincoln. Lincoln Cathedral is a glorious sight from the air, where one gets a better view of its main tower seen centrally between its two side towers—a view which is difficult to get from the ground, as the building is rather crowded in.

On return I immediately took over *Z.32*, and Lieutenant-Commander Blatherwick, our Number One, asked me to take him up for some instruction in piloting. I sat him in the pilot's seat and stood behind him telling him what to do. After landing he said there was much more in

* Voluntary Aid Detachment.

piloting an airship than he had thought—'you need ten hands and half a dozen pairs of eyes'. He is a natural comedian enhanced by the way he talks—he has no roof to his mouth. I remember once when 'Count' Cleary was holding forth as to what he would do in the event of being ditched, old Blatherwick said in his funny voice: 'Anyway, you'd be all right.'

Cleary asked 'Why?'—to get the crushing reply: 'Hard turds always float.'

Blatherwick was a great debunker. On another occasion a young officer was blowing the gaff about his father's prowess on safari. After sticking it for some time, Blatherwick interjected: 'Have you heard of the Dead Sea? Well, *my* father shot it.'

But to enjoy the full flavour of Blatherwick's humour, one had actually to hear him.

My next two flights were cut short by adverse weather conditions: first by sea fog when the surface near the coast was invisible from 400 feet, and the horizontal visibility less than a quarter of a mile although the wind was blowing at 15 knots; the second time I went out in company with F/Lt Sparrow in *Z.38* and when we reached the Wolds the wind was blowing about 20 knots. We had a hell of a time, being bumped about all over the place and making good about 5 knots. Sparrow got fed up and turned about. I was determined to get to the coast, as I thought conditions over the sea would not be so turbulent, but had only reached Beverley at the eastern edge of the Wolds when I was recalled. Ironically, by the time I reached Beverley the wind had died down.

In order to obviate the necessity of spending a comparatively large amount of flying time over land, a policy of mooring out the smaller ships near the coast had been inaugurated. *Z.32* had been allocated to a mooring-out station in a clearing in a wood near the village of Lowthorpe, situated about seven miles south-west of Bridlington. This made a beautiful shelter from the wind, but was without any cover. The great drawback to this particular site was that the prevailing wind blew directly across the opening into the wood. The ships' crews and ground personnel lived in bell tents and for meals there were small marquees.

CHAPTER FIVE

Howden—Mooring-out

We had made arrangements for two Zeros to be moored out in the woods at Lowthorpe: Sparrow's *Z.38* and my *Z.32*. As we were within five miles of the coast, it meant that all but a few minutes of our time in the air would be over the sea—and on the job.

My first flight from Lowthorpe was on the 9th May 1918. Fog was thick over the sea, but cleared north of Flamboro', whence I proceeded about thirty miles in a north by east direction and then turned in to Robin Hood Bay, proceeding down the coast to Scarboro', where my engine suddenly stopped. Miles, my engineer, found that the rocker arm of the contact breaker had stuck. He freed it and restarted the engine within five minutes. The fitting of the engine in the rear of the car was a great improvement over the B.E.2c tractors. If one's engine stopped in the tractor type, one had to swing the prop for restarting in the air from a precarious footing on one of the skids. With the pusher type, restarting was carried out from inside the car by winding with a starting-handle, *à la* motor car.

Off Scarboro' I passed *R.26*—one of the new Type 23 'Rigids'—heading north. I went in over the land in order to get an accurate check of the wind, and had the wind put up me by artillery carrying out firing practice. I quickly made for the safety of the sea, which, however, near the land was now covered in thick fog—extending some fifteen miles out, with a depth of about 500 feet. I skirted the edge of this fog bank for some miles, and then set course above it, intending to hit land at Hornsea. The wind must have blown me further south than I had allowed for, for I came out at Spurn Head, about twenty-four miles off target. Not a very good shot! I then proceeded coastwise up north, keeping very low on account of the fog and trailing my handling-guys in the water, much to the alarm of my young W/T op. Rook, who had replaced Sinclair. I landed at 4.10 pm in the buttercup-covered field by the wood, having covered approximately 220 miles in 9 hours 10 minutes.

When Phil Barnes, a young American pilot, a little later on landed here in the 'Zero' *Z.23* which we had sold to the US Navy, he told me he had written to his parents to say he had just landed in a field of gold, such was the impression the buttercups gave him.

On 11th May I patrolled north from Flamboro' Head for twenty-five miles. The clouds were low and I had to fly at less than 400 feet, where the visibility was about three miles with little or no wind. I turned westwards for land and struck it at Runswick Bay a little north of Whitby. Here I received a signal that a ship had been sunk fifteen miles east by north of Hartlepool. I set course for this spot and searched the area for about half an hour, but saw nothing. The wind having increased considerably and the weather thickened, I decided to return to base. I had just reached Saltburn at 11.15 when I received the 'Recall' signal. I carried on down the War Channel, but had to open up the engine to make any progress.

Howden was apparently getting a bit worried at my slow progress, for I received a signal at 12.20 pm asking for my estimated time of arrival. I replied: 'E.T.A. 2.45 pm'—and I would have made it within a minute or two, except that I had to cruise around the neighbourhood for over an hour, as all hands were engaged clearing away the mess of *Z.38* which had been blown into the trees and deflated as it was being taken out. I flew low round the countryside, giving entertainment to the local folk, eventually landing at 4.10 pm.

I spent all next day, which was a Sunday, helping Sparrow pack up *Z.38's* car and envelope for transport to Howden as, of course, there were no facilities for major repairs at Lowthorpe. The envelope was badly torn on a protruding branch of a tree which had been ordered to be cut off. On inquiry as to why this had not been done, I was informed by the PO in charge that they 'could not get to the branch'. I went out at 9 pm that night and did the job myself, but it was a hell of a sweat.

On 13th May I had got about as far as seventeen miles east of Whitby when I was recalled, so turned in for land, making same at Robin Hood Bay, where I spoke to a gunboat towing a kite-balloon—nothing to report.

I had just sent a message from off Scarboro', to say I would land at 11.30, when my transmitter broke down. I landed in a shower of rain at 11.40 am, a relatively short flight of four-and-a-half hours.

On the 16th May, when about eight miles south-east of Flamboro' Head, my operator, Rook, reported a loud Telefunken note, probably from a submarine; I passed on the report to Howden. Off Spurn Head I came up with a destroyer flotilla of nine vessels. We exchanged signals by flashlamp, but they had nothing to report. A little later, when about five miles north-east of Spurn, I sighted a great deal of wreckage, so it looked as if that Telefunken beggar had bagged a ship.

I proceeded up the War Channel to Flamboro' and Scarboro', but as the wind was getting up against me for my return, I thought it time to turn about, and found I had to open up the engine to make any headway. The engine also started to falter, so I got down well under the cliffs at the southern end of Filey Bay and made good progress round Flamboro', landing at Lowthorpe at 7 pm, after nine hours in the air.

I was delayed getting off next day by my accumulators having to be recharged. By the time I did get off the ground the Howden-based ships were all returning, having been recalled on account of thunder. I had scarcely got under way off Flamboro' when I, too, received the 'Recall'. My W/T op. reported atmospherics in his earphones, though it was a perfect day otherwise. I turned homeward, however, and thought I would pay a visit to our neighbours at the new RAF training station under construction at Driffield. I landed there and took the CO, a colonel, and the Adjutant, Captain Harold Balfour, up for a short trip. Balfour was a Sopwith 'Camel' stunt pilot whom I had met recently at Howden when he came there on a 'hedge-hopping' flight of 'Camels' flying in formation. This exercise of flying over the countryside at a height never exceeding 50 feet above the ground is officially called 'contouring'.

As Balfour and his chief enjoyed low flying, I took them low down over the main street at Driffield at about 20 feet above the house-tops. On coming in to land at the aerodrome my fore guys carried away the station telephone wires, much to the delight of my passengers, whom I then landed and took the ship and my crew back to Lowthorpe. In the afternoon two other officers arrived from Driffield, a Major Greig and Lieutenant Mills, both of the Royal Engineers. The Major was so disappointed at missing a flight in the airship that morning that he had commandeered a tender and rushed over to Lowthorpe in the hope of getting a trip from there. We took the ship out for his benefit and they got aboard, the Major especially being as happy as a sand-boy, shouting 'All aboard—any more for the *Skylark*!' when they embarked. I repeated the morning's performance, flying all the way to Driffield at or below the height of the telephone wires along the road. I put the wind up myself by flying low over the chapel spire, expecting any moment to hear it tearing through the bottom of the car. However, I cleared it by about a foot and then flew low over the Colonel's cottage to give him a chuck-up. I was pretty low as I zoomed up to miss the house and had to fly through a gap in the hedge through which my rudder plane passed unscathed. I seemed to have a penchant for carrying away telephone wires; this time I carried away those leading to the Colonel's cottage, to the great delight of the Major.

Incidentally it was Captain Balfour's daily exercise to fly round the church tower and see how close he could get to the flag pole without actually touching it—and, much later, it was he who, as an MP, took Major Draper to task for flying through Tower Bridge! The next time I met him was after the Armistice at Pulham, where he had been sent for three months' open detention for being one of a party who put a top-hat

R.1 landing at
iampino

ne airship station at
ıbagne, where *SR.1*
ıded on the way from
›me to Kingsnorth
ote the windscreens of
panded metal at the
ds of the shed to
eak the force of the
nd

ıe car of *SR.1* with
author at the window

R.33 moored to the mast at Pulham 1925

R.33 in the shed at Pulham. Lookin out of the car, *left to right*, Johnson, Scott and Irwin

on the statue of Eros in Piccadilly Circus on Armistice night. He is now Lord Balfour of Inchrye.

On 18th May, when about a mile off Flamboro' Head, I sighted a large patch of oil. I contacted a Shields trawler which was patrolling the War Channel, came down very low beside it, shut down my engine and shouted directions to the skipper as to the position of the oil. He pushed off at once to investigate, whilst I reported to Howden. At Whitby I took the wind over the pier by slowing down into it until I was stationary and reading the speed on the airspeed indicator. It was from north-west at 10 knots, having veered from west at 7 knots when I checked it at Flamboro' earlier on. I then patrolled south along the War Channel where I passed three paddle steamers busy sweeping the channel for mines; probably a convoy was expected. Only five hours in the air today, covering about 120 miles.

On 19th May I left Lowthorpe at 6.30 am. The wind at Flamboro' Head was from 255°T at 8 knots. I set course to the north, making good 20 knots with the engine doing 900 revs. When some twenty-seven miles east of Whitby I sighted a black patch on the surface some distance off which I thought might be a submarine; however, on approaching closer I saw it to be a shoal of fish. I tried to alight on the surface, hoping to collect a few; I skimmed the surface twice—like a seaplane, as Miles, my engineer, said—but each time I slowed down the engine the ship left the surface, being too light to settle on it. I did not wish to valve gas, as I intended to return to Lowthorpe for lunch and land light, so as to be able to take a 230-pound bomb up in the afternoon. This I did and left the ground again at 2.20 pm, going over much the same ground as earlier. I took bearings of Saltburn and Whitby which, on plotting, gave me a position seven miles north by east of Whitby. I took the wind in my usual manner and found it had backed right round to 130°T, blowing at nearly twice the strength of the morning, so I turned southward and proceeded slowly back to Lowthorpe, where I landed at 7.40 pm, having done a total for the day of 12 hours 5 minutes.

As it was a beautiful evening with the wind dropping almost to nothing, I decided to give the ground staff short flights round the gas-works of about ten minutes or so, just round the landing-field and down. This makes them much more interested in their work and was a reward for my having worked them pretty hard recently.

I had done about half a dozen of these short flips when the US 'Zero' appeared overhead. I decided to keep away while she landed. However, she also kept off, so I went in and landed. I was informed that *Z.23* intended to fly round for a little while, so I took off with another couple of the ground staff. I had gone round the field and was coming up to land when *Z.23* approached from above and to port. She would have cleared me easily, I think, but I remembered a lecture by Colonel Brabazon at Howden recently, instructing us never to fly under another ship; so, instead of landing, I veered off to starboard, my attention glued on the other ship meanwhile. My altimeter was showing 100 feet, so I assumed I had plenty of height and kept my attention fixed on *Z.23* to see which way she would turn. I failed to notice that I was approaching a small hillock surmounted by a clump of tall trees—the next thing I knew was that I had flown slap-bang into the top of one of them. There was the most almighty crashing and tearing sound and a terrific vibration from the engine as the prop splintered. I had to brush away the branches and foliage to get at the switch and stop the engine, after which we landed quite gently and the landing-party doubled over and hauled us back to the landing-ground.

The envelope was partially deflated by the prop splinters having been thrown up through it, but there was enough gas left in it to lift the car and engine on to the lorry. Then we unshipped the planes and deflated the envelope completely and rolled it up ready to dispatch to Howden when the lorry returned. This took us until 1.30 am. Was I hungry! I had had nothing to eat since lunch.

The damage done to the ship was pretty considerable. The envelope was holed in six places on the underside and two on top where prop splinters had gone right through. The propeller was smashed to smithereens; the radiator and piping carried away; the exhaust pipe broken at the junction with the cylinders; and two engine-bearer struts broken.

I felt very fed up at this happening, all on account of being overcareful. Had it happened whilst doing a stunt that didn't come off, I should not have minded so much. I was very sorry to lose my ship, too, as I had got so used to her that I felt I could do almost anything with her except loop the loop.

I was recalled at once to Howden and asked for a report in writing. I spent an unhappy Whit Monday morning writing it, and submitted it to the First Lieutenant, Lieutenant-Commander Blatherwick. I had put down exactly what had happened, but when old Blatherwick read it he said: 'Meager, old man, if I send this in as it is, they will hang you'—he was speaking metaphorically of course! 'Here, give it to me,' he said. 'I'll reword it for you'—which he did, giving the gist of my report but in less self-condemnatory terms. I signed it, he sent it off to Group Headquarters and I never heard any more about it. What a man!

That same afternoon, as I was going along one of the corridors between the cabins, my old Skipper at Capel, Squadron Commander A. D. Cunningham, popped his head through a doorway and called me into his cabin, greeting me with: 'Well, Meager, are you ready to go to Italy to fetch the "M" ship?'

I felt as proud as a fox with two tails. I had heard from John Barron, when he returned to Grottaglie from his visit with Lucas to Ferrara, that the Admiralty were going to buy an 'M' ship—and I had hoped that John would be selected as her Skipper and myself as Second-in-Command. To be selected as Captain myself was beyond my wildest hopes. After yarning for a bit, he told me to let him have a list of the crew I wished to take with me to fly her home.

The smashing up of *Z.32* did not affect my nerves or my keenness to fly. I was straight away given command of *SS Z.63*, a similar type of ship to my former one, and I kept my flying crew, Miles and Rook, who had flown with me in all my recent flights, and also my cox'n, Burrell, and rigger, Beastie, who had looked after the ship's maintenance so well on the ground. Cox'ns in SS ships did not normally fly, as the pilot himself did all the manoeuvring, control of engines and speed, maintenance of pressure in the envelope and equilibrium, and working out courses. In 'Coastals' and larger ships the cox'n worked the steering and sometimes the elevating, but usually the Captain or Second Officer did the manoeuvring of the ship and saw to the maintenance of height, pressure, equilibrium and speed.

I do not think I lost any flying days, for the weather was dud; I know I became soaked to the skin whilst helping Padre Edwards mow and prepare the cricket pitch.

On 25th May I took *Z.63* out for a short patrol of four and three-quarters hours over the usual course of Flamboro', War Channel to Robin Hood Bay and back to Lowthorpe. Then for the next fortnight the weather remained perfect and I had an intensive bout of flying. It would be boring and repetitive to recount the details of each separate flight, but some incidents of interest occurred during them.

On 26th May I sighted *C-Star 2** about three miles south of Flamboro' with both her engines stopped. I was closing her to see if she needed help when her engines were restarted and she carried on her normal occasions. An hour later I sighted a low-lying vessel to the southward; it was the destroyer *D.70*. At 10 am, when off Robin Hood Bay, the wind increased to about 20 knots and I received the 'Recall' signal.

I must have measured the direction of the wind pretty accurately, as I have a note in my log-book that the wind was from 'NE by E½E', which is 016¾° in the three-figure notation. More than likely I was showing off to myself how well I could 'box the compass'! As the wind was practically dead astern, I throttled down the engine and let the wind blow me home. When I arrived back at Lowthorpe I found that the wind was blowing strongly right across the entrance into the wood. Phil

* The 'C-Star' ships were an improved later model of the 'Coastal'.

Barnes in *Z.23* had decided it was too hazardous to try to get his ship through the gap, so he had pushed off to land at Howden, where he could expect to find a large landing-party and wide sheds. At Lowthorpe our landing-party was only about twenty men. I had the devil of a job getting the ship in, but managed it without damage.

As it was now daylight from about 2.30 am, I was getting under way early, hoping to catch a submarine on the surface recharging batteries and also with the intention of getting in two flights per day with a break in the middle of the day. Yesterday I left at 5 am and today, 27th May, at 4 am. About ten miles north-east of Whitby I came up with a convoy of forty ships and escorted them to the Tyne. Although we rarely if ever saw any enemy vessels, we had the satisfaction of knowing that our presence with a convoy kept the enemy submarines down under the water, for they could not see to let off a torpedo unless their periscope was above water, and of course they could not use their guns until the hull was awash. It is a fact that no vessel was ever sunk in a convoy escorted by an airship. In the early days of the war whilst the British Expeditionary Force was being ferried over to France, the transports were frequently accompanied by Airship *No. 4*—the Parseval—under the command of F/Lt G. H. Scott. I have met soldiers who were thus escorted who told me that when they saw an airship overhead they felt safe and could go below and get some sleep; otherwise, they stayed on deck all night with their life-belts on. There was also the evidence taken from logs of captured submarines, one of which I have already mentioned. So we did feel that we were doing something, however small, towards maintaining the food supply, and enjoyed a flush of satisfaction in seeing a convoy safely into port.

That afternoon I sighted a mine and went off in search of trawlers to deal with it. I found a batch about five miles away and then I could not locate the damned mine again. I picked up another convoy off Spurn and escorted it north, finally I landed at Lowthorpe at 9.35 pm, having spent a total of 15 hours 55 minutes in the air (8 hours 50 minutes in the morning; 7 hours 5 minutes in the afternoon), covering a distance of approximately 350 miles.

On 28th May I left Lowthorpe at 3.10 am and *C*4* was also out early, for at 4.15 am Rook intercepted a message to her: 'Trawler sunk 15 m. E of Flamborough.' I made for the spot and half an hour later spoke to a trawler in the vicinity, who confirmed the message and reported hearing a submarine on the hydrophone bearing south. I proceeded in this direction and soon sighted destroyer *No. 66*, who signalled: 'Submarine sunk here'—about ten miles south-east of Flamboro' Head. They had apparently got her with a depth charge.

I went in to Lowthorpe and landed, but left again almost immediately for Howden, as we had run out of petrol and gas at Lowthorpe. Unfortunately when taken into the shed at Howden I was jammed in behind a 'Rigid'—*R.26*—and an NS, so was a prisoner for the rest of the day. Fortunately the weather held good and early on the 29th May both *R.26* and the NS were taken out, leaving me free. These two ships required all the landing-party available, so I collected the crews of *Z.23*, an *SS* sold to the American Navy and manned by an American Naval crew, and my own ship, six in all, and with them took out first the American ship and got her off, and then my own *Z.63* likewise, and finally got off myself at 6.35 am. Fortunately there was a dead calm. About twenty miles east of Hornsea I sighted a large number of barrels floating about, but could see no sign of a ship or any other wreckage. I landed at Lowthorpe very light, so as to be able to take on a couple of heavy bombs in the afternoon.

I left again at 2.20 pm and proceeded up north to have another search for the proposed mooring-out station near Redcar at Kirkleatham. Here, it is not proposed to moor in a clearing in a wood, but to moor the ships in the shelter of a belt of high trees. I returned to Lowthorpe, having done nearly thirteen hours all told. Ensign Phil Barnes, USN, was still in the air in *Z.23* and eventually did a total of nearly twenty-six hours non-stop.

On 30th May 1918 I was again up with the lark or even earlier, as I left the ground at 2.45 am. When off Whitby I received a message reporting 'four enemy airplanes 25 m. E. of Winterton steering north'. Winterton is on the coast of Norfolk, so they had a long way to go before reaching my neighbourhood. On reaching Lowthorpe soon after 9 am, my game little W/T op., Rook, collapsed with exhaustion. The long hours were too much for the youngster, who was only a boy. During flight he had to be on watch all the time with no relief. I sent him to bed and told him to sleep all day, whilst I pushed off to Howden to pick up another operator.

At Howden I was ordered to locate a large American vessel with a valuable cargo and escort her in to Immingham, Grimsby. There was no W/T op available, so I took up the cox'n of *Z.23*, a tall, quiet, but very efficient USN CPO named Packham. I did not succeed in locating the ship, so I assumed she had reached Immingham safely.

A convoy had been formed off the Humber lightship and was just getting under way, so I proceeded north with it along the War Channel.

The War Channel from the Humber to Flamboro' Head consisted of a double line of red cone-shaped buoys spaced two to three miles apart. From Flamboro' to Scarboro' the buoys were red can-shaped buoys. Each buoy had a distinctive mark consisting of a white letter within a white square, triangle, or circle. I had not realised before I took a note of the letter on each one during this trip that they spelt out the name of a section of the Channel; thus from Spurn northward the lettering was S–P–U–R–N–T. I do not know what the T signified. Then followed O–R–B–M–A–L–F, which spells 'FLAMBRO' backwards. At either end of these lettered buoys was a spherical buoy with horizontal stripes and also a distinctive letter. At the Spurn end the stripes were red and white and the letter *Y* (this may have been the final letter of the Grimsby section). At the Flamboro' end the stripes were black and white with the distinctive letter P.

I finally landed at Lowthorpe at 9 pm, having completed fifteen-and-a-half hours in the day.

The day's rest had done little Rook a world of good and he was ready for the fray at 3.10 am, when we left the ground next morning. I have nothing to report during this flight between Flamboro' and Whitby and back, landing at 9.40 am. I had a good breakfast and set off again at 11 am, going north as far as Sunderland and the mouth of the Tyne. Off Hartlepool, Rook intercepted a message to *Z.62*—'Submarine sighted 6 m. NNE of Whitby'. I made for the spot at full speed and searched the area with *C.2*, *Z.62* and a pair of motor launches, but none of us saw anything, so I proceeded down the War Channel and landed at 7.40 pm, a duration of 15 hours 10 minutes and 350 miles for the day.

After flying for some hours during the morning of 1st June, the engine began to splutter. I wondered if I had run out of petrol, as the engineer found the petrol filter choked with mud, which usually happened when the tank was nearly empty. We have no gauges to tell us how much is left in the tanks—which are simply aluminium cylinders slung in a fabric cradle or sling fixed half-way up each side of the envelope. The petrol is led down by gravity through narrow pipes to the engine. The way we judge how much petrol is left is by knowing the consumption rate of the engine; we always go up with full tanks, change over tanks at regular intervals and note the time of each change. On checking the tanks after this flight, we found four gallons left in one tank, whilst the other was empty. As our average petrol consumption was four gallons per hour, it meant that we had only one hour's petrol left when we landed.

In the forenoon I took *Z.63* back to Howden, as she was due for engine overhaul. I was there given *Z.54* and asked to take an engineer officer, Sub-Lt Harris, up to Kirkleatham, which was then in commission as a mooring-out station. I had a 'Recall' signal when a few miles north of Flamboro', so landed at Lowthorpe. I left there early next morning and duly deposited my passenger at his destination, then proceeded on patrol southwards landing at Lowthorpe in time for lunch.

I was not destined to fly *Z.54* very much, for after lunch, as I was taking her out, a very strong gust of wind across the opening from the wood caught her bows just as she was emerging. Our small landing-party could not hold her, and though we very nearly got her clear, she was blown on to the trees and the envelope badly torn near the after end. I had no option but to rip her. So we had another awful job of packing up car and envelope for transport by road to Howden. I had to attend a Court of Enquiry, which exonerated me. I suggested that the opening to the clearing should be made more funnel-shaped by removing some trees near the entrance. The Court of Enquiry lasted all morning and in the afternoon I was asked to test and report on a new type of balanced, cutaway rudder that had been fitted to *Z.55*, which I then did. By now my former ship. *Z.63*, was back in commission, so I took her out for patrol on 5th June, first landing at Lowthorpe to pick up my codes. After an uneventful trip between Humber and Flamboro' during which the only thing of interest I saw were some trawlers carrying out diving operations over patches of oil, I flew her back to Howden.

Next day, 6th June, I took *Z.55* up again to test her new-type rudder for longer periods of flight. I left at 3.20 am, and when over the 'B' buoy of the Flamboro'—Spurn section of the War Channel I received: 'Submarine on surface 25 m. E'N of Whitby; proceed and search.' I immediately worked out a course for the spot indicated, making good about 50 knots with the wind behind me. I reached the position given at 6.25 am and found destroyer *D.57* making a square search. Together we thoroughly searched an area of about five miles square for nearly two hours, when three other destroyers arrived and joined in, followed by the airships *C.4* and *C*.4*

Soon after eight o'clock I left them to it and landed at Kirkleatham, near Redcar. There were, as yet, no facilities there in the way of mooring pickets, ballast or petrol, so I set off on my return in what turned out to be about the most ghastly flight of my career to date.

When I rounded the point at Staithes I caught the wind full in my face, blowing from south by east at about 20 knots. After struggling along for an hour, I received a message: 'Return to base at full speed', it being then 12.40 pm off Whitby. I opened up the engine, but found I was making very little headway even at 400 feet, so I came right down to a height of between 30 and 50 feet and kept close in to the coast. It took me quite a time to get across Robin Hood Bay, but by still keeping almost down to the surface I made better progress.

I recrossed the foreshore in Filey Bay, but had to go up to 500 feet on account of the height of the ground. The wind up there was blowing at 25 knots. Just as I left the sea there was a terrific clatter and banging. My first thought was 'Another ship gone west. Any way we won't be drowned!'—for I thought my prop had smashed and gone up through the envelope, but luckily it was only the exhaust pipe which had come adrift and the propeller was banging against it as it hung loose in the air. Fortunately for ship and crew it was the thick part of the prop near the hub that was hitting the exhaust pipe, and only a chunk of about 2 inches square was taken out of the prop. I yelled to Miles, the engineer to pull the exhaust pipe clear.

'I can't!' he yelled back. 'It's red-hot.'

So I whipped off my flying-gloves and yelled: 'Here, take these'; he put them on and pulled the pipe clear, leaving the engine with an open exhaust making a deafening roar.

We had an awful time crossing the Wolds, being tossed about unmercifully, as I had to keep as low as safety allowed to make any progress at all. The new-type rudder, or my inexperience in its use, did not make things any easier, as it was very slow to answer, but when it did, it swung the ship round very quickly. In bumps the ship was carried broadside with the wind before the rudder took effect; rolling, which is entirely absent with other types, was quite noticeable in these rough, bumpy conditions.

After literally creeping along over the Wolds, being bumped about all over the place, due no doubt to my flying so low over the uneven surface of the ground, I had reached as far as Market Weighton and was congratulating myself on having got over the worst of the journey, when the engine spluttered and stopped. As no petrol would flow through to the carburettor I thought we had run out of petrol; the wind was still pretty strong from the south, so I decided to make a forced landing.

I valved her down under the shelter of a belt of trees in Skelfley Park, near Market Weighton. In no time I was surrounded by some farm labourers, soldiers and land-girls. As I was a bit heavy, I told the engineer to let go a little water ballast; unfortunately he threw the closing-line adrift, and before I could yell at him to get hold of it and stop the flow, about half my ballast had gone. The ship immediately became light and started to lift my *ex tempore* landing-party off their feet. I quickly valved more gas from the bottom valve until the gas pressure dropped to zero; I then tried to valve gas from the top valve, but the lines got all tangled up inside the envelope, and all I managed to do was to tear off the patches where the lines entered the envelope. By this time more people had gathered round and were hanging on to the car after hauling her down with the trail rope and guys.

The envelope of course was now beginning to sag a little and lose shape. I told the engineer to start the auxiliary blower so as to blow some air into the ballonets and bring the pressure up. It broke down and its driving-chain came off its sprocket. We fixed the chain, but the engine still refused to function. Normally, air can be blown up a scoop and through the crab-pot valves into the ballonets, using the slipstream from the propeller; I thought I would see if the engine would give a last kick. Thank goodness it started at once and I blew the ship up to pressure.

One of the soldiers got me some rubber solution with which I patched up the tear-off patches for the top valve lines and while I was doing this the engineer took out the filter and cleaned it; it was choked with mud, though it is a wonder to me how the mud gets into the tanks, as the filling funnel has a very fine gauze filter with a loose covering of chamois leather over the top through which the petrol is poured.

Just as I was ballasting up with the intention of proceeding on my way, who should roll up in the station car but F/Lt Butcher and Lt Reggie Alderson, the Armament Officer at Howden, accompanied by Mrs Blatherwick and a friend. Butcher suggested I left my 230-pound bomb for them to take back in the car and so conserve my remaining water ballast. I thought this a very good idea, so we disengaged the bomb, having first set it to 'safe'. When I got back to Howden I learned that my bomb was still at Skelfley Park, as the ladies had refused to travel with it in the car. After dumping my bomb, I got away and very soon overtook *C*.2* which was also in difficulties as her after engine had stopped and she was limping home on her forward engine only, making good about 5 knots, which was about half my own ground speed.

It was now plain sailing or rather flying until I reached Howden. Here I had some more bother, but of a minor character. My engine, with its open exhaust, was roaring away like a racing car or traction engine as I came up to land; the noise must have misled the officer in charge of the landing-party into thinking I was coming in at an excessive speed, for before I had got anywhere near the landing-party, he started waving his handkerchief about. What he was trying to convey by this signal I could not make out, but I soon learnt, for when I came up to the landing-party he waved them away and would not allow them to take hold of my handling guys.

I was going slowly enough to yell out, when almost stationary over the landing-party: "What's the matter?"

I could not hear his reply owing to the din of the engine. Anyway, I went round again, the engine, of course, making the same clatter; he was going to wave the men away again. I said to myself, 'No you don't, old man!' and drove the car right down into the midst of the party and shut off the engine. We stopped short in our tracks, and all they had to do was hold on to us. The landing-officer came round to me and said: 'I did not land you first time as you were going too fast—you were doing 30 knots.'

I said I knew my speed over the ground was *not* 30 knots—the wind was about 25 knots and if I could have made 30 knots against that wind any time that day I should have been more than pleased; I had been lucky to make 12 knots and during most of the return journey I had only averaged 8–10 knots with the engine going all out. He finally 'deflated' me and made me properly fed up to the back teeth by saying: 'You should learn how to land your ship properly.'

This about filled my cup to overflowing after the bad times I had experience during the flight.

I was even more furious when I got over to the Mess to find that Butcher and Alderson had spread it around that they had saved my ship from destruction by their timely arrival. The only thing they had done was to make the suggestion about the bomb—which in the end they left for someone else to collect. However, I was very pleased and thankful to get back with a whole ship and a whole skin and with little or no damage done. I found on checking the petrol after landing that there was nearly four hours' supply left in the tanks.

On 12th June I went up to HQ to see 'Skipper' Cunningham about my Italian mission and soon after my return to Howden we received the sad news that 'Uncle Sam's' aerial navy was no more—for the time being anyway. What had happened was that Barnes, the pilot of the US Airship *SS Z.23*, had gone over the top to inspect the top valve and had only just escaped falling through the envelope, which had apparently become rotten with continued exposure to the elements; the ship was moored out at Lowthorpe when this happened.

At this time we had four young Americans attached to us at Howden: Pete Wolf; Phil Barnes from Minneapolis; Harrison Goodspeed from Grand Rapids, Michigan; and Pope. They were all ensigns in the US Navy, and all University graduates. Barnes, who became a great pal of mine, told me that their airship chiefs insisted that all their potential airship pilots must have degrees. Strangely enough none of them wore the naval blue uniform, all being dressed in khaki, but their ratings were in ordinary naval uniform. I remember their cox'n, CPO Packham, used to wear white ducks in the summer surmounted by the funny-shaped little white cap perched at a rakish angle over his forehead.

I was rather bucked to be informed that I had been appointed OC Kirkleatham Mooring-out Station pending my leaving for Italy. On 17th June at 3.15 am I set off from Howden in *SS Z.55* to take over my new command. I had with me my usual flying crew of Miles—Engineer—and Rook W/T op. On the way up I did a patrol, and when about five miles from Redcar I saw the waves breaking over a low-lying object. I made for it and found it to be one of our own submarines, *G.13*, surfacing.

After lunch at Kirkleatham, I patrolled northward from Redcar, escorting a northbound convoy. Off the Tyne I came upon a large fishing-fleet of 100 vessels putting to sea. I escorted a southbound convoy off Seaham and then received 'Return to base', so went in and landed at Kirkleatham.

This little out-station was simply under the lee of a wood—it was not actually a clearing *in* a wood; it had one advantage—there was no opening through which to take the ships in and out of the clearing, as the ships were simply moored to screw pickets under the shelter of a belt of high trees.

I was out at 3 am on 20th June; picked up a northbound convoy and escorted it as far as the Tyne, where it was very foggy, and I left the convoy, landing after six and a half hours.

During the night of the 21st/22nd June I was awakened by the roaring of the wind. I got up and went over to see that the ship was OK. The storm now increased in intensity and the wind was coming over the tops of the trees like a waterfall, forcing the ship's stern down. Then she started to bounce up and down, the car crashing down on the ground with an awful bump and then shooting up again. The car itself was not damaged, but the two after guys carried away; the ship swung round and practically stood on her nose. It was a frightening sight, with the tail right up in the air and the nose brushing the ground. Practically all the suspensions from car to envelope except the after ones were hanging in bights—in other words, all the weight of the car was being taken by these after suspensions—and the car was bumping about cruelly. However, we gradually got her in hand by tying down the stern guys securely and, though the wind still remained strong, she rode fairly steadily. After lunch the wind again got at her stern, and she developed a sliding movement backwards and forwards during the gusts. We altered the tension on the guys and I hitched two lines from the shackle at the after end of the car to two Scrulex anchors,* which prevented her surging. My Second-in-Command WO John Evason, was a tower of strength in helping to settle the ship, but I was very relieved when the wind died down towards evening.

Due to the buffeting-about the ship received in the gale, I was instructed to fly her back to Howden for overhaul. After inspection it was decided to fit a new car and this we carried out immediately by dint of working through the night.

I flew the trials in the morning and found her to be very nose heavy—10 to 15 degrees down—which could be serious in flight. The engine, too, was none too good, the oil pressure not being maintained. I decided to re-rig the ship and move the car a little towards the stern, but could not get any of the station riggers to assist me. Then I had a brain-wave—perhaps the planes were badly rigged. I measured their height and found that one was a foot higher than the other, but, worse than that, the

* This is a type of anchor, some 3 inches in diameter, which can be screwed into the ground to a depth of 2 feet.

trailing-edges of each were lower than the leading-edges by 10 inches. This meant that the whole plane was acting like a depressed elevator, thus tending to lever the tail up and depress the nose.

I decided to shift the position of the planes and level them off, which was a bit of a job, as I had the help of only one man and a boy. However, I did get some assistance from the fabric shop to remove the gaiters into which the planes are fixed. Unfortunately, they had only finished one side when they were called away to carry out a repair on *C.4*, so I was back where I started. Next day was Sunday and I managed to get one of the cox'ns from Lowthorpe to lend me a hand. While he and I were busy with the gaiter patches, who should walk into the shed but two former Anglesey men who had just arrived on the station and were having a look around—being Sunday it was a 'make and mend' day. They were in their Number One uniforms, but seeing me working practically on my own they asked me if they could help. Was I pleased? They were both expert riggers, one of them being a cox'n. They went off, got into working clothes and were soon back and on the job. To cut the story short, the job was finished by 9.30 pm and the ship ready for flight, thanks to the assistance of my two old Anglesey boys and the cox'n from Lowthorpe. This was an example of the *esprit de corps* at Anglesey. In 1969 I attended the forty-ninth reunion dinner of the RNAS Anglesey Old Boys' Association and one of the men who assisted me—Jimmy Lunn—was there; the other, Mallet, I am sorry to say, has died.*

I took the ship up for trials next morning, taking with me the Station Engineer Officer, Lt Seagram, as I wanted his advice regarding the oil pressure. As before, this dropped, but Seagram made some adjustments and it picked up. The adjustment of the planes had improved, but not entirely eliminated, the nose heaviness. However, I decided she was now flyable, came down and dropped Seagram.

I started off again with a new crew consisting of LM Gray as engineer and AM Hull as W/T op. I began to open up the engine at about 30 feet and must have reached the 'Speed of inversion'—ship acting oppositely to the controls—for down came her nose and she would have hit the deck had I not let go all my water ballast. As it was, I only missed a fence by a foot and had to steer between two tall trees. I landed straight away, filled up with water, getting away successfully at my next attempt, and proceeded on patrol.

I sighted some oil bubbles when about six miles off Whitby. I hovered over the spot for some minutes; the bubbles still continued to rise, so I dropped a hundred-pound bomb with delayed-action fuse to give

* Since writing the above, when attending the Anglesey Old Boys' 50th Reunion Dinner on 17th April 1970, I learned with profound sorrow and regret that Jimmy Lunn will not see this book as he has also passed away.

whatever it was a shake-up, but the only things that came to the surface were a lot of dead fish. A destroyer then came up and started netting the fish. I returned to Kirkleatham, having just previously been ordered to 'land as soon as possible'.

Next day, 2nd July 1918, I was out at 2.55 am in *Z.55* with the same crew. I joined a northbound convoy about twelve miles east of Whitby and saw it into the Tyne at 9 am. On the 3rd I was out at 3 am on a similar job—convoying—and the same again the next day, but failed to pick up a convoy in spite of zigzagging out and back about fifteen miles between Whitby, Hartlepool, Sunderland and Tyne. The weather thickened up and I could only just discern the land when I got back to the Tees. I received a rocket from Howden after this flight for going on patrol without a wireless operator; mine had gone sick and no replacement was available.

The wind got up on 5th July, but the ship rode as steady as a rock with our new method of mooring her tail to wind and tucked right under the trees.

The Spanish 'flu was spreading and I heard the sad news that Reggie Alderson had died of it; when I woke up the 6th July with a sore throat I feared I was in for it. John Evason also complained of similar symptoms. As there was no possibility of flying, I went to bed after lunch, put on my 'submarine frock'—as our heavy woollen sweater was called—piled on blankets and took three aspirins, with the intention of sweating out whatever infection I had picked up. And did I sweat? it simply poured off me and soaked my pyjamas and sweater. Towards tea-time, when I was having a pint mug of tea to replace some of the moisture lost, Evason and Coltman, cox'n of *Z.55*, reported that the top valve petticoat was sticking out. I peeked out of my tent and saw the top valve and petticoat like a large top-hat perched on top of the envelope. I sent Coltman up to lace it up and stick it down.

I ought to explain here what the top valve is like. At the top of the envelope, there is an open-ended concertina sleeve called a petticoat like a more elaborate version of the mouthpiece of a toy balloon. Around the rim of the valve is a series of threaded pegs spaced to coincide with eyelet holes in the open end of the concertina sleeve and the valve is inserted into the end of the concertina by threading the pegs through the eyelets and screwing them down tight with butterfly nuts. The petticoat itself can then be turned in on itself and concertinaed down to the eyelets by means of cord lacings running through eyelets on the edge of the concertina so that the valve sits snugly more or less flush with the top of the envelope. To ensure that the petticoat remains closed down tight against the envelope, a circular patch is solutioned around the valve rim, binding it and the petticoat to the envelope. The elaborate petticoat system allows a valve to be replaced with the envelope up to pressure; the drill is to tear off the solutioned or doped circular patch, loosen the lacings, thus allowing the concertina to expand, and tie off the neck of the concertina. The butterfly nuts holding the valve can then be unscrewed without releasing the pressure. Normally this operation and the insertion of a new valve would be carried out in a shed, the cox'n being let down on a bos'n's chair from the roof. Out in the open there was nothing to which we could sling a chair, so it had to be done by crawling over the top of the envelope.

Coltman got on top of the envelope by means of a ladder near the stern. He was just crawling up the envelope when there was an ominous tearing sound and he disappeared from view. The envelope immediately began to crease up. 'He's fallen through', I yelled to Evason.

Evason rushed over to the ship, while I slipped on a pair of trousers and rushed over after him. We got Coltman out in a couple of minutes or, rather, he got himself out, as he had to cut his way through ballonet and envelope. He was practically unconscious, staggered about and then fell down. I gave him artificial respiration as for drowning and he came to very quickly, pushed me aside, jumped up—saying 'I'm all right now, sir'—and then lent a hand with the ship, which had, of course, subsided over the car. We completed the deflation and spent the rest of the evening and most of the night packing her up for transport back to Howden. I was getting quite expert at this, as this was the third 'Zero' I had had to pack up at mooring-out stations since the middle of May. Anyway, I was quite cured of the flu and I travelled back to Howden on the lorry which came to fetch *Z.55*.

On arrival at Howden, I was immediately put in command of a 'Coastal', *C.4*, but I had no opportunity of flying her, as the weather went dud for a week.

I remember a conversation one day about then; Phil Barnes told me that Pete Wolf and he had been putting their heads together with a view to starting a commercial airship service after the war and he asked my opinion as to its paying possibilities. I said I did not think it would pay without its being government subsidised. 'What amazes us', he told me then, 'is the continued keenness on flying you fellows still show after four years of bloody war.'

He was not referring to me, personally, of course, but to all airship flying personnel, who were putting in as many or more hours on patrol as I was. I said I thought we were dedicated by the thought that we were doing our bit in furthering the war effort; that we were ensuring the safety of our food supplies, reducing the losses at sea, and making up in some small way for the terrific losses our army was suffering in France and elsewhere whilst we were in what we considered was a comparatively safe occupation. I don't think it ever entered our heads that we were engaged in a dangerous service, despite the large amount of a highly inflammable gas in the envelope overhead, or the tanks of explosive liquid comprising our fuel, to say nothing of the bombs which might send us sky-high if we hit the deck too hard. In spite of the loss of my friends Jackson, Dixon and 'Pay' Warlters by enemy action, which could easily have been my fate, as I did quite an appreciable amount of flying in the area in which they were brought down, I always considered we of the Airship Service were in the safest service in the war—one had only to think of the incredible losses in France and the useless sacrifice at the Dardanelles, where I had lost my eldest brother in the senseless attack on Lone Pine—4,000 men had been killed on a narrow front in *one morning*, and all to no purpose.

CHAPTER SIX

Appointed to Italian 'M' Ship

I was having a 'caulk' after lunch on 12th July when one of the office 'wallahs' woke me up and told me a telegram had just been received reading: 'Hasten Captain Meager's departure to London'; I was to catch the 2.30 pm train to London, the which I did, and reported at Dean Stanley Street first thing next morning, when I was given an outline of the programme. Our party was to leave London on the 22nd July; I was to stop off at Paris and Marsielles to see what landing facilities there were, and then proceed by rail to Ciampino for the inflation and rigging of the 'Semi-Rigid' 'M' type airship which the Admiralty had bought from the Italian Government. After trials had been completed satisfactorily, she would be formally accepted by Major Cochrane on behalf of the Controller of Aircraft Production; I was to take her over from him on behalf of the Admiralty and fly her home to England. Strangely enough the Admiralty, although handing over all RNAS personnel to the RAF, still retained the airships, and I was lent to them to deliver *SR.1*—as the new ship was to be known—in England. After seeing about my codes at the Admiralty, and getting what gear I needed at the Army depot at Millbank, I returned to Howden to clear up my affairs there.

On 22nd July 1918 I duly joined Rope, Williams and Cochrane at Waterloo on the 11.55 train for Southampton. We had a good passage to Havre, but a slow journey to Paris, stopping at nearly every station. At one stop I very nearly got left behind; I went over to a siding to get some water from an engine there and was just pouring out some of it for some WAACs on the train when it started off. I jumped on the footboard, which fortunately is low on French trains and made my way along them back to my compartment without mishap; 'Ropie' then set about making some cocoa by means of an electric gadget like a small immersion heater.

On arrival in Paris I called on our Naval Attaché, Commander Heaton Ellis, a fine old chap who took a great deal of trouble to put me in touch with the right people. One of these was Commander Sablé of the French Naval Airship Service, who took me to Issy-les-Moulineaux and St Cyr. If I landed at Paris it would be at St Cyr, which, according to Sablé, has a shed large enough to take an 'M'-type ship, whereas Issy has not.

Cochrane, Rope and Williams had gone on. I caught the night train to Marseilles and was met by a car which took me out to Aubagne, the French Naval Airship Station about ten miles east of the city. I did not much like the look of the place for landing, as it was surrounded by hills about a thousand feet high. I was informed that it was, in fact, a very difficult place at which to land and five ships had crashed there during the year. The shed there was too small to take an 'M' ship, but there were windscreens which should give adequate shelter; they were, moreover, latticed, which breaks up the wind and prevents the waterfall effect when the wind blows at right angles to their line.

Soon after leaving Marseilles, between St Raphael and Nice, we could see the woods on the slopes above were on fire. A mistral or northerly wind was blowing; this fanned the flames which we could see in a long line racing down the hillside—a fascinating, awe-inspiring and fearsome sight, as it could not miss the railway track. The question was: Could we get by before it reached us? The flames were leaping high above the trees and roaring louder than the rattle of the train; enormous clouds of smoke came rolling up over us and away out to sea. We were smothered with ashes and dust and at times almost choked with smoke. The driver was apparently trying to outrun the flames, for he increased speed, but he couldn't make it; the flames got very near; we could, in fact, feel their heat inside the train. The passengers, mostly French civilians, went hopping mad, running up and down the corridors, waving their arms, shouting '*En arrière; en arrière!*' as if the driver could hear. Finally the driver, almost in answer to the cries of the passengers, reversed thc train a short distance and pulled up just above Nice, whilst the flames crossed the track a little ahead and burnt themselves out on reaching the beach below. It was quite frightening while it lasted and the side of the train was scorched. Once we stopped there was a general exodus of passengers into Nice.

Eventually, after some delay while the fire burnt itself out, we went on through Ventimiglia to Genoa, where we had four hours to wait; enough to have a roam around the town, which has a very fine main street, colonnaded, with covered pavements on both sides.

When we stopped at Civita Vecchia, who should I see on the platform but Mezzadra, Second Officer of *M.6* at Grottaglie. We had a great natter together, he in broken English, I in broken Italian, during the remainder of the journey to Rome. I saw him on to his train to Taranto, and at the station met two other officers on their way back: Ferris Scott, our former Paymaster, and Pelligrini, a rugged, hoarse-voiced Tuscan whom I had instructed in SS flying at Grottaglie. Rome is certainly a happy meeting-place for me, as on my way to the Aeronautical Institute to see Colonel Crocco, its head, I ran into another ex-Grottaglie officer named Brucato. He was a very picturesque sight in the full dress uniform of the Artillery, and was having a last fling in Rome before proceeding to the front. On my arrival at Ciampino, who should greet me but Tenente Ilari, who had been the Acceptance Officer of the SS ships at Grottaglie. He welcomed me like a long-lost brother.

Inflation of our ship commenced next day, the 1st August 1918, at 6.15 am. Whilst the fitting of the girders and rigging of the car and planes was in progress, I took every opportunity of having trips in other ships stationed at Ciampino. On 2nd August Ilari took Cochrane, Rope and myself up for a couple of hours' patrol in *Pv.2*. On the 5th Cochrane and I were given a similar-length flight by Captain Menenti in *O.2*, a smaller ship of 127,000 cubic feet capacity with a boat car and two 120 hp Colombo engines side by side at the stern.

Cochrane wanted to have a look at the new large semi-rigid *A.1* of over a million cubic feet capacity which was stationed at Grottaglie. As there was little we could do except watch the work proceeding on *SR.1*, he and I went down there for a few days. We arrived to find the whole station, except the guards and Dr Saldutti, in bed. The reason for this was that *A.1* had been out all night on a bombing raid over the military installations at Cattaro and Durazzo. I was hoping to get a bombing flight in her, but the weather was against it, so I spent most of my time translating the logs of *M.6* and *A.1* for Cochrane.

Incidentally our old friend Vigliani, who had been at Kingsnorth with me, was one of the officers of *A.1*. He was lost in her on a subsequent raid when she was brought down by gunfire. He was such a nice cheerful chap, always smiling and always very friendly.

We were back in Rome by the 11th August and on the 14th Major Leone, Captain of *M.1*, offered me a trip in her. We escorted the mail boat from Civita Vecchia half-way to Sardinia; picked up the incoming boat and accompanied her back to Civita Vecchia. Overland we could see a heavy thunderstorm with much forked lightning. We kept clear of it by standing out to sea, and only experienced a little rain. This flight was of fifteen hours. The Second-in-Command of M.1 was Tenente Castruccio, a charming officer of the Engineers who was awarded the Italian equivalent of our VC for an act of conscpicuous bravery in one of the airships during a bombing flight.

The storm we had seen must have been a miniature tornado, for after we landed at Ciampino we found the roofs had been torn off the huts, and large trees were down all over the place.

I had two more flights in *M.1*. The first, on 18th August was a special flight put on for Sir Arthur Duckham and Mr Thornton of our Ministry of Munitions. We went down low almost on the surface of Lake Albano, then to Lake Nemi; on to Nettuno and the holiday resort at Anzio—later to become famous for the landings in World War II. The other, on 22nd August, we spent the morning patrolling the Tyrrhenian Sea between Anzio and the mouth of the Tiber. After lunch on board we went down to Monte Circe, Ponzia Island and back to Anzio, off the beach of which we alighted on the water.

The method of alighting on the water was to drop a large drogue—canvas sea anchor—into the water, force the ship down with the engines and, when near the surface, let go two large canvas bags which filled with water and held the ship down. To get off, the bags and the drogue were pulled inside out and emptied; the ship, thus being light, lifted off the water.

On alighting we were immediately surrounded by a crowd of small boats and bathing-belles. Someone in one of the boats produced a bottle of wine, out of which we drank the health of the people around.

After we left the water at Anzio, Major Leone took the ship again up to Lake Albano, where he attempted to alight on the surface without the aid of the drogue. He came down too low, however, and a gust from the surrounding hills caught us on the bow and blew us into the water, which came over the deck. All the water ballast had to be let go in order to get off the water and clear the hills. This flight lasted eight hours and Cochrane came up with us, in addition to the crew of eight.

One evening we were entertained by the CO of Ciampino, Major Biffi, and his officers to a dinner party at an inn overlooking the lake at Nemi—the lake itself is the crater of an extinct volcano, the slopes of which are covered in pine woods. The inn is perched about fifteen hundred feet up on a slope overlooking the water—a most picturesque setting.

Among our hosts was Professor Bianchi, who was in great form, telling amusing stories, half in English, half in Italian. I took to him at once. Biffi nicknamed him *l'Astronomo*, as he was a very eminent astronomer and mathematician. He used to come out to Ciampino to instruct the flying officers in navigation and astronomy. They then prevailed on me to make a speech in Italian, which I managed successfully with the aid of some of the very fine local wine produced by the landlord. A most enjoyable evening.

When not flying or otherwise engaged with the ship, Rope, Williams and I used to 'pole' off to Rome to have a look round the city. Cochrane came occasionally, but usually he spent his spare time at the British Embassy, where I believe his brother was staying—his brother had just escaped from being a prisoner of war in Turkey, where he had been captured whilst trying to get through the minefields in the Dardanelles in a submarine. Rope introduced us to friends of his named Englefield, a brother and sister. Mr Englefield was formerly the proprietor of the Hotel 'Laurati' and, when he sold it, he retained a very nice flat on top of the hotel from which one had a lovely view over the city. In his retirement Mr Englefield used to spend his time showing British soldiers on leave around the city. During our visits to the city we sampled many of the restaurants in Rome, including the 'Ulpia', a unique but dark establishment set in a cave-like apse at one end of Trajan's Forum, and the 'Castello dei Cesari', a sort of conservatory, built on the site of an Emperor's palace on the Aventine Hill, and many others. We always had tea at the 'Babington English Tea-rooms' in the Piazza d'Espagna, or at 'Old England' in the Corso, which were the only places, apart from Miss Englefield's, where one could get a properly made cup of tea!

At last SR.1 was completed. On 26th August 1918 she was taken out for a short flight by the trial crew to show she was capable of flying. Twelve people were on board, including Cochrane, Rope, myself, and CPO Owen. Although an entry in the log-book stated 'During flight everything functioned well', I was not very enthusiastic over it, as the SPA developed an oil leak, whilst the shaft coupling of one of the Italas ran rather hot; *SR.1* had three engines, a single SPA and two Italas, which were really Zeppelin Maybachs built in Italy under licence.

SR.1, with 441,000 cubic feet, was the largest airship apart from 'Rigids' ever possessed by the British Government, the later Parsevals being 325,000 cubic feet and the 'North Sea' ships 360,000 cubic feet.

Further short trials were carried out on 28th and 29th August, the flying crew, of course, being Italian, with ourselves as observers. I remember during one of these flights the Captain, Major Biffi and his Second Officer, Captain Menenti, had a terrific argument in the control car. They went too fast for me to pick up what the argument was about, but they went at it hammer and tongs, shouting and waving their arms about. Finally, Menenti snatched off his cap, threw it on the deck and jumped on it. End of argument!

During an interval of about a week between flights, whilst the engines were being prepared for speed trials, Cochrane and I went up to Ferrara and Campalto near Venice, which were both Italian operational stations. At Campalto was *F.5*—Forlanini No. 5—an airship which the British Government had agreed to buy before the war, but which had not been completed before war broke out. The Italian Government took her over and she was flown on many bombardment flights against the Austrians after the Italians had joined us.

F.5 was a 'Semi-Rigid' of 500,000 cubic feet capacity with a large internal triangular girder to which the envelope was attached. The base of the girder formed the bottom of the ship and a walking way throughout its length, as well as providing storage space for tanks and equipment. The envelope was rather unusual in that it consisted of an inner and an outer skin both made of silk; the inner one contained the gas and was compartmented, then there was a layer or cushion of air between the inner and outer envelopes. The ship was powered by two Isotta—Fraschini engines of 250 hp each.

On our return to Ciampino we took part in the speed trials of *SR.1*, during which she obtained a top speed of 51 mph, with both Italas at 1,400 rpm, Pitch 5 on the variable-pitch propeller, and the SPA at 1,500 rpm. Running the Italas at 1,200 rpm, Pitch 1, and the SPA at 600 rpm, the speed was 32 mph. After a few more short test flights we went up in *SR.1* to carry out further speed trials and an endurance test. We had done about an hour and a half at full speed when we got a terrific bumping-about while flying over hilly country near the coast. The tail went up; the plane cage nearly disappeared from view and whipped about in an alarming fashion. Menenti, who was piloting, slowed down at once and decided to call it a day and land in order to inspect the planes for damage; but we were lucky and none was found when we got back to the shed later.

Next day, 21st September, we succeeded in carrying out our speed and endurance trials, being up from 6.25 am until 6 pm. We commenced by doing two and a half hours at full speed, followed by three hours at two-thirds speed, at the end of which one of the water jackets on the starboard Itala cracked and the engine was stopped; the flight was continued, however, and I took the steering-wheel at 2 pm and carried on until we landed. I found her difficult to steer at slow speeds, taking a long time to answer, but when she did she got a hell of a swing on, similar to the new 'Zero' rudder which I had tried at Howden. At a good turn of speed I found I could keep within 2½ degrees of any course—or within one division of the compass dial.

On 24th September we met Ian Struthers in Rome; he was on his way to take command of a new Airship Station in Malta. We invited him to Ciampino for the morrow, when we were giving a spread in the Mess. I had last seen Struthers at Wormwood Scrubbs when he had landed there with *NS.6*.

Our 'spread' was a great success and Frailik, who was Messing Officer, put on an excellent dinner. After the meal we had a sing-song and dancing with Captain Sapio at the piano. Frailik and Williams did a very funny dance together—Williams with Frailik's cap and sword; Frailik with Williams's cap and walking-stick. They did an exaggerated goose-step parade and were really very funny, both being a bit 'on'. It was extraordinary how these two hit it off together, as neither spoke a word of the other's language.

Struthers performed the Highland Fling, and the doctor and others sang some rather risqué songs, while an officer from Milan sang a Milanese drinking song which goes to a rollicking tune as follows:

Bevi, bevi, compagno—se non, ti ammazzaro.
Non m'ammazzar', compagno—che addesso bevero.

Drink, drink, comrade—if not I will kill you.
Don't kill me, comrade, for I will now drink.

Melso bevuto tutto, e non mi ha fatto malo;
L'acqua fa male, e il vino far' cantar'

I have now drunk it all, and it has done me no harm.
Water makes one ill, but wine makes one sing.

Another went something like this:

Singer: *Io vorrei la cameriera.*—I would like the waitress.
Chorus: *E che n'e feresti tu?*—What would you do with her?
Singer: *Io vorrei i suoi occhi.*—I would like her eyes.
Chorus: *E che n'e feresti tu?*—What would you do with them?
Singer: *E per guardar'gli, mattina, sera, gli occhi della cameriera; gli occhi della cameriera;*
E per guardar'gli mattina, sera, gli occhi della cameriera che non si retrova piu.—To look into them, morning and evening, the eyes of the waitress; the eyes of the waitress which cannot be found elsewhere.

And so on.

The following evening after dinner, a deputation from the Petty Officers' Mess invited me to a celebration they were having. I was quite overwhelmed with their *Evvivas* as I entered. They also had a sing-song and I discovered that one of my engineers, PO Tomlins, was an excellent pianist. Just before I left I formed the whole crowd into a circle, and with crossed arms swinging, we sang 'For they are jolly good fellows', etc., the Italians picking up the tune, if not the words, very quickly.

Revenons à nos moutons: on 30th September the wireless and armament were to be tested, but very soon after we left the ground the starboard engine stopped. It was soon restarted, but ran groggily with smoke coming from the top of the cylinders, accompanied by a cracking sound. The engine was stopped and four cylinder water jackets were found to be cracked, so none of the tests were carried out. Another try was made a few days later, but the wind got up and the pilot, Menenti, decided to land before it got worse. He made a bit of a mess of it, as he reversed the Italas too soon, declutched, but then found that the SPA by itself was not strong enough to manoeuvre the ship, resulting in our very nearly being blown on to the shed. However, all's well that ends well, and we got down safely.

After the flight, Rope felt ill; he developed a high temperature of 104 degrees and the doctor diagnosed flu. As there were no medical orderlies on the station to look after him, I got him into the ambulance and took him to the English Nursing Home at Santo Stefano Rotondo; they could not take him in, so I took him along to the Italian Military Hospital at Celio, where they found him a bed, although they were already crowded out. The hospital is run by nuns, the doctors being army medical men.

Ropie was very ill indeed, but his wonderful constitution and saintly manner of living pulled him through. I used to visit him on every day that we were not flying. I don't think Cochrane realised how ill he was, for he sent him along some highly technical work to do, but Rope was too ill to tackle it. In fact, when he did get out of bed for the first time he collapsed. He told me his legs were like water and down he went.

The effects of the Spanish flu in Rome must have been on a par with those in London during the Great Plague or the Black Death of an earlier period, for people were dying like flies. There were too many deaths for burial services and lorries full of dead people were leaving the city by night, taking them out to communal graves outside the city, at the rate of five hundred a day.

I remember on one occasion, when we were on our way back to Ciampino late one night, our tram crashed into the back of a lorry filled with coffins of flu victims. One of the coffins, that of a child, was thrown into the roadway by the impact. No one would venture to pick it up and put it back on the lorry for fear of catching the infection, so I did it myself, as for some reason I had no fear of catching it.

I used to keep fit by going for long walks with Cochrane or Williams to Albano, Castel Gandolfo, Marino, Frascati and Rocca di Papa, all very picturesque places in the Alban Hills, from which magnificent views were obtainable over the Campagna Romana.

On one of these occasions, on a very hot day, we were absolutely parched with thirst. 'The next house we come to,' I said, 'I'm going to ask for a drink.' We duly came to a large white house, knocked on the door and asked the maid for a glass of water—I could speak enough Italian for this. She said she would ask *la Padrona*. The mistress herself then came to us and asked us if we were Americans.

'No, English,' I replied. At this she was all over us, sent the maid for a bottle of wine and glasses and poured us out a tumblerful of the most delicious local wine. It turned out that she had been lady's maid to a lady in England some years before. We wended our way back to Ciampino walking on air, such was the delayed action of the wine.

On 8th October we were to have done our final trials, including W/T and armament, but the artillery experts failed to put in an appearance. Four days later we did the final W/T tests, but cancelled the armament, as it was decided to remove the cannon, and carry only one Fiat machine-gun for the flight home. This would mean a saving of well over a hundredweight. During this flight the transmitters functioned all right, but the receivers were dud; they were, in fact replaced by new sets before we finally left for home.

Cochrane then took up the ship as pilot for acceptance trials with an entirely English crew, plus a young Italian officer named De Rossi who had been designated to fly home with us. We carried out turning circles at various rudder angles and speeds; also ascending and descending trials and further speed trials. These trials lasted nearly six hours, for about half of which I was on the elevator control. Cochrane was satisfied with the behaviour of the ship and formally took the ship over on behalf of the Director of Aircraft Production; I then took her over on behalf of the Admiralty.

It was not until a week later that I had my first opportunity of taking the ship up as pilot. This was on 20th October with the following crew:

Pilot: Self. *Second-in-Command:* Captain T. B. Williams, AFC. *Cox'n:* PO H. Lee. *First Engineer:* PO H. Leech. *Second Engineer:* PO R. Tomlins. *W/T Op:* AM R. J. Rook. *Observer:* Major R. A. Cochrane. *Observer Engineer:* CPO Owen.

This flight was more to familiarise the crew with the ship, and for practice, than for any specific trial; it lasted an hour and a half. We made rather a fast landing owing to the engineers not reversing the props when I gave the signal—one accidentally stopped his engine by catching his sleeve on the switch; the other kept his engine going ahead, not having understood the signal. (After this we had a dial fitted with pointer to show what pitch was required.) During the landing we dragged three men along the ground hanging on to the trail rope, bruising and grazing them.

We made another short flight of the same duration on 23rd October, with CPO Clarke and PO Burrell as cox'ns, and an Italian with the camera for test; the rest of the crew were as before. The engines were behaving badly; the SPA developed a knock, so it was stopped, and then the starboard Itala started missing and was found to have a broken valve spring, which was quickly replaced. I got the ship beautifully into equilibrium and made a very good landing on the handling-guys—that is without dropping the trail rope.

We were now only awaiting suitable weather reports from England and France before embarking on our journey home. We began to think the 'met' people were scared to chance their arm in case they would be held responsible should the ship be lost, as day after day passed without 'Suitable conditions' being received. I had an idea, too, that Cochrane was seriously thinking of packing the ship up and sending her home by train. So far, no aircraft of any kind had flown from Italy to England or, in fact, the other way either. All the aircraft sent out to our seaplane stations in Italy or the Middle East, as well as our reconnaissance planes, had previously made the journey in packing-cases, being re-erected at their destination; none had ever been flown home. So it is not to be wondered at that even our own airship people were quoting odds of ten to one against our making the flight successfully and the American naval airship people quoted six to four. I did not hear of this until after we had finally made it, when Nixon, who was on the Airship HQ Staff, was congratulating me and mentioned the fact that I had won him a 'tenner'.

At last, on 24th October, we received the first 'Suitable' from England for a month. On the 25th we made another short local flight for camera tests during which we flew over Rome and took some photographs.

I think I have mentioned the practice before landing an airship of what is called 'ballasting up', which means getting the ship more or less into equilibrium, neither light nor heavy. On this flight we had gone up ten bags of sand light, say 300 pounds, in order to pierce the inversion of temperature—it is warmer at a height than it is on the ground. In addition, we had used a little fuel and the sun was nearly overhead and thus superheating the gas; in my opinion we were very light indeed. In order to redress this, I was valving gas, as I considered the ship to be too light to land properly.

Cochrane said: 'Stop valving; you are heavy already.'

'I don't agree', I replied. 'The ship is very light.'

'Look at your tail', he said. 'It is down.'

'So it may be, but I know we are light.' However, I desisted from valving, slowed down as we were approaching the landing-party, reversed the props and dropped the trail rope. The result was that, being light, we shot upwards with the trail rope hanging out of reach of the landing-party and we had to go round again with it hanging down. On the way round the rope carried away a couple of local telegraph wires. I'm afraid Cochrane did not view this in the cheerful way the CO and Major Greig had done at Driffield, but was furious. Anyway, I completed the circuit and came in very low with a good length of rope on the ground, so that when I reversed and the ship slowed down, a goodly number of men could man it and not be carried off their feet. This they did and we landed without mishap.

I couldn't help thinking of the Biffi-Menenti episode I have described earlier, though there was no gesticulating or cap-jumping!

I had one final disagreement with Cochrane. He had already sent home the spare riggers on the ground of the expense—a proper 'Fifer'. He now said we needed another engineer on the flight, to which I quite agreed, as the SPA needed constant attention; what I did not agree with was that Burrell was to stay behind to clear up stores whilst CPO Owen went on the flight as Chief Engineer. I agreed with taking Owen, but stressed the point that we should need another cox'n even if only for his assistance on the ground, as we would be landing two or three times on the way in a foreign country. Cochrane was adamant and nothing would budge him; Owen was to go and Burrell was to stay. When I broke the news to poor Burrell it very nearly broke his heart—and mine. He was such a good man at his job, besides being such a lovable character. We missed him badly on our various landings *en route*.

The next two days were pretty hectic preparing the ship for the great adventure. We were under no misapprehension as to the risks involved and we took out of the ship everything not required for the flight. Theoretically we should have had a disposable lift of about 9,600 pounds made up as follows:

Total gross lift	13,000 kilograms
Dead weight of ship	8,640 kilograms
Disposable lift	4,360 kilograms = 9,592 pounds

Actually the disposable lift was always less than this, as we usually left the ground with sufficient air in the ballonet to allow us to reach flying height without having to valve gas. In the end, I calculated our load as follows:

Fuel	738 gallons —	5,535 pounds
Oil	64 gallons —	576 pounds
Water ballast	106 gallons —	1,060 pounds
Spares		300 pounds
Armament (one machine-gun and ammunition)		40 pounds
		7,511 pounds
Crew (9)		1,400 pounds
	Total	8,911 pounds

At an estimated consumption of forty gallons per hour, we had enough fuel for eighteen hours' continuous flying at full power—much longer, of course, at cruising speed or with an engine in reserve.

All was now ready for our great attempt. We realized that it was going to be no cake-walk.

CHAPTER SEVEN

SR.1's Flight Rome—England

On 28th October 1918 we were hauled out of the shed at Ciampino and ballasted up about two men light, as we anticipated the usual morning inversion. At 4.25 am the order 'Let go' was given. It was pitch dark, but a searchlight beam was shone on to the shed.

We found the anticipated inversion all right, for at a height of 200 feet we commenced to fall; to avoid being blown on to the shed, I let go most of the water ballast and opened up both Italas, which gave us some forward movement and elevator control for some dynamic lift. I was not worried much about the lack of ballast, as I knew we should consume a great deal of fuel on the way and could, in an emergency, jettison some of it. Moreover, as the day wore on we should probably experience some superheating from the sun.

On board were the following personnel:

Captain and Pilot: Captain G. F. Meager. *Second Pilot:* Captain T. B. Williams, AFC. *Italian Observer:* Tenente R. De Rossi. *Cox'n:* CPO G. T. Clarke. *Chief Engineer:* CPO R. G. Owen. *First Engineer:* PO H. Leech. *Second Engineer:* PO R. Tomlins. *First W/T Op:* LM B. Bocking. *Second W/T Op:* AM R. J. Rook.

So away we went over the Eternal City of Rome; there was no black-out and the many twinkling lights presented a very attractive sight as we set course for the coast, which we crossed at a little place named Ladispoli at 5 am. We found the wind to be from the north-east at 10 knots. Half an hour later, off Civita Vecchia, we ran into some very bumpy weather and the ship danced about a bit. I feared for our planes, so slowed down the engines and veered away from the coast. After another hour or so we reached Giglio Island off Cape Orbetello, at 6.45 am, with Monte Cristo to port: by now it was almost daylight and conditions were much calmer.

We passed between the islands of Elba and Pianosa—two opposites in appearance; Pianosa, as its name implies, being low and flat, whilst Elba is rocky and mountainous—it looked very forbidding, even though the sun was now shining brightly in a completely blue sky.

We found the wind at Elba had gone round a little, being from east-north-east at 15 knots. This helped us considerably after passing Cape

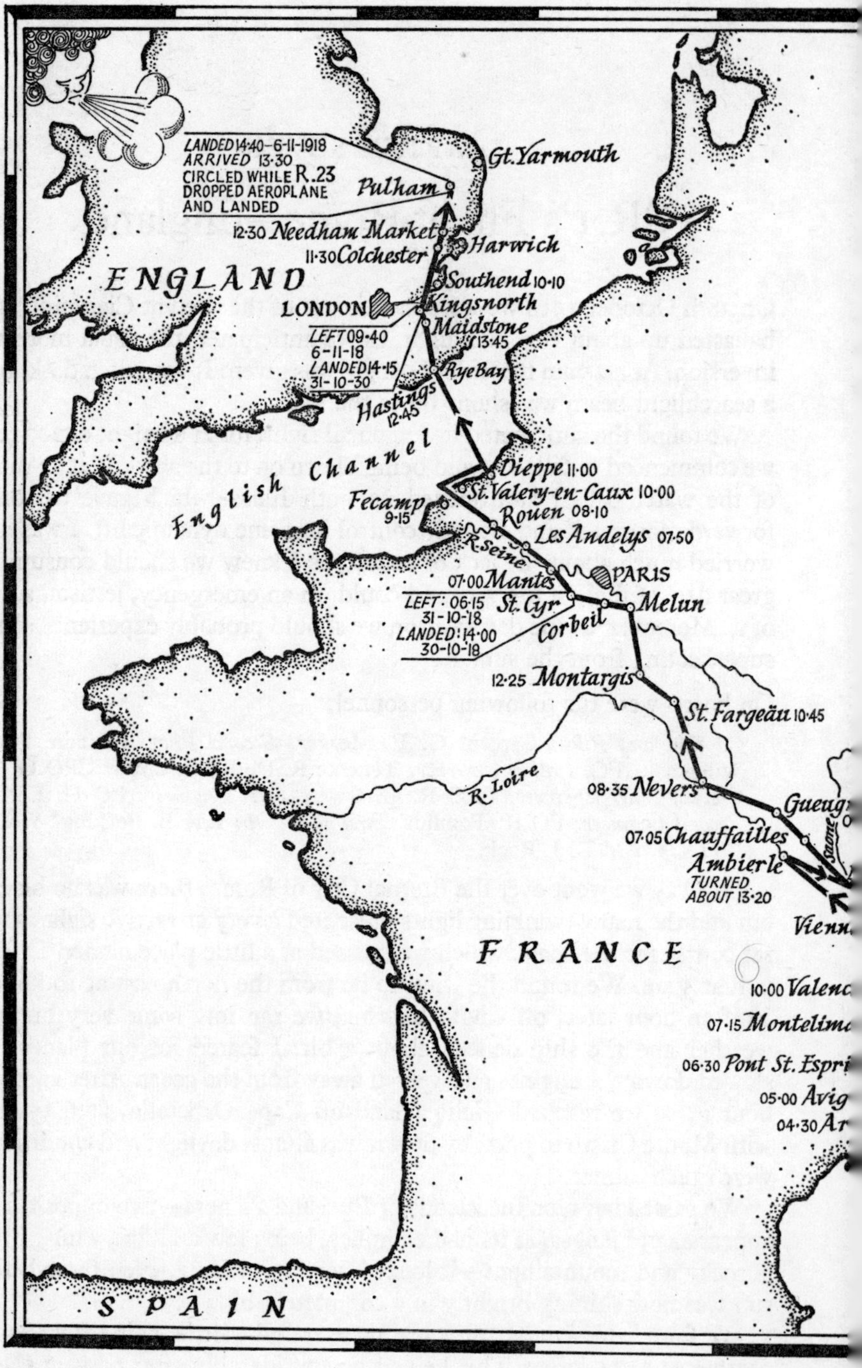
LANDED 14·40–6-11-1918
ARRIVED 13·30
CIRCLED WHILE R.23
DROPPED AEROPLANE
AND LANDED
Pulham
Gt. Yarmouth
12·30 Needham Market
11·30 Colchester
Harwich
ENGLAND
Southend 10·10
LONDON
Kingsnorth
Maidstone
LEFT 09·40
6-11-18
LANDED 14·15
31-10-30
13·45
Rye Bay
Hastings
12·45
English Channel
Dieppe 11·00
St. Valery-en-Caux 10·00
Fecamp
9·15
Rouen 08·10
Les Andelys 07·50
R. Seine
PARIS
07·00 Mantes
St. Cyr
LEFT: 06·15
31-10-18
LANDED: 14·00
30-10-18
Corbeil
Melun
12·25 Montargis
St. Fargeau 10·45
R. Loire
08·35 Nevers
07·05 Chauffailles
Ambierle
TURNED
ABOUT 13·20
Saone
FRANCE
SPAIN

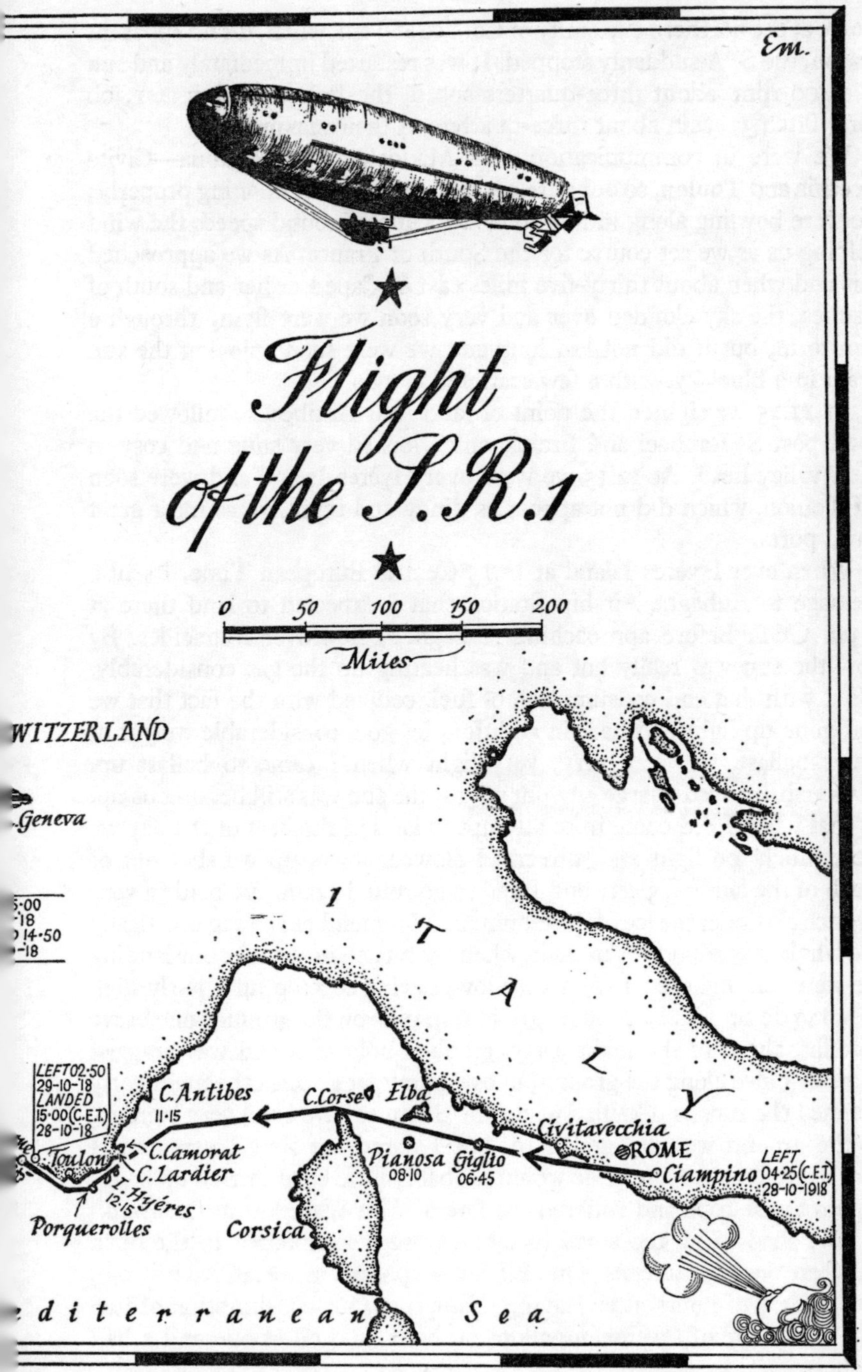

Em.
Flight of the S.R.1
0 50 100 150 200
Miles
I T A L Y
LEFT 02·50
29-10-18
LANDED
15·00 (C.E.T.)
28-10-18
C. Antibes
11·15
C. Corse
Elba
Civitavecchia
ROME
Ciampino
LEFT
04·25 (C.E.T.)
28-10-1918
Toulon
C. Camorat
C. Lardier
I. Hyéres
12·15
Porquerolles
Pianosa
08·10
Giglio
06·45
Corsica
editerranean Sea

Corse at the northern extremity of Corsica at 9 am, when, for no apparent reason, the SPA suddenly stopped. It was restarted immediately and run at 1,400 rpm, about three-quarters speed, the Italas running at 1,300 rpm, Pitch 3, again about three-quarters of their maximum.

We were in communication with Maddalena—in Sardinia—Civita Vecchia and Toulon, so our wireless sets were now functioning properly; we were bowling along in fine style at 42 knots ground speed, the wind helping us as we set course for the South of France. As we approached this and when about thirty-five miles east of Cape Lardier and south of Cannes, the sky clouded over and very soon we were flying through a rainstorm, but it did not last long and we were soon enjoying the sun again in a blue sky, with a few scattered clouds.

At 11.15 we sighted the point of land near Antibes, so followed the coast past St Raphael and Frejus which looked very snug and cosy in their valley head. At 12.15 we were over Hyères Island and were soon off Toulon, which did not appear as dingy and repulsive as most great naval ports.

When over Hyères Island at 12.15 Central European Time, I sent a message to Aubagne Airship Station that I expected to land there at 3 pm CET. Before approaching Aubagne, I flew over Marseilles. By now the sun was really hot and was heating up the gas considerably. What with that and consumption of fuel, coupled with the fact that we had gone up light and had, in addition, let go a considerable weight of water ballast, we were very, very light when I came to ballast up. Although I valved a large amount of gas, the sun was still heating us up, so that when I did come in to attempt to land in the heat of the day we were much too light and, directly I slowed down, up we shot out of reach of the landing-party and I had to go round again. We made a very wide circle under the lee of the mountains; I remember valving practically the whole way round; even then, when we turned in to make our landing we were still light, so I went very low, having to keep up a fairly high speed to do so. I had a good length of trail rope on the ground; one brave matelot, ahead of the main party, grabbed hold of it and was dragged some distance along the ground, but wouldn't let go until the main party manned the rope and hauled us down. He must have been very bruised, as the ground was dry and hard, but I dared not slow down until I reached the main party or he would probably have been carried up hanging on to the rope and suffered the fate of Tim Waterlow at Cranwell.

The shed being too small to take us, we were moored in the open between the windscreens. Our ETA was spot on, as we landed at 3 pm, ten and a half hours after leaving Ciampino. Our consumption of fuel was at the rate of seventeen gallons an hour, and oil at one and a half an hour.

Then we all set to on the job of refuelling and gassing up, the whole of the crew working like Trojans. With the willing assistance of the trained French Naval Airship personnel we took in 302 gallons of petrol —we had used 310 gallons—and seventeen gallons of oil, and gassed up 74,000 cubic feet of gas from 350 tubes of 6 cubic metres each of compressed gas. Imagine the stacks of cylinders, which measured about 5 feet long by 8 inches in diameter, cast iron, and weighting about two hundredweight apiece. Fortunately we did not have to lift them, as the French matelots stacked them in pyramids alongside the windscreens.

With a short break for a meal we finished filling up by 11.30 pm. Williams and I had a hot bath, which refreshed us very much, whilst De Rossi had a couple of hours in bed.

On returning to the ship we found the crew stretched out on the deck of the ship fast asleep. We did likewise; I remember using my service cap resting on the cox'n's boots as a pillow—talk about 'hard lying'; had we been still part of the Navy, we should have claimed it. In this fashion we enjoyed an hour's well-earned rest.

We all turned to at 1 am, hoping to get away at least by 2 am, but it was so cold and damp that we had much difficulty in starting the engines. It was not until nearly three o'clock on 29th October that we left Aubagne, again in pitch dark, carrying the same crew with the addition of Lieutenant-de-Vaisseau Picard, a French airship pilot, to assist with the navigation across France and after landing.

The weather forecast was for northerly winds in the Rhône Valley as far as Lyons, with south-east winds elsewhere in France. If we reached Lyons in reasonable time, we might expect a favourable wind afterwards and could push on direct to Paris.

Soon after leaving Aubagne, and when at a height of a thousand feet, I nearly had a fit on looking out of the control-car window to see in the blackness below the tops of some fir trees only a few feet away. We increased our height and proceeded in a west-north-west direction, picking up the River Rhône at Arles at 4.30 am, and followed it to Avignon at 5 am. The city itself was in total darkness, but just beyond it was a brilliantly lighted factory going full blast!

We continued along the Rhône, which was a wonderful guide in the dark, passing Pont St Esprit at 6.30 and Montelimar at 7.15 am. Up to this point we had used 108 gallons of fuel—roughly twenty-seven gallons an hour.

The northerly wind down the Rhône Valley was increasing, and we were making very poor progress. Once when flying parallel with the main road we could not outdistance a column of heavy lorries travelling at about ten miles an hour.

There was one very ticklish spot about five miles beyond Montelimar where the river flows between two hills, with a high, rocky island dividing the river. We were flying very low to mitigate the strength of the wind as much as possible; De Rossi was steering and Williams was on the elevator; both did an excellent job in keeping over the water flying between the hill and the island. To make matters worse, just then the SPA stopped with the carburettor frozen up and the oil congealed. Owen said he could get it going again, but it took him an hour and a half to do so. He must have been nearly shrammed to death working in the open with the ship heading into a bitterly cold wind. He came down into the car after getting it going, completely plastered from head to foot in oil.

To make better progress, I opened up the Italas to full speed, in spite of which, and flying at as low an altitude as we dared, our ground speed was no more than 7 knots. At one point we were so low our aerial trailed the ground and the weight was carried away.

Lieutenant Picard told me it was always like this during the morning in the Rhône Valley, the cold air from the Alps flowing down the mountainsides into the valley, which acted as a funnel. He expected that after Valence there would be an improvement. But it seemed that we would never get there. However, we did eventually, nearly three hours after Montelimar—a distance of twenty-three miles. By now it was 10 am; with the SPA going again, we made better progress, but received some rare old bumps off the mountains, which rocked the plane cage. We could see no damage from the control car in spite of our having omitted to trice it up before leaving Aubagne.

All this time we had been asking Lyons for the Paris weather report, but had received no reply at all.

As forecast by Picard, the wind decreased somewhat after passing Valence, but we still did not make good more than 30 knots, though we kept as low as safety permitted. Flying like this, of course, requires unremitting vigilance.

At noon we could vaguely see the city of Lyons almost hidden in a pall of fog. We were now making a better ground speed of 35 knots, so I decided to carry on to Paris; we expected the wind to be from the south-east as forecast. However, after proceeding for an hour and a half, we were only just past Ambierle and the wind was still contrary; I decided, after consulting Lieutenant Picard, to turn about and land at Bron just outside Lyons. Picard had divulged that he had not brought the night recognition signals, so we should have been in trouble had we reached Paris after dark, and in addition I was becoming a little worried about our petrol supply, as we had used over half of that with which we had left Aubagne.

When we got back to Lyons the fog had cleared, and we made a good landing at 2.50 pm at the airship and aeroplane emergency landing-ground at Bron. We had used 427 gallons of petrol—thirty-five and a half per hour—and seventeen gallons of oil—one and a half gallons per hour—during the twelve hours' flight.

Bron was not an airship station—in fact, it was not even an aeroplane station either, being merely an emergency landing-ground with supplies for both types, manned by Territorials; these were not the equivalent of our 'Territorial Army', but were mostly old men and army reservists, more the equivalent of the Home Guard of the Second World War. They were completely ignorant of airship practice. In fact, we were the first ship that had ever landed there, although we did not know it at the time.

It is not surprising that we had the greatest difficulty, first in mooring the ship out on the landing-ground and then in replenishing fuel and gas.

We solved the mooring problem by tying the ship to a three-ton lorry filled with hydrogen tubes, and the guys to screw pickets. Fortunately the weather was an absolute calm, so the ship itself gave us no anxiety.

Lieutenant Picard was a great help in organising the transport of supplies, for it all had to be brought over to the ship. To assist with the replenishing we were given about twenty third-line troops in charge of a young but intelligent corporal who fortunately understood a little English. We did not know until they started to do the job that not one of them knew anything about it, for at first there was absolutely no order or method at all—complete chaos. In their enthusiasm over having a job to do, the whole party tried to get hold of a key with which to turn the gas full on. The result was that in next to no time six of the twelve nozzles of the only filler pipe were blown off their connection. I soon saw that if things went on like this we should be left with plenty of gas in cylinders but without any means of getting it into the ship; I stopped operations, buttonholed the corporal and told him to form his men into teams—one to take off the metal tube caps; another to attach the fillers; another to turn on the gas *slowly* when told to do so by CPO Clarke; and a last group to connect the ship's filling-pipes, one to each compartment. The corporal quickly grasped the idea and henceforward things went along much more smoothly. No more nozzles were blown off; but the loss of six of them meant that the time needed for replenishment was doubled. It was now that we felt the loss of Burrell's assistance and know-how; far too much was on the shoulders of Clarke the cox'n, good though he was, for ballast had to be taken in as well.

Whilst all this was going on the engineers were occupied in filling up with petrol and oil. The oil gave no trouble, but some idea of the magnitude of filling up with petrol may be gained from the fact that 397 gallons were put in from small cylindrical tins containing about a quart each. Each one of these had to be lifted or thrown up to a man in the ship, opened and emptied into the tanks in the car and then pumped up into the tanks in the keel. The size of the task may be gauged from the enormous stack of empty tins about 10–15 feet in height near the control car.

I cannot speak too highly of the way all the crew worked on these various jobs. The secret was that they all pulled together, everyone willing to lend a hand at any job whether it was in his own particular field or not. There was no 'who does what?'; the fact that a man was an engineer or W/T op did not prevent him turning to and lending a hand to the Chief Cox'n when his own particular job was done. Bocking and Rook lent a hand to the engineers after they had seen to their accumulators being recharged. Williams and De Rossi worked as hard as the others and I was lucky to have such men with me. The fact that they were officers made no difference; they lent a hand with any job there was to do and were a great help to Clarke, who was on his own with the gassing up.

At 7.30 pm we had a short break for a meal which we all had to take together off bare trestle tables in the men's dining-hall. The meal was very rough, but we were so hungry that we enjoyed it. After the meal we carried on with the work straight away, but at midnight I could see that young De Rossi was practically all in, so I sent him off to get a little rest. The remainder carried on right through the night, getting in 300 tubes of gas (63,000 cubic feet), and the 397 gallons of petrol mentioned earlier, by 3.30 am next morning, when we were all aboard and ready to go.

It was a very cold, damp night, the temperature on the ground being ½°C with the moisture simply streaming off the envelope and rigging. The result was, of course, that the engineers had the devil of a job getting a kick out of the engines. The oil had congealed to a jelly and would not circulate. The engineers took it in turns to reach down bare-armed into the oil tank trying to force the oil through the pipes with their fingers or thumbs. We did not try to start the SPA; even the Italas, which usually started without any trouble, took an hour to get going. We ran them for half an hour on the ground to warm up and then, at 5 am on the 30th October 1918, I gave the order to 'Let go'—having, of course, ballasted up pretty light, more than 300 pounds in fact. At a height of 30 feet we lost sight of the ground, so dense was the fog. We reached no higher than 60 feet when the starboard engine stopped, and the ship commenced to fall. I let go some water, but felt our guys drag twice over some objects, probably huts at the edge of the landing-ground, but could see nothing, so let go all the remaining water ballast, 1,060 pound in all. We then rose quickly, but still could see nothing on account of the darkness and fog. Then to cap it all, the control-car lights failed, but we managed to see our instruments with the aid of some feeble hand torches. What a night!

At a height of 1,200 feet we were clear of the fog, and the ship started to dry off. Then, as the moisture evaporated, we became so light that we found our solitary engine was insufficient to keep her at a constant height. I did not wish to valve or lose any gas by blowing off at this early stage in the flight. At 5.50 am the SPA was got going, stopped after a few seconds, but started again very quickly. As it warmed and we could open it up we soon had sufficient punch to use our controls to keep us at a constant height, which, by this time, had risen to 2,100 feet. Very occasionally we saw the ground, but mostly it was obscured by fog or low cloud.

We set a course to hit off the River Saone, which we made at 6.20 am, by which time the starboard Itala had been started. Picard, who was again with us, tried to persuade me to return to Lyons, but I decided to carry on, as I doubted very much whether we should have been able to locate Bron in the fog. We crossed the Saone at Villefranche and rose to 3,500 feet to get over the mountains bordering the river. At a place called Chauffailles, above the noise of the Italas, we heard a clanging and banging from the SPA above. The exhaust pipe had broken off and fallen on top of the petrol tank in the control car. Williams, Owen and Leech promptly climbed on top of the car and pushed the red-hot mass overboard. In doing this Leech burned his flying-gloves; later, when he handed in his gear at Pulham, the Stores wallahs there charged him up with their value!

We carried on with an open exhaust on the SPA, which kicked up such an awful roar that all of us became temporarily deaf—except the W/T ops, who were sheltered from the noise in their enclosed cabin.

At 7.45 am we were over a small town called Gueugnon, soon after which we lost sight of the ground, hidden by low cloud. We reached the River Loire at 8.20 and followed it to Nevers. From there we set course across a wide expanse of heavily wooded country with few landmarks. Poor Picard was completely lost and was worried that we might find ourselves over the Marne and on the wrong side of the enemy lines. I told him not to worry, as we should strike some recognisable landmark sooner or later. We did, in the shape of a single-line railway. Thinking it must lead to a town I told the cox'n to follow it—only to find that it petered out in a quarry. Moral—stick to your course!

Very soon after we passed over a small, picturesque and typically French town which seemed to consist entirely of buildings with circular turrets of what appeared to be grey slate—rather like the Grosvenor Hotel at Victoria Station. There was a small station just outside the town, so we came down very low to read the name. Picard had the glasses and said it was St Marceau. We searched the map for a place of that name and finally concluded that it must be St Fargeau. All this time we had been bowling along at about 50 knots with a wind of about 20 knots helping us; measuring our speed from our shadow on the ground, I found we were doing 52 knots.

At 12.25 we reached a large town which should have given us our position without any doubt, but there was a difference of opinion as to what it was: Picard said it was Montereau; De Rossi plumped for Melun. Actually it was neither—it was Montargis. From there we followed the river and railway past Fontainebleau in its huge forest and came to Melun, a clean handsome-looking city on an island splitting the river into two channels. Picard seemed to have the Marne on the brain, for he was convinced that the river below us was indeed that river. However, Melun was unmistakable, and so the river had to be the Seine, which we followed past Corbeil and, a little later, we sighted Paris in a haze of mist and smoke.

We flew right across the city and I recognised many places, although it was too misty to see them clearly. At 3 pm we made a good landing at St Cyr, where we were welcomed by Commander Sablé, the charming French naval officer whom I had met earlier when on my way out to Rome. He told me that the measurements he had given me then were incorrect and that the shed was too small to house our *SR.1*; he said that he had sent a wireless message to this effect, advising me to go on to Havre, where there was a large shed. We had not received the message; in fact, we had had no communication at all since leaving Aubagne—probably as a result of the mountains *en route*.

So once again it was moor out, refuel and gas up in the open.

To increase our worries, we were informed that both gas and petrol were in short supply—at first we were given only 43,000 cubic feet of gas and 200 gallons of petrol, although we had consumed 300 gallons on our ten-hour flight from Bron. I calculated that our fuel supplies, now 600 gallons, would be ample for the flight to Kingsnorth. But the gas supplied gave us insufficient lift for the water and petrol we had taken in. I managed to wheedle a further 16,000 cubic feet which gave us sufficient lift without having to jettison anything in order to take off.

One of our visitors whilst we were moored was Lieutenant-Colonel Lestrange Malone, our Air Attaché in Paris, who later became an MP, specialising in air matters.

Filling up here was much easier, as the French naval ratings assisting us were all experienced hands and worked with a will. Just the same, we still had to gas up from cylinders, which takes much longer than from a gas-holder, even with experienced personnel, so it was close on midnight when we had finished. We all had a little much-needed sleep that night; I had an hour and a half in Sablé's bed and Williams a couple of hours.

Poor old Bill was looking very washed out and I feared he was going to crack up, but he's a tough nut and the short rest did him a world of good—though he was more asleep than awake when he returned to the ship at 3 am to find me dozing, seated on the tool-box in the control car. It was too cold and wet to get a proper rest, as it rained on and off all night. I thanked God it was again a calm night.

Of course, the rain made everything soaking wet, which meant that the engines were again difficult to start. In fact, we had not started the SPA when we left the ground at 6.15 am, on 31st October 1918 on the last stage of our flight to England—Paris to Kingsnorth; Lieutenant Picard was left behind in France.

At the rate of consumption from Bron to Paris (thirty gallons per hour) we had an endurance of some twenty hours, which was plenty. It was still raining when we left the ground—without an inversion for a change. We rose to a thousand feet, where the wind was blowing at 15 knots from the south-west. We set a compass course of 285 degrees making good 310 degrees true—practically due north-west. We were running on the two Italas, and those slowly, in order to get them properly warmed up.

We passed Mantes at 7 am, the SPA having been started a quarter of an hour earlier. At 7.30, near Les Andelys, we ran into thick fog and only saw the ground clearly once more before reaching the coast. Then the pointer of the aneroid—our altimeter—broke off at the centre, but De Rossi had a brilliant brain-wave; he simply turned the dial round 180 degrees so that the blunt end of the pointer indicated the height within a few feet.

It was properly nerve-racking as we strained our eyes trying to see the ground through the fog. We could scarcely see the forepart of the ship, let alone the ground. Fortunately it was flat country over which we were flying, so low at times, that Williams, who was on the elevators, swore he once saw a cow looking at him through the car window! It must have been a pretty tall cow, as the window by the elevator is between five and six feet above the bottom of the bumping-bag! But perhaps Bill was simply seeing things, for by the time we landed at Kingsnorth he had temporarily lost the sight of one eye through straining to pierce the fog.

At 7.55 we saw a large river bearing south-west and a quarter of an hour later we made out a fairly large river bearing east and west. This was undoubtedly the River Seine to the south of Rouen. The fog closed in again almost at once and the ground was invisible from 300 feet. However, I still kept the ship very low, as I did not want to find myself over the sea and not know where I had crossed the coast. Providence was certainly with us when we did actually reach the coast at 9.15 am, for we found ourselves flying between a line of brown-coloured cliffs which loomed up on either side. By incredible good fortune we must have struck a break in the coastline and flown through it—a proper miracle.

It was a little clearer over the sea, though there were still patches of thick fog or low cloud, and it was only with difficulty that we followed the coast in order to get a pin-point. I myself must have had an hallucination on one occasion—as we came out into a clear patch, I saw on our starboard side what appeared to me to be a town on the coast. I indicated to the cox'n to steer towards it before I realised that what I saw was a high, vari-coloured sandstone cliff.

At 10 am we sighted a small harbour formed by two moles which we took to be St Valery en Caux. Continuing further up the coast, we came to a much larger port which Bocking recognised as Dieppe, having flown there with 'Rosey' Warner in *SS.11* from Capel. I sent a W/T message to the Admiralty giving our position and received in reply: 'Land at Kingsnorth.'

I took the wind in my usual fashion and found it to be 17 knots from south-west. When slowing down, the SPA blew out an oil-pressure cock which hit Williams on the head; his flying helmet probably saved him from being knocked out.

We left the French coast at 11 am, setting course direct for Kingsnorth and making good 37 knots. Most of the time over the Channel we were flying through fog and rain, but on approaching the English coast the weather cleared. We were very bucked and excited when at 12.25 pm we saw the English coast at Beachy Head. Bill Williams turned to me with a beaming face and said: 'We've done it, George.'

We shook hands, and then I told him that perhaps we had better wait until we were at Kingsnorth before we started congratulating ourselves!

At 12.45 pm we crossed the English coast at Rye Bay near Hastings and made an uneventful journey across Kent via Maidstone to Kingsnorth Airship Station, where we completed our flight home at 2.15 pm on 31st October 1918, three and a half days since leaving Ciampino, and eight hours since leaving Paris—somewhat longer than by jet plane.

When we landed we were all as deaf as a post from the noise of the engines, especially from the SPA with its open exhaust. I remember Johnny Wheelwright coming to the side of the control car as we came to rest and offering his congratulations; I couldn't hear a word he said! As mentioned before, Bill Williams was partially blind for a short time after we landed and all of us were dog tired; during the three and a half days we had been on the journey, the most sleep anyone on board had had did not total more than six hours and some of us had made do with much less. And this after ten to twelve hours flying each day, followed by strenuous work from the time of landing early in the afternoon and throughout most of the night. How we all stuck it beats me. I have no words adequately to express my admiration and thanks for the way every member pulled his weight both in the air and on the ground.

As the bluff old former Prime Minister of New Zealand, Bill Massey, used to say: 'I can say without fear of contradiction' that but for all their willing help and devotion to duty we would not have won through.

Soon after we were safely in the shed the CO, Captain Woodcock, RN, invited me into his office and asked me to give him a short description of our voyage. At the end of it he said: 'You must have had a special Providence watching over you.' I heartily agreed with him—plus the devotion of the personnel who fully justified their selection.

Soon after our arrival at Kingsnorth, I received a telegram from General Maitland, CMG, DSO, AFC, Head of the Airship Section: 'Hearty congratulations on successful conclusion of flight from Italy in *SR.1*.' He followed this up with a visit to see the ship, accompanied by the representative of the Deputy Controller of Aircraft Production, Mr Given.

I remember the pleasant shock I received next morning to be called by the female voice of a WRN steward—'Your bath is ready, sir'—there had been neither WRNS nor WRAF at Howden when I left!

The weather now completely broke for a week and delayed our journey to Pulham, Norfolk, which was our ultimate destination. On 5th November we had a visit from Maitland's senior assistants at HQ, Wing Commanders A. D. Cunningham and D. Harries—the former accompanied us on our final flight leg to Pulham. We left Kingsnorth next day at 9.40 am for our final station at Pulham, my old station of 1916–17.

There is not much of interest to record on this flight. The starboard Itala again gave trouble, vibrating badly if run at more than 1,000 rpm. When over Hadleigh at 12.05 pm I sent my ETA to Pulham as 2 pm. We were within sight of the sheds at 1.25 when we received a message by Aldis lamp: 'Can you wait till two o'clock to land?' I replied 'Yes' —and circled the landing-ground whilst *R.23* was brought out to try the experiment of dropping an aeroplane from her in flight. This was carried out successfully, the dropped plane being a Sopwith 'Camel' piloted by Lieutenant Keys. We in *SR.1* had a grandstand, or rather bird's-eye, view of this event, the first of its kind.

We landed at 2.30 pm, having taken five hours for the journey, an hour of which was spent circling the Pulham district.

For some reason or other our reception at my old station was the reverse of cordial. Only three of my former shipmates were still there: The PMO, F/Surgeon Harris; the Padre, Rev. Jones; and the Stores Officer, Captain Robbins. The place was full of non-flying majors, satellites of Captain F. L. M. Boothby, RN, the CO, a number of whom appeared to be there mainly for social duties; it was no longer the 'happy station' I had known during my previous sojourn. To add to our bloody-mindedness, Williams and I were immediately lurked into doing Duty Airship Officer on alternate days!

The day after we landed we made a short flight of forty-five minutes to give the CO and Major Little—*R.23*'s Captain—a trip. On landing, Fred Boothby immediately initiated schemes for pulling the ship to pieces. Pulham was now an experimental station and I suppose they had to justify their existence; actually some of the proposed schemes were, I I must admit, excellent—a new enclosed car and new planes amongst them—but my anticipation of doing some really long patrols was knocked on the head.

We had arrived back in England too late to be of much use in the war effort, for less than a fortnight after our arrival at Kingsnorth the Armistice was signed. What a day the 11th November 1918 was at Pulham. When the maroons went up at 11 am the whole station went daft.

For the previous two months an SS ship had been moored out in the open on the edge of the landing-ground opposite to the men's hutments. Some cute fellows among the party out there thought they were being left out of the station festivities, so they poked some holes in the envelope with a pole. It was reported that the ship was deflating, so Major Scott, who was Chief Experimental Officer, buttonholed me in the Mess and told me to get a handling-party and bring the ship in.

I went over to the hutments and got hold of the station Sergeant-Major. 'They won't carry out any orders from me, sir,' he told me. 'They're all tight.'

I got hold of the station band and marched the whole of the station personnel, excluding officers, some 800 strong, in a long column across the aerodrome to the mooring-mast with the band at their head. Leading them were the Chief Cook, in his whites, wearing a black bowler, and myself, rather more conventionally dressed.

Never in the history of airships had an *SS* such a mighty handling-party. We draped a Union Jack over the car and, with the band leading the way, at first playing a dead march, but soon breaking into a more lively tune, we traipsed across the aerodrome and into the shed. Then the band moved off again, with the men behind in a huge column of fours, myself and Cookie at their head, with some 'Wrens' carrying a large White Ensign and CPOs on either side, and we marched past the Officers' Mess back to the men's quarters.

Two days later the C.O. asked me to get *SR.1* ready for a demonstration over London. We had already taken the plane cage and cylinders down preparatory to fitting 'North Sea' type planes and we had a deuce of a job getting the springs back in the cylinders. Then came the job of getting the whole paraphernalia of the plane assembly back on the ship—they are the most impracticable things ever invented; everything inaccessible and difficult to work—a proper Harry Tate* show. We eventually fitted them in position on the ship only to find we could not work the elevators; so off they had to come again. We finally finished the job at 3 am, and then the London flight was cancelled on account of a high crosswind making it impossible to get the ship out of the shed. As there was little likelihood of flying for some days, I requested leave and went up to Town. This was four days after the Armistice, but people were still dancing in lines up and down the Strand, with no road traffic possible at all.

I had no sooner got home than a telegram arrived recalling me to Pulham, as *SR.1* had been detailed to proceed to Harwich for the surrender of the German submarine fleet.

Not counting our flight from Italy, this was perhaps the most interesting flight of my career up till then. We were instructed to rendezvous at 1030 at the South Cutler Buoy a few miles off Harwich. We left Pulham at 9.50 am on 20th November 1918 and duly made the South Cutler, where we joined *R.26* and a flotilla of destroyers, four cruisers and the first batch of twenty submarines to be surrendered. The latter hove-to in line ahead, on which, thinking the surrender had been completed, *R.26*, under Major Watt, pushed off. A motor launch then ran along the line of submarines, dropping a British crew on board each submarine in turn; a few minutes later a White Ensign was run up. When all the submarines had a White Ensign hoisted, the cruisers and destroyers, with *SR.1* overhead, escorted them into Harwich Harbour. The surrendered submarines were then moored to buoys in the centre of the River Stour above Parkestone Quay, four deep each side of a lane of water now called Submarine Avenue.

Although we had been searching for them for the past three or four years, this was our first full view of a German submarine and we were thrilled, though we could imagine the feelings of their crews—some members of which, we heard later, lost their calm bearing and shed tears. The personnel on board *SR.1* for this truly historic flight were: myself; Williams; Clarke; Burrell; Leech; Holden; Bocking; Beasty; and Potts, a photographer; there were also two passengers: Captain Robbins and a young American pilot, Ensign Baehr, USN.

We were to have repeated the exercise the following day, but conditions were too foggy. A party of us went by road to Harwich to see the last batch of submarines surrendered and hoping to be able to board one. We managed to get hold of a motor-boat and witnessed the last batch of

* He was one of the great comedians of the day.

submarines to come up the river and moor. We tried one or two, but were not allowed to board. Eventually we met the officer in charge, who said we could go over *U.151*, the original *Deutschland*, and enjoined us only to take such things as we could get into our pockets! We also went below in *U.155* and while we were aboard her a motor-boat drew alongside which contained the Admiral of the Port. We all had the wind up, wondering what to say if he came below and found us. Luckily he remained on deck, whilst we lay doggo down below. We were greatly relieved when he left. We must have presented a funny picture with our overcoats bulging, making us look more like a lot of pregnant women than naval or RAF officers. One of the chaps with us—an Australian parson in private life but a RNVR officer for the war—made me laugh when he said: 'Do you know, I'm sinking lower and lower, and now it has come down to looting a ship!'

On 7th December we carried out a short flight of three and a quarter hours over the sea off Lowestoft to try dropping marker buoys. On this flight we carried two officers—Captains Heath and Shepperdson—who had been picked up by the Military Police in London on Armistice night for, among other things, climbing up Eros in Piccadilly Circus and crowning him with a top-hat. With them under open detention at Pulham for this episode was Major Harold Balfour, whom I had last seen at Driffield before leaving for Italy; he it was who put the wind up me in an Avro with his antics, 'Immelman' turns, vertical banks, and diving, rolling and side-slipping almost to the ground. The people on the ground sent for an ambulance as they thought he must crash, but he was just keeping his hand in as chief of the Aerobatic School at Feltwell, North Norfolk.

On the same day as this flight there was a notice in *The Times* saying that the Italian Government had given me the Croce di Guerra. The *Morning Post* printed an abbreviated account of our flight which I had submitted to the Admiralty and I also received the following personal letter from General Maitland:

Airship Dept.,
4 Dean Stanley Street,
London, S.W.1.
Dec. 1918.

Dear Meager,

Many congratulations on receiving the Italian 'Croix de Guerre' which is a well merited reward for your perseverance in bringing *SR.1* over to this country in spite of the enormous difficulties you met with.

You are certainly the first Airship Officer to receive a foreign distinction of this sort, which is richly deserved, and I congratulate you very heartily on it.

Yours sincerely,
E. M. MAITLAND.

Shortly afterwards I received the following commendation from the Admiralty:

Admiralty,
London, S.W.1
12th Dec. 1918

With reference to the recent voyage of airship *SR.1* from Rome to Kingsnorth under the charge of Captain Meager, RAF, who was lent by the Air Ministry for this duty, I am commanded by My Lords Commissioners of the Admiralty to request that this officer may be informed that his Report has been read by them with great interest and that they are of the opinion that the Flight reflects very creditably both on the Captain and the Crew.

R. R. SCOTT,
Secretary.

The Secretary,
Air Ministry.

On the strength of this, and probably on a recommendation from General Maitland, the Air Ministry awarded me the Air Force Cross.

On Boxing Day, being at home for Christmas leave, I went to Constitution Hill to see President Woodrow Wilson make his entry into London and visit HM the King and Queen. I climbed to the top of the gates of Green Park and so had a grandstand view. The President seemed very pleased with his reception, beaming on the crowds and waving his top-hat in response to the terrific cheering of the largest crowd I have ever seen. In spite of his beaming face, I thought he looked very pale and not very robust.

After he entered the Palace, the crowd became colossal, filling the space in front of the Palace, around the Victoria Memorial, and reaching along the Mall; all up Constitution Hill was a sea of heads splashed with the colour of the ladies' hats. When an aeroplane came over it became a sea of white faces upturned to admire the evolutions of the planes shining like silver in the sun. In response to the continued cheering, the King and Queen, the President and Mrs Wilson, and the Duke of Connaught all came out on to the balcony. I felt that the occasion, together with the surrender of the German submarines, for us marked the end of the war and the end of an era.

CHAPTER EIGHT

Peacetime Flying

On 21st January 1919 I had my first flight in a 'Rigid' airship, going up in *R.26* to assist Mr Frazer, who was carrying out investigations into airship handling for the National Physical Laboratory at Teddington. Her Captain was Major Watt and her Second Officer Captain S. E. Taylor; amongst others on board were my former Captain on *C.27*, Captain Dudley Barton, and Sergeant Sinclair, my W/T op on *SS.32*. One of the riggers was Corporal Moncrieff, who later on became one of our cox'ns on *R.100*. This trip was cut short by one of the engines breaking down.

There was a very marked contrast between the conditions in the control car of *R.26* and in that of *SR.1*; In *R.26* one could carry on a conversation in an ordinary tone of voice, and there was ample room, with a chart table for navigation. Next day, with *R.26's* engine repaired, I again assisted Mr Frazer with his various investigations. To take the required readings meant that I spent practically the whole of the flight in the keel; so the only places I saw during the five-hour flight were glimpses of Norwich and Bungay.

The year following the end of the war was not an easy one, with unemployment and strikes very much in everyone's minds. The station rank and file personnel caught the general 'strike fever.' They refused to return to work after lunch one day, and formed up in a mass outside the Officers' Mess; their real grievance was the delay in demobilisation. The Army and the Navy, whose demobilisation was much more advanced, were picking up what few jobs there were available.

Fred Boothby took a strong line, but asked anyone with a grievance to step forward and he would deal with it—only one man did so. What had started the present trouble was a youth of eighteen years of age who was under arrest for insubordination; the spokesman told Boothby that the men were not going to allow him to be taken off the station for court martial.

Fred said that he had his duty to do and would carry it out; he was seeing them now only with regard to demobilisation. Strong measures were taken to maintain discipline; the Military Police and a party of Marines were sent for, and the station NCOs were armed with loaded revolvers and bayonets.

In the end the station settled down again without recourse to more drastic measures. Major Cochrane now became Chief Experimental Officer, replacing Major G. H. Scott, who had gone to the Beardmore Works to become Captain of *R.34*. Cochrane was much more affable now than he had been in Rome and gave me various responsible and interesting jobs to do. On 30th May 1919 *SS T.14* left the ground under the command of Captain S. E. Taylor, DSC, with myself and Lieutenant Purton as co-pilots; AC Sheldrake as engineer; and AC Cowin as W/T op, for an endurance flight and water-recovery trials. *T.14* was a twin-engined SS ship of 100,000 cubic feet capacity, with the engines carried on gantries built out from the after end of a boat-shaped car; they were Rolls-Royce 'Hawks' of 75 hp each. This type of ship had separate steering and elevating wheels at which we did two-hourly spells with two hours stand off.

We went out over our old routes with *C.17* and *C.27* to Cross Sands, Newarp, Would and Haisboro' light-vessels. Near the latter we tried out an experiment of picking up water. At first we had difficulty getting the canvas bucket into the water, but after a time we became quite expert and on this, as well as on several attempts later, we picked up a considerable amount of water. Our method was to fly low, with the wind more or less on the beam, turn head to wind, slow down till we were practically stationary, and then a man in the bows would let down the bucket, tipping it as it struck the water, so that it filled. In this way we collected 180 pounds of water at our first attempt.

We proceeded northward to Grimsby and Hull, where it was very bumpy and we were very light, so went out to sea a little and picked up 300 pounds more water. We then went in to our old mooring-out station at Lowthorpe, but saw it was now deserted. We went low over the village and I saw Miss Winn, the postmaster's pretty daughter, run out into the garden. I dropped her a note of greeting which fell beside the little fountain in their garden where an ancient leaden swan spouts water from his broken beak. I also dropped notes to the local Padre, and to the estate agent, Mr Hawes, both of whom had been very hospitable to me when I was at Lowthorpe.

We then flew on to Redcar and visited our other mooring-out station at Kirkleatham, which we found likewise deserted. When off Newbiggin-by-Sea, we were in wireless telephone communication with Pulham, a distance of some 200 nautical miles. At that time this was the greatest distance ever talked over by wireless.

With the setting of the sun we became somewhat heavy, so we let go some of the ballast water we had previously picked up. We proceeded southward during the night, and by 6 am on the 1st June had become quite light from the consumption of petrol, so we took in some more water. While we were doing this a thick blanket of wet fog formed over the sea; the moisture on the envelope very nearly bore us down on to the surface, but we opened up the engines just in time and rose above the fog to 1,200 feet, where the sun was shining brightly.

During the afternoon we sighted a steamer off the north coast of Norfolk, closed her and found that although she had a German name, *Weissenfelde*, she was manned by a British naval crew. As we were getting a bit short of grub, we went down low beside her and semaphored asking for a loaf of bread. Even before the message was finished we saw a steward running below and by the time we had turned over the ship's stern he had returned with a sack all done up. We let down a bucket on the end of a length of cod-line which broke directly it was hauled in by those on the ship. We then let down our spare wireless aerial to which they hitched the sack. Inside was a loaf and half a dozen oranges—a very welcome addition to our larder.

A little later, when off Yarmouth, we came up with an Italian warship, the *Libia*. By a quirk of memory, I remembered she had been stationed at Taranto when I was at Grottaglie and her commander's name then was Villarey. I told our operator to signal '*Buon giorno*, is Captain Villarey on board?'

We received the answer: 'Captain Villarey is on board and sends his best wishes.'

The excitement in the ship was very amusing to watch—men were waving their caps at every vantage-point and porthole, whilst others shinned up aloft to get a better view.

We proceeded south as far as Felixstowe, which we reached at 9 pm, and here the port engine stopped: we had emptied one of our four petrol tanks, which were slung about midway up the side of the envelope in pairs. We then estimated that we had about six hours' petrol left. At 11 pm, however, when near Southwold we cleared out another tank so we decided to make for home, as we had used more petrol than estimated. When full, each tank held forty-five gallons.

It was a pitch-black night, but I got a good back bearing on the red light on Southwold pier. We then steered for Pulham entirely by compass, as it was too dark to see any landmarks. When half-way there, the station beacon light flashed out.

We reached Pulham at 12.45 am on 2nd June and were just approaching the landing-party when the engine stopped—which meant that three of our tanks were now empty. We turned over to our last tank and restarted at once, but the engine stopped almost at once—all the main tanks were empty. As we were drifting away from the landing-party, we flashed a message saying we were going to make a free balloon landing. In the meantime the engineer started an engine on the emergency tank and we came round and landed safely at 1.30 am on 2nd June 1919, a total time in the air of fifty-two and a quarter hours, a record for a 'twin' at that time. After landing we found we still had sixteen gallons of petrol left, enough for four hours on one engine.

This was my first flight in a twin SS and my longest continuous flight to date. The ship was exceptionally easy to control and stable on her elevators, though we found her steering somewhat difficult at first; once we had got used to it, we could steer an accurate course by compass only.

We had by now dismantled the SPA and removed it from *SR.1*, so future flights were with the two Italas only. On 2nd July 1919 the ship left Pulham at 9.45 am for a demonstration over London in support of the 'Victory Loan'. By one o'clock we were over the huge crowd around the Stock Exchange and Mansion House where the Heralds read the Peace Proclamation; they then proceeded in procession to Buckingham Palace. We followed overhead and were over Trafalgar Square as the procession was passing through Admiralty Arch when both our engines suddenly stopped, caused by a blockage in the petrol supply. Being light, we rose to a height of 5,000 feet, and only checked our going higher by valving gas. The blockage was soon cleared and the engines restarted.

We were very thrilled to pick up wireless messages from *R.34*—Major Scott—which was on its way from Longside, near Edinburgh, to the USA, the first east-to-west crossing of the Atlantic by air. We had, only a few minutes before, seen her sister ship, the recently launched *R.33*, under the command of Captain G. M. Thomas.

We had a slow journey back to Pulham with a contrary wind of about 15 knots, through many rain squalls, whilst the W/T op reported very bad atmospherics, indicating thunder. We landed at 7.55 pm, having completed 10 hours 10 minutes and consumed 294 gallons of petrol.*

We were detailed to carry out Victory Loan propaganda, dropping leaflets over South Wales on the 6th July. We left the ground at 10.10 pm with 806 gallons of petrol and the same crew as before, but without any passengers.

We proceeded westward throughout the night, which was very dark with low cloud. After passing over Bedford we had only fleeting glimpses of the ground, but eventually located our position at 4.30 am, 7th July, as over Evesham, very prettily situated in a 'U' bend of the River Severn. We were only five miles off course, which was not bad considering we had been flying blind most of the night. As we were very near where my

* On board were the following: *Captain (Pilot):* Captain G. Meager. *First Officer:* Captain T. B. Williams. *Chief Cox'n:* F/Sgt G. Clarke. *Second Cox'n:* Sgt H. Lee. *First Engineer:* Sgt H. Leech. *Second Engineer:* LAC A. Holden. *Rigger:* LAC T. Cheadle. *W/T Op:* LAC Baird. *Passengers:* Captain R. Gibb; Sgt-Major Allan; F/Sgt Ford; and Cpl Glenn.

elder sister—she has the old Anglo-Saxon name of Etheldreda—was living, I thought I would pop over and give them a sight of my ship. Her husband, Jim Holden, was farming the Home Farm at Beckford Hall, under Bredon Hill, for Captain Case, and although it was about 5 am I knew they would be up and about. I dropped a short note which was received all right.

At 7 am we were over Cardiff, a fine modern-looking city with the remains of an old castle close by. Here we had 734 gallons of petrol left, sufficient for twenty-six hours at full speed, but very much longer at the rate we had been using—eight gallons an hour. We proceeded past Caerphilly and Pontypridd and then up the Rhondda Valley, a very depressing-looking place consisting of numerous coal-mines and slag-dumps, with row on row of small cottages clinging to the hillsides—a very poor uninviting sort of country.

Fog or low cloud now began to develop and only occasonally did we see the ground; I did not like it a little bit amongst the high hills on either side. We pushed on as far as Merthyr Tydfil, where the visibility was so bad I decided it was useless proceeding further. Our object, after all, was to advertise the Victory Loan—but few people would see us in the fog. I decided to call it a day, turned about and made our way down the Neath valley, passing over Aberdare, Neath and Swansea to Kidwelly, but did not see Llanelly, which was completely hidden by fog or low cloud. We went up the River Towey to Carmarthen, which was the farthest west we made; then back to Swansea, across Swansea Bay to Aberavon and down the coast to Nash Point, whence we set course across the Bristol Channel to Minehead, which we reached at 2 pm on 7th July.

Over the recreation ground at Minehead I noticed a group of boys playing, so I dropped a note amongst them addressed to May Atkins, my former WRN steward at Pulham, where she was known as 'Peter Pan'. She lived with her parents at Dunster and had just recently been demobilised. I later received a cutting from the local paper to say the note had been delivered to the addressee at 2.10 pm—pretty prompt delivery, without a 5d stamp!

We then proceeded up the Bristol Channel past Weston-super-Mare to Bristol, soon after which the starboard engine started missing. The engineers found a valve spring broken, replaced it and restarted the engine. We were now proceeding over the beautiful Cotswold country with its many fine mansions and cosy grey stone villages. At 6.25 pm we reached the lovely city of Oxford, with its cluster of grey stone colleges, passed Aylesbury, Luton and Hitchin and changed course for home at Bury St Edmunds at 9.40 pm. We cruised around the neighbourhood of Pulham for nearly an hour while a landing-party was being mustered, finally landing at 11.30 pm on 7th July 1919.

The duration of the flight, 25 hours 20 minutes, was, up to this time, a record for an 'M' type of ship, the previous best having been 18 hours by De Bei in *M.15*. We used 434 gallons on this flight at an average rate of seventeen gallons per hour.

For the first time I can remember we carried parachutes on board, one for each member of the crew. They were not the modern type of free-fall parachute, but were in a container hung to the keel.

Soon after this flight our Chief Cox'n, Clarke, received a letter from our former engineer, Tomlins, who had been demobilised and was working for Vauxhalls at Luton:

> I was so bucked at seeing the old ship over Luton that I went and celebrated, having a whisky with old Meager and one with Williams, and eight pints of Government ale with 'Nobby' Clarke himself and the rest of the crew—in fact, got properly blind-o!

We were ordered to prepare *SR.1* for another Victory Loan demonstration and leaflet-dropping on the 12th July, but it poured with rain the whole day and flying was cancelled. Next day, Sunday, 13th July, was a great day at Pulham, for *R.34*, with 'Scottie' in command, landed there on her return from the first double crossing of the Atlantic, being beaten by just a month for the first ever non-stop crossing by Alcock and Brown, whose Vickers 'Vimy' aircraft alighted in Ireland on 14th June, 1919

R.34 landed at 8 am and I was in charge of a section of the landing-party. I've never seen such a crowd of pressmen and photographers, all milling around Scottie when he reached the Mess for breakfast.

After the triumph of *R.34* a tragedy happened two days later when *NS.11* was lost in a thunderstorm off Cley on the north coast of Norfolk. She was struck by lightning and set on fire. Her Captain, W. Warneford, Elliott, her First Officer, and crew of six were all lost. A coastguard said there was a long, dirty black cloud stretching eastwards from Blakeney. A few minutes later there was a great flash of flame followed by a terrific explosion, but he saw no lightning. An old lady writing from either Stiffkey or Cley, I forget which, said that a flash of lightning from a very heavy black cloud seemed to strike near the ship's tail, followed by a great flash of light from the ship. This was at 1.10 am on 15th July 1919. Elliott was another old Anglesey boy and he had married an exceedingly pretty Llangefni girl.

That morning I had received the following telegram:

> Buckingham Palace. 15/7/19.
> To Captain George Meager, Airship Station Pulham, Norfolk. Your attendance is required at Buckingham Palace on Thursday, 24th instant at ten fifteen o'clock a.m. Service dress. Please telegraph acknowledgement.
>
> Lord Chamberlain,
> London.

At the investiture you advance up a slope to the dais where the King is standing; halt, turn left, salute, advance two paces and stick out your chest; the King hangs the decoration on to a brass hook previously fitted to your left breast. His Majesty then shakes you by the hand, saying, 'I'm very pleased to present this to you.' Thus I received the Air Force Cross in recognition of *SR.1's* flight from Rome to Kingsnorth.

On 6th August I was asked to assist Messrs Pannell and Frazer of the National Physical Laboratory with turning trials at various angles and speeds. These trials were carried out in *R.33*,—in design she was a copy of the Zeppelin *L.33* which had landed almost intact at Little Wigborough, Essex, after having been brought down in an air raid. Her crew had set her alight after landing, but the hull had remained intact.

We left the ground at 9.45 am, but owing to engine trouble we could not begin our observations until one o'clock—she had five 250 hp Sunbeam 'Maoris'. My job was to take readings of the compass during turns at intervals of fifteen seconds. The flight lasted for eleven and a half hours, the ship being commanded by Captain G. M. Thomas, with five officers, twenty-two crew, two passengers, two NPL experts, and myself.

Mr Pannell was a large man standing about 6 foot 4 inches, with a huge head and body frame. Amongst us he was known as 'Mr Pannell of sliding fame'; whether the 'sliding' was a play on 'sliding panel' or on his use of the slide rule I cannot say—perhaps a combination of both. He was amongst those lost in the *R.38* disaster over the Humber—while carrying out similar tests to those in which I took part in *R.26* and *R.33*.

Three days later we were visited by members of various crack Indian regiments, including the Ghurkas—a fine body of men comprising the Indian Peace Contingent. *SR.1* was detailed to make a flight for their benefit. We left the ground at 2.45 pm, cruised around for a bit and our Second Cox'n, Sgt H. Lee, made a parachute jump from a height of 2,000 feet. The parachute opened quickly and he landed 4 minutes 20 seconds after jumping out of the ship. The parachute was of the fixed type, the modern free-fall type not having been invented. After this demonstration we proceeded to the coast, flew over the sea from Winterton to Yarmouth. We turned inland over the familiar countryside up the Waveney Valley to Bungay and Harleston, taking photographs of Flixton Hall and Gawdy Hall which I later presented to their respective owners as a small token of thanks for their hospitality to me while I was stationed at Pulham. After being in the air for 5 hours 20 minutes we landed, having completed what turned out to be *SR.1's* last flight, for I received orders on 29th August 1919 to deflate the ship.

The crew for our last flight consisted of myself, Williams, Clarke, Lee, Leech, Baird, Holden and Cheadle, with eight passengers: Captain

Robbins; Lieutenants Bolam and Watkins; Corporal Speed; and Aircraftmen Flynn, Miles, Nason and Treacher.

On 12th–13th August I was up assisting Pannell and Frazer in *R.33* with their experiments, reading the compass as before and taking readings of the petrol gauges on tanks in the keel at one-minute intervals.

We were back over Pulham at seven o'clock next morning, but did not land, as we picked up a distress call 'SOS' from the steamship *Englewood* which had struck a mine off Black Deep near the Sunk light-vessel in the Thames Estuary. Captain Thomas immediately set course to try to locate her, but we did not find her, as she had already been towed into port. We then flew over France for a short while, accompanied by a French airship; carried out further trials over the Channel, and finally landed at 7.45 pm, having completed twenty-seven and a quarter hours. I did not fly in *R.33* again until 1925, six years later.

Shortly after this we were honoured with a visit from General Trenchard, head of the RAF. He came over to the shed, inspected the ship and started interrogating the crew. He asked Clarke what his job was: 'Coxswain, sir.'

Trenchard scratched his chin being a bit out of his depth. He had another shot at Lee, but the answer was 'Second Cox'n, sir.'

This completely nonplussed him, so he tackled Leech. On Leech answering 'Engineer, sir', you could see Trenchard's relief, as he was now on sure ground and started talking engines.

On 6th September Major Elmsley landed a new wooden-type ship, *R.32*. This was of 1.5 million cubic feet capacity with five Rolls-Royce engines of 250 hp each. She was based on a Schutte-Lanz-ship, being similar to the one brought down at Cuffley in September 1916, and was built by Messrs Short Brothers at Cardington. She made almost an aeroplane landing, and an engineer officer named Coleman and I just prevented the after car bumping on the ground. Elmsley must have seen the danger, for he let go about a ton of water from the stern tanks and the car started to rise; all who were now hanging on to it, except myself, let go altogether, leaving me hanging on to the handling-rail, and up we went for about 75 feet. I thought of poor old Tim Waterlow as I hung there in mid-air. It didn't enter my mind to shout to those in the car to haul me in. Fortunately for me the landing-party had held on to the handling-guys and they hauled the ship down; I was OK—much to my relief!

A week later Elmsley asked me to go in *R.32* as navigator. With him was Scroggs, who had given me some of my first airship instructional flights at Anglesey. The object of the proposed flight was to make a demonstration over the Aircraft Exhibition then in progress at Amsterdam; we were to be accompanied by *R.33*. After an hour's delay she joined us and we both proceeded east. *R.33* was flying faster than *R.32* and soon outdistanced us. We crossed the North Sea from Southwold to the Hook of Holland and when over Ymuiden we received a W/T message saying that *R.33* was coming up from the southward. We foregathered near Scheveningen at 6 am on 11th September at which time the temperature in the control car was 74.F, whilst that of the gas in the envelope was 2 degrees higher.

We lined up astern of, and much lower than, *R.33*, proceeding thus to Amsterdam. We circled the city, which is very beautiful from the air, with its canals and main streets bordered by trees. There are large docks with many ships. We saw three large floating docks with ships in them. One very useful sign for aircraft was A ↑ M painted on top of a large gasholder, the arrow indicating north.

The control car of *R.32* was completely free of engine noise and we could hear distinctly all the usual ground noises such as dogs barking, children shouting and, as Scroggs described it, 'the familiar squeak of a tram-car going round a corner'.

Elmsley wrote a note to Colonel Snyders, who was in charge of the Exhibition, and gave it to me to drop out of the gun cockpit in the point of the tail. The note was in a fabric envelope to which was attached a miniature parachute. We then set course for home, *R.33* having left some time earlier, and without further incident landed at Pulham at 5 pm after twenty-one hours in the air.

We completed the unrigging and deflation of *SR.1* on the 19th September 1919, using our own crew, now reduced to six men. Demobilisation and the end of my airship career seemed to be very near. We had carried out some useful flights, but I cannot claim that the ship was an unqualified success. I had looked forward to being some help in combating the U-boat menace. Instead of this, directly we arrived at Pulham, Boothby was full of ideas for pulling the ship to pieces, replacing car, controls and engines. But although my airship experience was not quite over, this was the end of my piloting life; I only flew once more as captain, and that was some years later when I carried out the trials of *AD.1* for her Airworthiness Certificate.

On 25th September a letter arrived from Group HQ that all Direct Entry officers were to be demobilised forthwith—what a kick in the pants after nearly five years of endeavour. This order was rescinded next day, but only postponed for six weeks in my case, as Mr Pannell had requested that I be retained to assist him and his colleagues of the NPL with their investigations.

So it was that on 20th October I made another flight in *R.32* as observer for Pannell. For this flight they had rigged up a magnetic compass and a sundial in the gun platform at the top of the ship and this was to be my place of observation. One reached it by climbing up a fabric tube through the centre of the ship; fortunately winter was not yet upon us and it was not too cold. Two days later I went up again as observer for Mr Pannell and Mr Simmons of the NPL. Before starting on their investigations, an experiment was carried out over the aerodrome of dropping five parachutes with dummies simultaneously. We then went out to sea, crossing the coast at Dunwich. We completed our readings over the sea, returned to Pulham and landed after seven and a half hours, this being my last flight as a serving officer. For both these flights the Captain of *R.32* was Major I. C. Little with Captain Scroggs as First Officer.

My last job at Pulham was to assist at the first mooring of *R.24* to the mast, on 7th November. It went off very well, taking only ten and a half minutes from the time the ship's wire was dropped to when secure on the mast. During the hauling in the ship overrode the mast a little and very nearly knocked Cochrane off the top. I was finally demobilised on 8th November 1919, and left Pulham, as I thought, for good, on 11th November, exactly a year since the Armistice. On totalling up my log I found that I had flown 1,036 hours, covering an approximate distance of 27,500 miles.

CHAPTER NINE

R.33 and the Gordon Bennett Balloon Races

I was acting as an Assistant Traffic Inspector for the Auckland City Council in New Zealand when I received a cable from the Air Ministry offering me a position as an Airship Watchkeeping Officer with the new experimental ships. I accepted and on 9th June 1925 I reported at Pulham once again, for flying duties in *R.33*, which was then under repair, after having broken away from the mooring-mast in April of that year. *R.33* was being reconditioned mainly in order to carry out some flights to obtain certain information regarding pressures on the outer cover during flight. In addition, it was intended to carry out the experiment of releasing an aeroplane and flying it back on to the airship in flight.

The first pressure experiments were carried out in a nineteen and a half-hour flight during 5th/6th October 1925, with Captain Carmichael Irwin as Captain, Squadron Leader R. S. Booth, AFC, as Second Pilot, under the overall supervision of Major G. H. Scott.

Booth had brought the ship back to Pulham after it had been blown away from the mooring-mast and carried across the North Sea to Holland with him and the Duty Watch aboard; he had done this with her bows all smashed in and her forward gas-bag deflated—one of the finest salvage feats ever achieved.

The make-up of a 'Rigid' airship was pretty well standardised by this time. The lifting agent, hydrogen gas, was contained in huge fabric containers shaped like enormous cheeses, of which there were nineteen in *R.33*, placed within the hull between the transverse frames where they were spaced apart by the longitudinal girders. The total capacity, with all bags full, was 1,960,000 cubic feet. She had five Sunbeam 'Maori' engines of 250 hp each; one in each wing car approximately amidships; two on the centre-line in the after car, one tractor and one pusher; and one pusher in the rear part of the forward car. The control cabin formed the front portion of the forward car.

For the pressure tests the outer cover of the ship was pierced by numerous small holes of a quarter-inch diameter connected by rubber tubing to manometers in the keel. We carried out the tests over the

Maplin Sands, turning circles at various speeds and rudder angles. The idea of these tests was to obtain information as to the stresses imposed on the envelope and hull during turns. This problem had been highlighted by the *R.38* disaster—she had broken in half when carrying out somewhat similar turning trials over the Humber in 1921. An airship is more vulnerable to this type of damage than one might suppose—and it is worth remembering that a destroyer can also overdo high-speed manoeuvring and similarly break its back in a fast turn at sea. The information obtained was to be used in designing the hulls of the two new ships of 5 million cubic feet that the Air Ministry proposed to build and designated *R.100* and *R.101*.

For this flight practically the whole of the *R.101* design, calculating and drawing office staff were carried, but conspicuous by their absence were any representatives of the design staff of the Airship Guarantee Company, who were to build *R.100*. No doubt the information obtained was passed on to Messrs Barnes Wallis, Temple and Norway, who were to lead the design team of *R.100*. A shorter pressure-testing flight of four and a half hours was carried out on the 9th October 1925.

A much more interesting flight was carried out on 15th October. This was to test the feasibility of an aeroplane slipping itself off the airship and hooking itself on again during flight. For this a small trapeze bar was slung a few feet below the centre of the ship and to this was hooked a light aeroplane, a De Havilland DH53 with the pilot, Squadron Leader de Haga-Haig, already in the cockpit.

At a height of 3,000 feet the aeroplane was slipped; it then flew round and attempted to hook itself on again before the signal was given from the ship. It was going too fast and tipped up its nose as the parrot-beak fender struck the trapeze; the propeller went into a stay wire smashing itself, and severing the wire; de Haga Haig immediately unhooked and glided down to the ground safely.

The second attempt was made on 28th October with F/Lt Junor in the plane. He slipped correctly at a height of 2,500 feet but in hooking on he carried away the trapeze—probably again approaching too fast.

The method of hooking on in flight was for the plane to fly about 50 feet below the airship—the trapeze was lowered the same distance—and at a slightly greater speed than the airship; the pilot aimed the nose of the plane at the trapeze, so that it rode up over a kind of parrot-beak guide mounted in front of the prop and so into a spring-loaded slot.

It was not until the 4th December that the next attempt was possible. This time it was completely successful. The trapeze, with plane attached, was lowered 50 feet and successfully slipped. The plane then flew round and hooked on again without mishap, and repeated this successfully five times. The last time the trapeze with plane hooked on was hauled up by a winch in the keel so that the wings rested against pads on the underside of the ship's keel, where it was secured. The speed of the airship during the hooking on was 45 knots; the height at which the experiment was carried out was between 3,000 and 4,000 feet. The ship was then ballasted up and landed with the plane attached. This series of experiments being completed, the ship was deflated. We did not do any more research work of this kind until the following year.

R.33 was then re-inflated, being now registered as a civil aircraft with her registration mark *G-FAAG* painted in large letters on her side.

On 21st October 1926 she was taken out of the shed at Pulham with two Gloster 'Grebe' aeroplanes of a ton apiece attached in tandem along the base. The engine of the after 'Grebe' was started when we were at a height of 2,000 feet and soon afterwards her pilot, Flying Officer A. Ragg, released her. We then carried out some acoustic experiments which could have ended in disaster, as fragments of a bomblet which was let off pierced the airship's outer cover, fortunately not piercing the gas-bags.

After the pilot of the forward plane—F/O Mackenzie-Richards—had released his machine and flown clear, we came in and landed at Cardington rather heavily; both cars hit the deck and broke connection struts and the bottom 'G' girders. Major Scott was in charge of this flight, with Squadron Leader Booth as acting Captain, Squadron Leader Johnston as navigator; myself as First Officer; a crew of twenty-three; the Director of Airship Development, Group Captain P. F. M. Fellowes; the two plane pilots with Wing Commander Walsh in charge; and a mechanic; the acoustic experiments were carried out by Mr Whateley-Smith.

On 17th November 1926, with the struts replaced and the girders repaired, *R.33* left the ground to do a plane-dropping demonstration for the Dominion Premiers. Again we had the two 'Grebes' slung underneath, but they were not released, as the cloud height of 500 feet was considered too low for a sufficient margin of safety, so the flight was cut short to an hour and a quarter.

On 23rd November the ship was taken out of the shed, her mooring-wire shackled to the wire from the top of the mooring-tower, and the functioning of the new mooring system was tried successfully three or four times. The engines were then started up and the ship was slipped from the tower head at 13.42 hours.

Again we carried 'Grebes', which were flown off by Squadron Leader Baker and F/Lt Shales, after which we flew back to Pulham. It might be of interest to note that the person in charge of parachutes during this flight was Leading Aircraftman Dobbs, the inventor of the inflatable rubber dinghy. He was known in the service as 'Brainy' Dobbs, as he was of a remarkably inventive cast of mind, always bringing out some new gadget.

In the middle of carrying out experimental work with *R.33*, I was offered a nice change from airship flying; I was asked by the Royal Aero Club to be one of Great Britain's representatives in the Gordon Bennett International Balloon Race to be held at Antwerp on 30th May 1926.

Originally Squadron Leader Booth had been selected as my aide, but he could not get leave, so F/O Maurice Steff took his place. Steff was at that time an officer in the Kite Balloon Section of the RAF at Rollestone Camp, Larkhill, but was temporarily at Pulham doing some experiments with kite balloons in conjunction with 'Bill' Bateman of the NPL. Bateman was one of the three survivors of the *R.38* crash.

We found the city of Antwerp *en fête* when we presented ourselves to the Committee of the Belgian Aero Club to receive our log-sheet, weather report, map, and rules of the competition. A reception was held at the *Hôtel de ville* by the Burgomaster. We were presented by the British Consul, who afterwards took us to the Consulate, where he had collected the British colony, and presented us with a memento of the race from them, in the shape of a handsome bronze plaque.

The balloons, fifteen in number, were taken out to Wilryck Plain, just outside Antwerp, on Saturday, 29th May, and plonked down, with basket, net and groundsheet, on the space previously allotted to each team. We had been allocated three Belgian soldiers to assist us, but after a few minutes they were called away to assist another competitor whose net had become all tangled up. So we were left with the expert help of Mr R. F. Dagnall—the founder of RFD Company, of Guildford—who had been engaged by the Royal Aero Club to assist us with the preparation and inflation.

We very soon had our balloon laid out on the groundsheet, spread our net over, and inserted the valve. We then discovered that only empty sandbags had been supplied and we were expected to fill them ourselves, which we did with the aid of the three soldiers and Commander Perrin, Secretary of our Royal Aero Club, who had come out to see how things were going. We left the balloon all ready for gassing, surrounded by sandbags, at 7.30 pm.

Steff and I were out on the plain at Wilryck at 3 am next morning. Inflation of all fifteen balloons commenced simultaneously at 3.30 am. At 5 am we were relieved by Mr Dagnall and went back to Antwerp to get breakfast. A very willing voluntary helper, Captain Rupert Preston, had left the hotel to go out to the plain, before we got back. There were no trams, buses nor taxis to be had and we were thoroughly wet, as it had started to rain before we left the plain.

Whilst having breakfast we had a shock when Mr Dagnall telephoned to say he had deflated the balloon as the net had broken badly, and he was afraid it would burst through the net if inflation was continued. So it looked as if we were out of the race before it had started.

I immediately got hold of the Secretary of the Belgian Aero Club, Monsieur Jules Moselli, and asked him if he knew where we could obtain another net. He said he did not think there was another net of the necessary size in the whole of Belgium. Luckily, M. Vandenbemden, who was there, assistant to M. De Muyter the leading world balloonist, overheard this and broke in to say that it was not so, as he had an old net for a 2,200 cubic metre balloon at his house in Brussels, which we could have if we liked to fetch it. M. Moselli gave me a note for the President of the FAI—the organizing body—M. Georges Hanrez, stating what had happened. The President told us to get the net and in the meantime he would call a meeting of the Race Committee to decide whether we should be allowed to inflate and take part in the race. Through the good offices of M. Olieslagers, who was the official looking after the interests of the British entries, a car was placed at our disposal and I was driven at top speed over the thirty miles of cobbled road to Brussels. We set out at 10 am; picked up the net, and reached the plain again at noon—pretty good going considering the roads and the weather, which had scarcely let up since the morning.

I informed the Committee I had brought back the net. Then arose a terrific argument as to whether we should be allowed to inflate. One man in particular was strongly against it, his argument being that we should have an unfair advantage over the other competitors in that we should have fresher gas. He forgot that the other balloons, being now three parts full would be drying out, now the rain had stopped, whilst the *Bee*, our balloon, was still lying in pools of water, and had become sodden. It was decided to allow us to inflate so as not to waste more time and a final decision would be given at 2 pm. I had to give an undertaking to pay for the gas used and to pay 250 francs for the hire of the net.

We spread the fresh net over the thoroughly soaked balloon, fixed the valve, and recommenced inflation at 1 pm. The borrowed net was certainly an old one. Steff, Dagnall and I spent all our time walking round as the balloon rose to shape, repairing broken or stranded meshes.

At 2.30 pm the Committee gave its verdict that we should be allowed to compete on condition that we left the ground in our proper turn—we were to be Number 7 in order—the first of the British balloons. The first balloon was due to leave the ground at 4 pm. Allowing a ten-minute interval between each starter, we had until 5.10 pm in which to get ready.

During lunch-time Captain M. A. Giblett, the Director of the Airship Meteorological Section at the Air Ministry, discussed the weather map with Steff and myself. The forecast was for a strong south to south-west wind; heavy low cloud; rain and storms.

We returned to the plain at 4.15 pm to find the *Bee* very nearly inflated. The first balloon to go was being hauled to the starting-position.

It had started raining again, so that our net was thoroughly soaked. Being made of hemp, it shrank so much that it was only with the help of Mr Allen, of Spencer Brothers, and his men, who were assisting with the inflation of Mrs John Dunville's balloon *Banshee III* and various other helpers, including Rupert Preston and, of course, Mr Dagnall, plus a strong supporter of ours, M. van Kolhoven, the Dutch aeroplane inventor, that we managed, after a struggle, to get the net lines fixed to the hoop and basket.

At 5.15 a message was delivered to say we had twenty minutes before it was our turn to leave; if not ready by that time, we would be disqualified. We were in the act of fixing the basket and had just got it toggled on when along came the handling-officer with his party to take us to the starting-point. We had no time to fix up the instruments or put the inside of the basket ship-shape. All our gear, including instruments, food, water, trail rope, grapnel, coats and sandbags, was dumped into the basket in one unholy jumble.

It was now pouring again and heavy squalls were blowing across the ground, so that at times the balloon was lying over nearly horizontal and the handling-party had all they could do to hold it. Our coats were at the bottom of the heap in the basket, so that by the time we got away at 5.38 pm we were already pretty well soaked.

We went up very light so as not to have to bother with throwing out sand, but could concentrate on getting our instruments fixed up. We quickly rose to 1,500 feet, entering the heavy rain cloud at 1,000 feet. The rain was pouring into the basket in small cascades which ran down the leading-lines of the net. With the weight of water in the basket, plus that on the balloon and net, we very soon lost our initial lift and commenced to fall. Usually when one has reached the limit of initial rise, if there is no inversion of temperature, one can maintain height with a few handfuls, or scoopfuls, of sand, but we had to empty out no less than three bags weighing fifty pounds each to check our first fall.

We had our work cut out to maintain a constant height owing to the continued inflow of rain-water, but we managed to get our instruments fixed in the rigging, and our trail rope over the side during our ascents.

I think the net we had hired must have been for a 60,000 cubic feet balloon—the *Bee* was 80,000—as by now it had shrunk so much that it pinched the balloon in and brought the neck almost down to the hoop; normally it is four or five feet above it. This pinching effect must have forced gas out of the neck, for very soon we were falling fast from a height of 3,000 feet. Whilst Steff threw out sand, I cut a hole right through the bottom of the basket, which was now inches deep in water. By this time we were down to 700 feet and still falling heavily, despite our spilling out thirteen bags of sand. This did not check our fall, and we came hurtling down in the middle of the village of Vrijhoeven Cappelle, two miles from Waalwijk in Holland. We hit the roof of the school and carried away a few tiles; from here we were swept along at thirty miles an hour on to another roof, off which we bounced into the midden in a farmyard. We were so heavy that twelve farm labourers could not lift the balloon and basket over a fence on to clear ground, so we ripped her. Fortunately we were in the lee of some large farm buildings, so the balloon did not kite about in the wind.

None of the locals who quickly gathered round knew a word of English, French or Italian, and neither of us spoke Dutch. The crowd clambered all over the basket and got away with our rations, instruments and field-glasses.

Very soon two officious police officers came along and wanted full particulars from us. They had not heard of the Gordon Bennett Balloon Race, and were not satisfied either with our passports or the Royal Aero Club Certificate requesting assistance from military and civil authorities. We were told we would be detained until we had paid for any damage done, plus twenty-five gulden for the help of the labourers when landing, plus the same amount for storing the balloon. They said we would have to go with them to the police station two miles away. We did not fancy marching for half an hour between two policemen with a crowd of five hundred gawking, clog-shod yokels clattering along behind, so declined to go unless they provided a vehicle.

Luckily at this juncture there arrived on the scene a gentleman in a motor car named Oerlemans who spoke very good English. He managed to satisfy the police of our bona fides, but could not offer us a lift, as he was bound in the opposite direction. To our great relief M. Oerlemans returned a little later, picked us up, took us to his home, gave us dry clothing and a large drink of Schnapps. This last probably saved us from pneumonia, as we had been shivering with cold and wet ever since landing. We had come down at 7.20 pm and it was nearly ten o'clock by the time he rescued us from the police. We could not have met with greater hospitality than the Oerlemans family showed us. The firm of Oerlemans & Zonen were forage contractors and had supplied large quantities of hay and forage to the British Army during the South African War.

Next day we spread out the balloon to dry, made up the net, folded up the balloon as soon as it was dry and stuffed it and the net and our other gear into the basket, had it transported to Waalwijk station and caught a train back to Antwerp.

I met Van Orman, the winner of the race, when we returned to Antwerp. He said he had found that the rain had collected round the top valve in such quantities that instead of throwing out sand, he would pull the valve line, and a shower of water would come out of the neck of the balloon. We must also have experienced this without realising it; this, and the water that had run into the basket off the rigging, was quite enough to have made us so heavy.

My next effort was at Wolverhampton Flower Show: free balloon flights were still a great attraction at most of the big flower shows. From Wolverhampton, I took up Messrs Spencer Brothers' balloon *Cecil*, (of 40,000 cubic feet), taking two passengers. We landed at Craven Arms, under Wenlock Edge in Shropshire, about 30 miles south-west of Wolverhampton. Captain Tom Willows also took up a balloon. He was a link with the first SS ship—his small 20,000 cu. ft airship was taken over by the RNAS and in 1915 it was fitted with a 39,000 cu. ft envelope and called *SS.1*. It was burnt when landing at Capel under the captaincy of Sub-Lt R. S. Booth, RN.

Booth and I took up another of the Spencer balloons, the *Duchess of York*, during another flower show, this time at Shrewsbury; we left 'The Quarry' at 7 pm on 18th August and landed at Edgmond, eighteen miles away, the balloon being required for next day's show.

Next day, we studied the weather map carefully and came to the conclusion that with the wind then blowing—west-south-west 40 mph—we should be taken in the direction of Nottingham. We prevailed on someone to drive Booth's car to that city, to avoid having to return to Shrewsbury to pick it up. We left 'The Quarry' at twenty minutes after seven in the evening, passed over Stafford, Derby and Ilkeston and landed at Hucknall Torkard, about five miles north of Nottingham, to a party of very nice miners who were taking part in the General Strike of 1926 and seemed heartily fed up with it, hoping to be back at work in a fortnight. In the one and three-quarter hours we had taken over the journey, we had travelled seventy-five miles at a rate of 40 mph. We duly picked up Booth's car in Nottingham and returned to Pulham, having dispatched the balloon and basket to Spencers' factory in north London.

The method of piloting balloons from these shows was somewhat crude, as we carried no instruments. For a statascope—the rise-and-fall meter—we used scraps of torn-up tissue-paper which we occasionally threw over the side of the basket—if the scraps fell away downwards, we were rising; if they rose upwards, we knew we were falling!

My next ballooning venture was to represent Great Britain again in the Gordon Bennett Balloon Race, this time from Detroit, USA. My aide for this occasion was Squadron Leader Ralph Sleigh Booth, with F/O M. Steff to assist on the ground.

We crossed the Atlantic in the RMS *Antonia* from Southampton to Quebec. On the way we passed a huge iceberg and I thought of the *Titanic*! In the Gulf of St Lawrence we nearly ran into a whale.

We had a look around Quebec and were not at all impressed, except with the magnificent and picturesque 'Chateau Frontenac'; we went to see the Montmorency Falls, which are higher than Niagara, but with a much smaller volume of water. Then we went on to Montreal, where we had the thrilling experience of shooting La Chine Rapids. Even in a steamboat this was exciting, as it was fairly shot along amid the swirling and foaming waters, with rocks visible just beneath the surface and only a few feet away, on both sides of the boat.

From Montreal, we went on to Toronto, where we visited the International Exhibition. John Barron, who lives in Toronto, looked in on us and drove us down to Niagara Falls, which we saw at night, all illuminated by various coloured lights. We went to the Rapids, where Captain Matthew Webb lost his life in attempting to swim across around the end of the last century. And I don't wonder; he was a brave man to make the attempt! It is quite a narrow stretch which constricts the current until it is faster than a boiling, tumbling mill-race.

We got to Detroit at last, where the brothers Carl and George Fritsche looked after us—they were directors of the Metal Clad Airship Company. George had lost an arm in the war, and the way Carl looked after him, and his devotion to his elder brother, impressed us very much.

We located our balloon, which had already been delivered at the Ford Airport at Dearborn just outside the city. Mr Henry Ford—the original Henry Ford—gave a lunch to the competitors at the Ford Motor Works. We had a long chat with him and his son Edsel and I was much impressed with their quiet gentle manners. Mr Ford, senior, told us that his father was an Englishman born in Ireland—Dublin, I think. His wife was English from Warwick and he seemed proud of the fact of being half English, saying that the backbone of the United States was its English stock. We were shown over the Ford Motor Works, which were in a spotless condition; no smoking was allowed and one could have eaten off the polished parquet floors.

Our party was joined by the Hon. Arthur de Moleyns—now Lord Ventry—and Mr Griffith Brewer, the Chairman of the Royal Aero Club and himself a foremost British balloonist and competitor—he had broken his annual visit to his great friend Orville Wright at Georgian Bay to come down to Dearborn for the race. It was Griffith Brewer who vindicated the Wright brothers' claim to be the first man to build and fly a controllable powered aeroplane. Wright's precedence, and also certain valuable patents which he had taken out were challenged in America by another aviator; Griffith Brewer delivered a famous address, to the Royal Aeronautical Society in London, 20th October, 1921, completely proving the claims of the Wright brothers.

Another former shipmate of mine who came to renew his acquaintance was Harrison Goodspeed, who had been one of the four young American SS pilots at Howden in 1918. He had come over from Grand Rapids, Michigan.

We had no trouble with our new net during inflation and we were the third to leave. Just before taking off we were presented with a bouquet of flowers by our Lady Sponsor, Miss Paula Dilling, a very attractive American girl.

At 4.10 pm on Saturday, 10th September 1927, we let go and proceeded south over Lake Erie and Fort Clinton. The clouds were building up to the southwards with occasional lightning; one flash was not far from the balloon, so we dropped ballast to get above the clouds. We then had a wonderful experience bumping along the top of the clouds; we would emerge from the top of the cumulus cloud under the impulse of the up-current in it and then, having lost the impulsion, we would sink back into the cloud, to be pushed up through the top again. This went on for most of the night until we finally emerged into brilliant moonlight and saw a complete rainbow encircling the moon, a beautiful sight. As we were in or above cloud all night, we did not have the faintest idea where we were. For one period of about an hour we must have been practically stationary, for we heard during that period, the continuous bump bump of a pumping engine. At 6.40 am on Sunday morning I dropped a message 'From Balloon *Bee* at 8,000 feet, above dark clouds travelling south'. It was picked up at Flatwoods, West Virginia.

During the morning the sun heated up our gas and we rose to 15,000 feet. Then we came over the large forest area on the Allegheny Mountains, which cooled us down, and we were soon down to 6,000 feet. We must have overchecked her fall, as in next to no time we were up to 17,000 feet, where the heat was terrific and I remember putting an empty sandbag over my head as protection. We were now over the foothills south of the mountains, and passed over a town on a fairly wide emerald green river. Booth, who is an excellent map reader, soon located it as Lynchburg on the James River.

Shortly after this we came down with the intention of doing some 'trailing', as we had not very much ballast left. Unfortunately our net caught in the branches of a tree and, try as we might, we just could not get it free, so we decided to make our landing; this was in a recently cut tobacco plantation at 13.30 hours on 11th September 1927, 21 hours 20 minutes after leaving Detroit, and a distance of 450 miles. This was near the village of Cove, five miles north-east of Clover, Virginia, which is eighty miles south-west of Richmond. The race was won by Hill with

Van Orman, the previous year's winner, second. The distance covered was of the order of 700 miles.

Next morning we packed up the balloon and basket and went by train to Richmond, where we were met by a Mr Leverty, a representative of the *Times and Despatch* newspaper. Scenting he had a 'scoop' for his paper, he whisked us out to the Varsity Club for the night. After getting our story of the race he took us to see his editor. Here we were shown the printing works where the morning's edition was being made up incorporating our recent venture, and very interesting it was, too—unknown to us, this was partly to keep us from being quizzed by the rival paper!

Next morning we were shown over the Lucky Strike cigarette factory, where they turned out ten million cigarettes a day, all by machines attended by girls.

We went on to Washington and had a good look around; then on to New York, where Booth's sister was doing social work; from here we returned to England in the *Lancastria*, on which we were pleased to hear that Webster in a Supermarine Napier S5 seaplane had won the Schneider Cup for Britain.

On returning to Pulham I joined the Norfolk and Norwich Aero Club and started to learn to fly an aeroplane—actually an Avro—but before I got very far I was transferred to the RAW* at Cardington and sent on a three months' meteorological course in London—which I passed with flying colours, getting a mark of 83 per cent.

On 21st April 1928, I attended Booth's wedding as best man, and a week later was myself married to Griffith Brewer's daughter Betty, at the Brompton Oratory. I have to thank the Gordon Bennett Race for this, but it prevented my representing Great Britain a third time!

* Royal Airship Works.

The start of the Gordon Bennett International Balloon Race, Antwerp, 1926

The Balloon *Bee* with Flying Officer Steff (*left*) and the author aboard, Antwerp, 1926

The frame of *R.100* under construction at Howden. The centre girder can be seen with the gasbags stowed over it

R.100 with her outer cover on

CHAPTER TEN

Appointed to R.100 and her First Flight

Booth and I were given the choice of which of the new ships we would like to be appointed to; we had no real preference at that early date, so both of us said we wished to be posted to the first ship to fly. At that time there seemed to be no question as to which ship that would be—the hull of *R.100* was practically complete, whereas only about one frame of *R.101* was on the stocks. As it turned out, however, the organisation under Mr Gerrish at Cardington was superior to that at Howden, where *R.100* was being built, and so it transpired that my next actual airship flight was in *R.101*, but of this later. In the meantime, Booth and I were appointed to *R.100*, as Captain and First Officer respectively, and were both sent up to Howden to get to know the construction of the ship.

It would take a book in itself to describe in detail the construction of *R.100*, so I will try to compress it as much as possible. The girder work employed a novel method of construction evolved by Barnes Neville Wallis,* her Chief Designer. Each girder consisted of three parallel metal tubes joined by lattice work to form a triangular section. The tubes were made of flat duralumin strip wound helically and riveted at regular intervals through the overlap; this meant that the tubes could be made of any length up to 70 feet—considerably more than if actual tubing had been used. The same construction was used for both longitudinal and transverse girders. Another ingenious construction was the connecting joint between the transverse frames and the longitudinals; a 'V' at the end of each transverse girder interlaced with a 'Y' at the end of the longitudinals. The centre of the arms of the 'Y' formed a centroid of the joint for the purposes of calculating stresses, which was where Nevile Shute Norway† came in, as he was Chief Calculator. Neither *R.100* nor *R.101* were built empirically—that is by trial and observation—as were

* Now Sir Barnes Wallis and famous for, among other things, the 'bouncing bomb' he developed for the 'Dam-busters' Raid' in World War II.

† After the airship programme was discontinued, he became joint founder of the Airspeed firm and designed the very successful Airspeed Oxford; he was still better known as Nevile Shute, the author. At this time, he had not yet published any of his novels.

most of the ships of Zeppelin construction, but both were scientifically stressed,* hence in my humble opinion they were much stronger than those of Zeppelin-type construction. Compare the US *Shenandoah*, which was based on actual Zeppelin designs and broke up when flying through a line-squall, with *R.100*, whose hull structure was undamaged in similar circumstances.

Another innovation was a triangular tubular girder running from Frame One in the nose-piece, through the centre of the gas-bags, to the cruciform girder of the plane structure at the after end; this was attached to the slack wiring system at the centre of each transverse girder. The central girder replaced the central wire fitted in Zeppelins and in our own previous rigid airships. The other great design achievement was that in the whole construction of *R.100*'s hull only fifty standardised parts were used, as given by the Air Ministry to the press in 1929.†

The gas-bags, fifteen in number, were made of cotton, lined with goldbeaters' skin—of membrane. When full, they contained 1,156,000 cubic feet of hydrogen gas. The outer cover consisted of strips of linen stretched longitudinally between transverse frames, machined together and taped over inside and out, the inside tape being eyeleted to take the zigzag wiring for attaching the cover to the hull. This was done by threading the wire through the eyelets and passing it over a series of wires fitted to the longitudinals at intervals right round the circumference of the ship, called circumferential wires.

Power was supplied by six reconditioned Rolls-Royce 'Condor 3b' engines of 650 hp each. They were fitted tandemwise in three cars: a pair of wing cars amidships and an after car in the centre-line. The after engine of each pair was reversible.

Inflation commenced on 30th July 1929. Booth, myself, Chief Cox'n T. Greenstreet, Assistant Cox'ns Long, Hobbs and Moncrieff showed the Airship Guarantee Company's staff the method of inflation for the first two bags and then handed over the control to them, though we still took a very active part in the evolution. Cox'n 'Jerry' Long assisted Mr Norway at the fore end of the bag at the top of the ship, and Cox'n Tommy Hobbs at the fore end of the axial girder. I was with Mr Horrocks, the Chief Draughtsman, on the top of the ship at the after end of the bag with Chief Cox'n Greenstreet on the axial girder below.

* Although the two ships were similar in appearance, their internal design was completely different. The frame of *R.101* was the work of Colonel Richmond.

† My recollections on this point not being very clear, I wrote to consult Sir Barnes Wallis. He replied: 'I have now checked that the number of separate parts (excluding extruded stranded wire bracing) was eleven. In arriving at this number I ignored differences in gauge, that is to say a tube made in 16 gauge material and one made in 22 gauge would count as the same part for the purpose of estimating the number of eleven, as they would be made on the same machine.

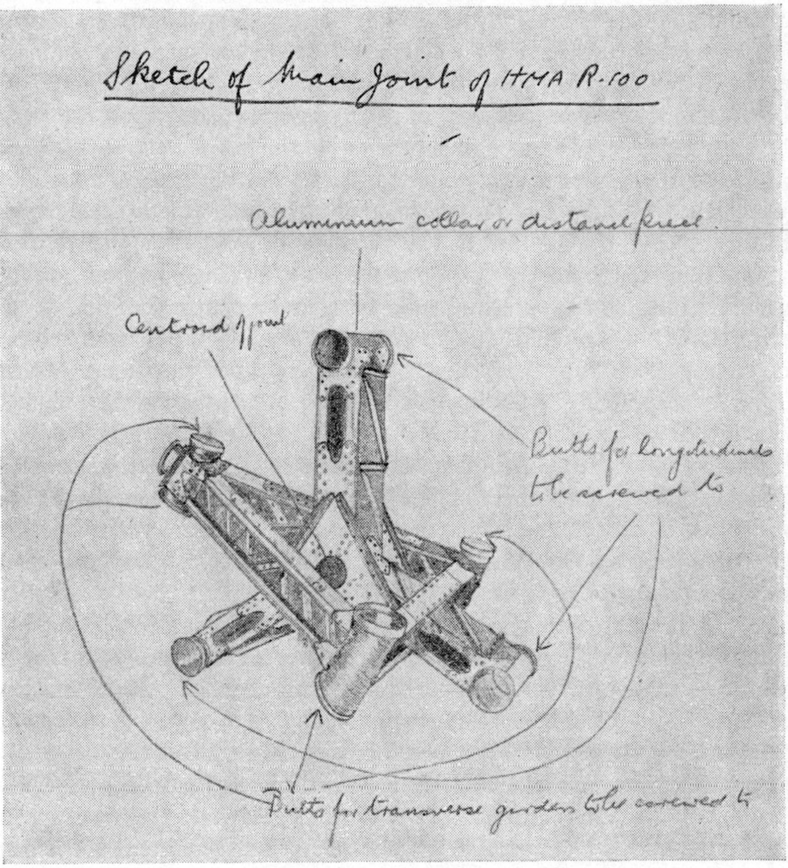

R.100's Main Joints connecting longitudinal girders to transverse frames

This ingenious joint was so designed by Barnes Wallis (now Sir Barnes Wallis, F.R.S.) that N. S. Norway, the Chief Calculator, could work out the strains of tension and compression forces on wire cables swaged into the centre of the joint.

In effect this joint consisted in interlocking of the capital letters 'V' and 'Y', the ends of the arms of each letter being the points into which the ends of the girders were screwed; the ends of the 'V' took the transverse, and the ends of the 'Y' the longitudinal girder. The centre of the interlock was the 'centroid' which held the wires.

Great care had to be taken until the bag was half full to prevent it creeping along the axial girder due to the ends drawing to the centre. To prevent this, three AGC riggers, Deverell, Wiseman and Williams assisted those at either end of the axial girder. These men, later on, became very valuable members of the flying crew.

Care had also to be taken to get the top of the bag correctly positioned in the wire mesh netting panels, attached to the upper girders, by which the lift of the gas was transferred to the hull. If a difficulty arose in this placing, the gas flow had to be stopped. To do this, orders were at first shouted by those at the top to those supervising operations on the ground. This led to some confusion from many people shouting at the same time; but Mr Wallis quickly devised a method of passing messages down a speaking-tube from the cat walk at the top of the shed. Another difficulty experienced in the early stages of the inflation was that of slowing down or stopping the inflow of gas. We were inflating with silicol gas which came direct from the generating plant into the ship, and this meant that once a charge had commenced we had to take all the gas generated by that charge, whether we wanted it all or not. Inflating from a gas-holder is a much simpler business, as you can take as little or as much gas as you like, the supply being regulated by a hand valve. By inflating direct from a silicol plant, if you stop the gas from flowing you run the risk of blowing up the gas plant. Major Teed, who was in charge of the gas plant, however, soon devised a means of slowing the generation of the gas if necessary, and this greatly facilitated our work at the top of the ship in getting the gas-bags correctly positioned.

We had only one setback during the inflation and that occurred when No. 4 bag was being inflated: a huge rent, 15 feet in length, was torn in the bottom of the bag owing to the line anchoring the bottom of the bag to the corridor not having been cast off or slacked out as the bag filled out. However, Chief Cox'n Greenstreet set to himself and with the able assistance of his assistant cox'ns completed a magnificent repair by 7 pm the same evening, the tear happening at noon.

After this little setback, inflation went ahead with a swing, two bags a day being inflated, so that within ten days we had completed as far as No. 14 Bag; No. 15 was left uninflated until just before the ship was ready for airborne trials.

The huge airship, weighing over a hundred tons, was now floating in the air, held down by crates full of weights and by large oil drums full of earth slung through blocks in the roof, thus acting as balancing weights. Although the airship was airborne, the bridles to the roof were not entirely cast off from the top of the ship in case they should be wanted in an emergency.

The engines were being run whenever possible preparatory to the airborne engine trials, which were eventually started on the 25th September. For these trials the airship had to be well and rigidly held to the shed, the nose being buttoned into a socket in the 'front door', while the doors at the after end were opened to allow for the rush of air. During a preliminary run the back doors had been only partially opened, with the result that a stream of air struck the doors, bounced off the roof and fell in a cascade on to the tops of the fins, beating the tail down in an alarming manner.

The airborne trials consisted in running each pair of engines at three-quarters speed for an hour and a half, the final five minutes of which was at full throttle on both engines, and then the after engine only was run astern for half an hour.

The noise inside the shed during these trials was simply deafening—you could shout at the top of your voice into a person's ear and not be heard. One rather alarming sight early on in these trials was the static electricity generated by the propellers, which were only a few inches from the concrete floor of the shed. I thought at first it was blue smoke from the exhaust which was following the swirl of the slipstream. At times, in addition to the blue spiral from the floor aft of the propeller there would be a blueish halo to the circle swept out by the propeller tips like St. Elmo's fire. This static effect was overcome by spraying water on the floor in the vicinity of the car—we then saw the phenomenon of miniature waterspouts or tornadoes being whisked up off the floor.

A far more alarming occurrence happened while the port engines were being run; this was a split in the fabric outer cover of the airship abaft the port car. It started as a split about 18 inches long, but before the attention of those running the engine could be attracted by observers on the floor the cover had split the entire distance between two frames. It is an ill wind that blows no good, and this was no exception, for it had the effect of ensuring a better liaison between observers on the ground and those running the engines in the car, for after this misfortune someone was always stationed in the control car to keep a constant watch for signals to stop from observers; he would immediately ring through on the engine telegraph to stop or slow down.

These trials must have been a great anxiety and a big responsibility to those in charge, Mr Wallis and his staff; it speaks volumes for the thoroughness and efficiency of their arrangements when it is realised that between the top of the airship and the shed there was only about 3 feet of clearance, while the tips of the propellers cleared the ground by a little more than 1 foot. It must have been a nightmare for those responsible, though to describe the airship as surging up and down, and the cars as leaping and straining at their drag wires, as did Norway in *Blackwood's Magazine* of May 1933 is, from my recollection, a little exaggerated—'straining', yes, but 'leaping', decidedly not! There was no room for leaping.

The engine airborne trials having been completed satisfactorily, we were then looking forward to the final completion of all the odds and ends of the ship.

Meanwhile *R.101* had been completed and flew her first trial on 14th October 1929, with Squadron Leader Booth an interested observer on board. Shortly after this I had to go to Cardington in connection with stores and rations and while there was offered the opportunity of a trip in *R.101* during her next flight. I did not want to miss this, so I slept two nights in the airship—and found it exceedingly cold and draughty.

R.101 left the shed at 5 am on the 1st November 1929 and was secured to the mooring-tower at Cardington. At 09.40 the same morning she was released from the tower and flew for eight hours. In the course of this flight we were able to give Their Majesties King George V and Queen Mary a chuck-up at Sandringham, and were very bucked to see Their Majesties come out on the gravel path to look at the airship. Amongst those on board was Sir Samuel Hoare and as a tribute to him the airship was taken over his home near Sheringham. It was a very quiet flight and nothing exceptional was tried. My general impression of the ship was that she steered well, but was somewhat sluggish on her elevators. Instead of returning at once to Howden, I remained at Cardington another day on Major Scott's instructions, as *R.101* was standing by to carry out her full-speed trials. This flight was carried out during the night of 2nd/3rd November, the airship being slipped from the tower at 20.40 hours on the 2nd, and was secured back to the tower at 10.40 the following morning. I was again taken as an observer and to gain experience in handling a large airship.

We proceeded south and passed over London in clear weather. The myriads of lights of the metropolis are an amazing sight at night. The main thoroughfares can easily be distinguished by their more brilliant lighting, but it is no easy matter to say which road is which if you do not happen to strike the city at a familiar point. It was rather amusing to hear passengers pointing out places they recognised—or thought they did—when we were nowhere near them.

On the south side of the river the weather became somewhat foggy, but we were able to get a very good back bearing on the red light at Croydon, and then made a south-westerly course for Portsmouth and the Isle of Wight. Portsmouth Dockyard was a blaze of exceptionally brilliant lights, but I personally was much more thrilled to cross over to the little old Isle of Wight and pass over its town of Newport, where I spent my early boyhood. The lights of the town had, however, already been extinguished, so we could discern little except the River Medina, but I do remember picking out the swing railway bridge over the Medina near the station. We crossed the island to St Catherine's and then set course for the Needles.

The triangular course, over which the speed trials were to be held, was Needles—Durlestone Head—Poole—and back to Needles. We had just completed the first leg from Needles to Durlestone Head with four engines at full power, and were in the act of turning for the second leg when one of the engines broke down and could not be restarted. This put an end to full-speed trials on all engines for this trip. The airspeed attained with all four engines at full power was 55 knots—or 63 mph. The course was traversed on three engines at full speed, and the speed through the air was 51 knots or 58.6 mph. The ship behaved very well during this flight and maintained a comparatively even keel. The wind was fairly strong over the sea, but was not gusty, and the general atmospheric conditions were stable; there were no sudden gusts or vertical currents.

Unfortunately, when attaching the airship to the tower the bow fouled the top of the tower and dented one of the tubes, while one of the yaw guys dragged against the bow and buckled a reefing boom; however, the damage was so slight that it was all repaired by the evening. I spent the afternoon and evening in the ship at the tower lending a hand gassing up. Owing to the fact that the ship's lights were cut off whilst gassing operations were being carried out, this was a most difficult job in the dark with the aid of hand torches only.

The next day I had a change from the big 'Rigids'—I had been detailed to go to Cramlington, Newcastle, to fly the trials of the small 'Non-Rigid' airship *AD.1* for her Certificate of Airworthiness. I was to fly the trials on 6th November. I have never spent such an anxious night as that before I did this flight. It was some ten years since I had piloted a 'Non-Rigid', which is a vastly different matter from piloting a 'Rigid' or 'Semi-Rigid'. I do not mean that it is more difficult, but it is a more personal job; I had violent indigestion all that night and, due to nerves, scarcely slept a wink. Strange to say, directly I was seated in the cockpit of the little 'Blimp' I felt at home at once, as if I had never given up flying an SS. She was of 60,000 cubic feet capacity with a car somewhat like the SS B.E.2c of 1915–16, with an ABC 'Hornet' engine of 75 hp. I spent an hour and a quarter testing various things, but could not go higher than 1,500 feet, as the engine kept spluttering and threatened to peter out when I did so. She was a very handy little ship in the air and it was a great pity when she had to be packed up. One thing I noticed about her was that she had no anti-rolling guys, which meant that when handled on the ground the car was a little wobbly sideways. There was, however, no unsteadiness in this respect in flight. When landing, the trail rope release failed to function; I have never seen a man jump so quickly out of his seat on to the handling-rail on the side of the car, and jam his foot on the bar holding the trail rope as did the cox'n, Sgt J. W. Long, a former RNAS airship cox'n of great experience. I allowed the pressure to drop rather low on landing, but beyond a wrinkle showing amidships the envelope kept very good shape, showing her rigging was well designed. I may say that this low pressure was due to the setting of the air valve at 25 m/m by AID* instructions, which meant that one could not blow in a slight excess of pressure up to say 30 m/m on coming up to land, as was our usual practice during the war; on slowing speed and being hauled down, this excess was enough to ensure that one landed with the full normal flying pressure of 25 m/m. Beckford-Ball—or 'Bingo' as I knew him—the pilot of *AD.1*, told me that he had pointed this out to the AID, but they were not to be convinced that in flying as well as in landing this low setting of the valve is a handicap, and could lead to danger.

Within a week of my return to Howden the lift and trim trials of *R.100* were carried out. This was done on Armistice Day, 11th November; there was some consternation when the useful lift amounted to only 57 tons instead of the estimated 64: a deficit of seven tons requires a good deal of explaining, and if the weather had not been so cold there would have been many wet towels and much ice required to cool the heated brows of those racking their fertile brains for a plausible theory as to where the seven tons had disappeared. I believe it was finally put down to excessive dampness absorbed by the cover and bags—I doubt it, said the carpenter, but shed no bitter tear.

The ship could now be said to be finished, and only the formality of taking her over remained to be completed. This was delayed for some days on account of No. 5 Bag leaking, which led to much worse damage, as it was allowed to deflate above the axial girder, with the result that the bag was nipped by the radial wires where they all come together at the centre of the ship, and a 10-foot hole was torn in the bag. None of us was surprised, as we had deferentially suggested that this might happen, but had been assured that no such thing could possibly occur.

To rub in the fact that *R.101* was the first to fly, she flew over Howden during her duration trial on the 17th November. She certainly looked a beautiful sight.

We eventually took over *R.100* provisionally, on 22nd November 1929, by which time a large party of MPs were impatiently awaiting a flight in *R.101*, but the weather was too bad, so they had to be content with tea on

* Aeronautical Inspection Department.

board at the tower. It was now necessary to have a spell of fine weather long enough to unship *R.101* from the tower and put her into the shed, and for certain of the personnel to come to Howden for *R.100*'s flight south. *R.101* was put in the shed on the last day of November, but it was not for over a fortnight more that the weather was settled enough to give our baby an airing. An absolutely flat calm was necessary, for it must be remembered there was a clearance of barely a couple of feet between the top of the ship and the shed; and there was only a matter of 10 feet on either side when going through the doors.

At last the weather becomes anti-cyclonic with dead calm nights, thick with mist. On 14th December Mr Peters, the Meteorological Officer, who had been on duty at Howden for some weeks, told us that we might expect the weather to remain settled for some days; on 15th December Wing Commander R. Colmore, Director of Airship Development, Major Scott, Assistant Director (Flying), Squadron Leader Johnston, Navigator, F/O Steff, Second Officer, and Mr Giblett, who was in charge of the Airship Division of the Meteorological Office, arrived on the scene, so it really looked as if things were going to happen at last.

Booth and I had spent all day and most of the evening in the shed getting everything ship-shape for going out. I finally went to bed at 11.30, but slept badly, being continually awakened by numerous people clumping along the passage. Finally Booth came in at 4 am to say the Army had arrived. So we turned out and went to the shed, where we found a convoy of lorries crammed with soldiers of the York and Lancaster Regiment from York. These were to be our handling-party—and a very excellent one they made, as it turned out; they did exactly what they were told and kept silence, which is a golden rule for airship handling-parties. I spent a busy early morning before dawn, getting our stores packed on a lorry to go down by road.

I had just completed this and was making my way over to the ship when I saw someone in the half light whom I thought I recognised; I could not for the life of me put a name to him. A little later it came back to me with a rush that it was Major Rennie, who had entertained Booth and myself at Brough and shown us over the Blackburn aeroplane works there. I looked around for him, as I should have liked to have taken him over to the control car for a few words with Booth, but unfortunately I couldn't find him again. In the meantime the engines were being warmed up under the supervision of Mr Angus, our Chief Engineer.

Before the soldiers were allocated to their positions, Squadron Leader Booth gave them a short lecture on what was expected of them. It was a great treat the way they carried out their duties, with officers in charge of parties, in striking contrast to some other landing-parties we had with *R.100* later.

At 07.20 on 16th December *R.100* was ballasted up and walked out of the shed at Howden. When the ship was about three parts out of the shed my heart went into my mouth, as a slight puff of wind blew across the mouth of the shed and the ship started to move off the centre-line. The soldiers, however, did their work well and held her up to it, whilst keeping her moving. In a few moments, at 07.30 to be exact, what a relief it was to hear Johnston's voice sing out: 'All clear forrard!'—she came out tail first. A great cheer went up from a large crowd which had sprung up from the Lord knows where.

The ship was taken well out on to the landing-ground before the final ballasting up was carried out, and at 07.53 hours the order was given by Major Scott, who was in charge of the trial flight, to 'Let go!' We rose gently and slowly on an even keel into the air, amid more cheers and horn blowing. After rising statically for a minute, the engines were rung to 'Slow ahead', and *R.100* slowly gathered way.

We cruised around the vicinity of the aerodrome for some minutes and had just set a course for York when the port forward engine was stopped owing to a crack in the water jacket. However, this gave us no worry at all, as we still had five others.

At 09.00 we were over York, that delightful city which to know is to love. I did not see the city, as I was up in the keel superintending the crutching of the bags over the corridor.

We flew around York slowly for a quarter of an hour and then set our course for Cardington, in glorious weather albeit somewhat hazy on the ground. We maintained a height of 1,700 feet, and with a north-westerly wind of from 10 to 15 mph to help us on our southerly course, we were bowling along at about 70 mph, running with only two-thirds of our available power.

We reached Kettering at 10.50 and were over Bedford in less than two hours from leaving York, 135 miles away. As the flight was to be of short duration, we did not carry out 'watch' routine, so I spent most of the time climbing about the interior of the hull, inspecting the functioning of various items like gas-bags, outer cover, valves, fins and controls.

Away down aft in the vicinity of the fins the bases of the gas-bags looked like being damaged, as they were being blown about by the rush of air through the ventilators in the bottom of the outer cover. It was therefore thought advisable to blank off, partially, some of the ventilators, and this was done temporarily during the flight. The cover itself developed extraordinary undulations which, however, did not flap about but stayed rigid. At first sight this wave formation looked most alarming, but on drawing Squadron Leader Rope's attention to it he was reassuring, saying he thought there was nothing to worry about so long as there was no flapping or movement in the cover. However, I did spot one split of about a foot in length developing in the cover just by the corridor abaft the passenger accommodation, and put a rigger on to patch it up immediately, before it spread.

For an hour or so we cruised in the neighbourhood of Bedford and Cardington, and eventually dropped our mooring-wire at a few minutes before 13.00 hours. Our cone was secure in the cup on the tower at 13.30.

My point of duty during the landing operation was on the winch platform up in the nose of the airship. I had with me Cox'n Hobbs and two other members of his Number Two Watch. Our duties were to pay out the main and yaw-guy wires on receipt of instructions through the speaking-tube from the control car. During the period of waiting on fine weather we had practised this evolution many times in the shed at Howden, so we experienced no difficulty. In order to ensure the wire running freely through the cone, one of the riggers had to haul away on the bight of the wire through a trap-door underneath the winch platform; when the weight of wire below the cone was sufficient to outweigh that of the wire from the back-haul to the winch, he would let the bight go. The wire would be paid out for about 150 feet as a preliminary, and we would then await orders from the control car before letting out more.

Looking out through the hatchway in the nose of the airship we had a wonderful view of everything below on the landing-ground as we slowly approached the landing 'T' and little knot of men round it, some 700 or 800 feet downwind, on the leeward side of the tower.

We make straight for this party and as soon as we cross the boundary of the aerodrome *Clang, clang* goes the gong and the order 'Pay out main wire 600 feet' is received from the control car.

This I repeat back; and the man working the winch repeats it again, paying out the wire by easing his brake lever gently.

The wire goes clattering over the fairlead, then up over the pulley above the cone, and so down through the cone until 600 feet are paid out.

'Stop main.' I call.

'Stop main; brake on.' says the man on the winch.

Clang, clang to control car: 'Main wire out 600 feet, sir.'

'Main wire out 600 feet, thank you,' comes back Squadron Leader Booth's voice.

A short pause and *Clang, clang* goes the gong.

'Pay out main to stopper. Stand by to pay out port yaw guy.'

I repeat the order, and the main wire goes clattering out while a couple of riggers ease out the port yaw guy through the hawse pipe, letting the eye out first and holding the bight towards the ship's bows with a hook until the slack has all been fed out. One must not let the eye swing free, or the yaw guy will in all probability twine itself round the main wire, and hold up the whole evolution while it is disentangled. Whilst preparing the yaw guy, the main wire will have been paid out until the stopper rests in the cone.

The last few feet, after the stopper has left the winch drum, are a ticklish business; the wire has to be slowed right down, and the stopper eased up over the rollers of the fairlead through the hatchway, up over the pulley and down into the cone. If it is given its head it will, in all probability, stick momentarily on the fairlead, then fly over it and whip about on the bow tubes holding the cone.

This did happen once and was a most frightening experience, the wire taking charge and the stopper whipping about free on the triangle of tubes, damaging them.

The stopper finally disappears down into the interior of the ship's steel cone, which hangs pendulous from the extreme point of the bow, and with a muffled rattle and bang seats itself into the base of the cone. This fact is reported to the control car and on looking through the hatchway we see the bunch of men at the landing 'T' run forward and drag the end of our main wire towards the 'T', where they shackle it by means of a Thomas Block to the 25-ton wire led out of the mooring-arm on the top of the tower. Immediately the wires are coupled together a white flag is held up by the foreman in charge of the coupling. Meanwhile, the airship has been slowed up to a standstill by reversing the after engine of each wing car. The ship will now be trimmed slightly bow up, so that she will pick up the slack wire. As soon as the Captain of the ship is satisfied as to trim, he will order a white flag to be shown from the control car as a signal to the officer in charge of the mooring-tower, that he may commence to haul in on the main winch. As soon as he gives the order to haul in, a white flag is also shown from the tower platform. If for any reason either wishes the evolution to stop, a red flag replaces the white.

During the evolution of trimming the bow up, the Mast Officer must be on the *qui vive* and ready to pay out on the main winch in order that there will be no snubbing of the wire or snatch on the bow at the moment the main wire becomes taut. In the meantime both yaw guys will have been paid out, and when the airship has been hauled down to a height of 500 feet the main winch is stopped until both the yaw guys are coupled and hauled taut. The Mooring Tower Officer now assumes responsibility and control of operations. The airship is hauled down on all three wires, the function of the yaw guys being, as their name implies, to prevent the airship yawing from side to side and, their lead being set well aft, they also prevent the airship overriding the tower head.

When the ship's cone is 50 feet from entering the cup at the end of the telescopic mooring-arm at the top of the tower the yaw-guy winches are stopped, the ship being hauled in the last 50 feet on the main wire alone,

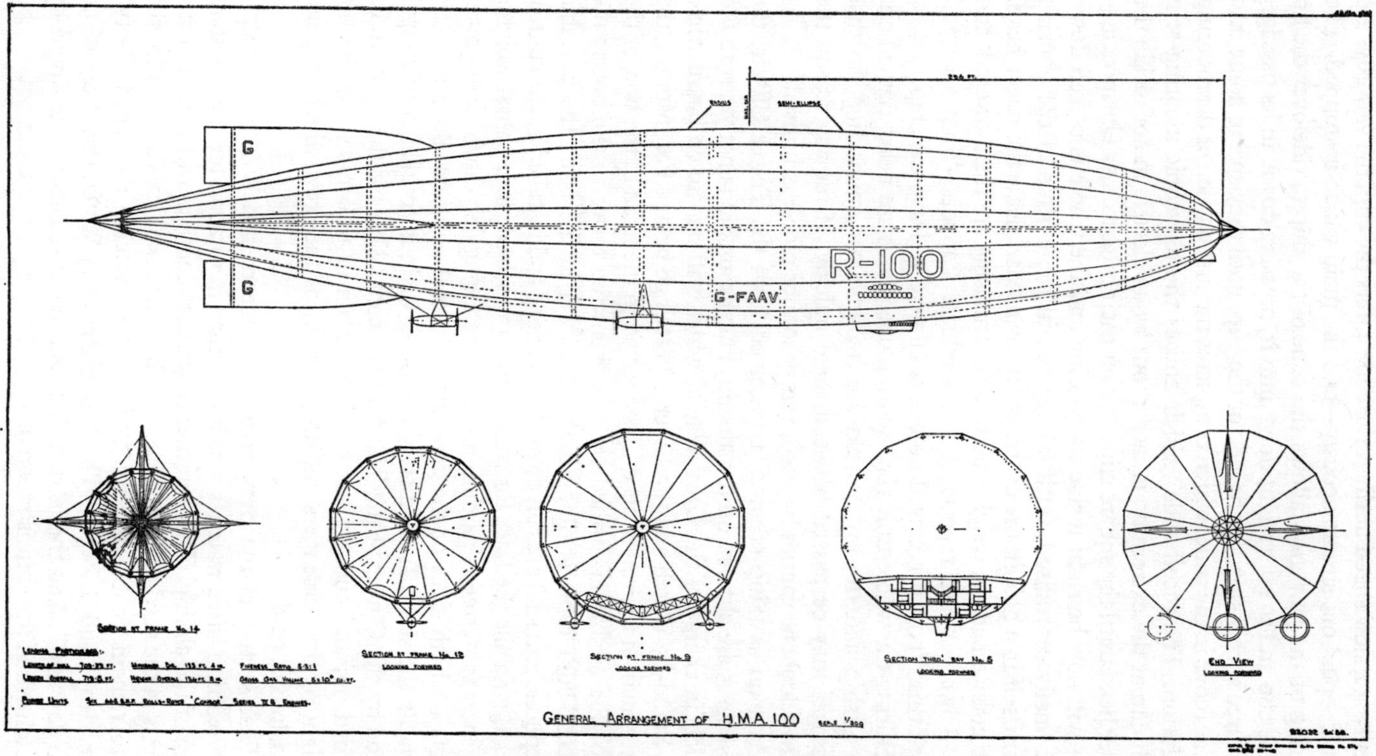

R.100 from a blueprint sent to the author by Sir Barnes Wallis 1970.

usually at a slow speed until, as the cone enters the cup, the yaw guys are veered—paid out simultaneously—and the main winch is stopped. The veering of the yaw guys allows the cone of the ship to ride over the lip of the cup and so go straight down into it, pressing down, in its passage, the three spring stops in the side of the cup, until they spring home into their groove in the cone, which completes the first portion of the mooring evolution. The recoil slide, which houses the telescopic mooring-arm with cup at the extremity, is racked out by an electric motor inside the tower head until the square clips fit over their projections. The mooring-arm will now be right inside its housing and the whole is racked down and finally centralised, until a large pin in the bottom of the housing seats itself in a hole in the centre of the iron floor inside the tower head. The counterbalance weights used for centralising are then lowered, and the Tower Officer reports to the airship's Captain—'Ship secured.' Until this report is received no one is allowed to leave the ship.

During the whole time the mooring operations are being carried out the airship and the tower head are in radio communication, so that messages may be passed between them quickly. If for any reason the radio-telephone cannot be used, semaphore or morse is utilised.

As soon as 'Ship secured' is received from the Tower Officer, the passengers are allowed off the airship, but the airship is not yet ready to be left in charge of the Duty Watch, which will remain on board while the Stand-by Watch and the Liberty Watch go below. For instance, the water main at the tower head is connected to the main in the bow of the ship; the airship is earthed by wire from the tower to the bows; the electric-light cable is plugged into a socket in the bow; the portable telephone and lead are run down the corridor and installed in the control car. Meanwhile the lines for connecting up with the four ballast weights—generally termed 'garden rollers'—are being let down from main joints on both sides of the corridor at several positions along the keel towards the stern. Immediately the water main is coupled a request is made by the Officer of the Watch in the control car for the water to be turned on, and enough water will be taken in to compensate for the weight of the passengers and the portion of the crew which will not remain on board.

Each section of the crew, riggers, engineers, and W/T operators, is divided into three watches which take turn in rotation for the maintenance of the airship. This rotation of watches continues whether the airship is in the shed or at the tower, so that there is no confusion as to who is to remain on board after a flight. The watches are called 'Duty', 'Stand-by', and 'Liberty'. The tour of the Duty Watch lasts from 08.00 one day until 08.00 the next, being relieved for meals by the Stand-by Watch when the ship is moored.

The Stand-by Watch work ordinary working hours when the airship is moored, relieve the Duty Watch for meals, and is the next watch for duty. It is also liable to be recalled to the ship in case of emergency, e.g. when storm routine is in force. The Liberty Watch is free from the time it is relieved until 09.00 the following morning, when it becomes the Stand-by Watch.

The Chief Cox'n and Chief Engineer do not keep a watch, but are responsible that the riggers and engineers respectively in the different watches understand their duties and carry them out in an efficient manner.

The Watch-keeping Officers keep step with the crew, Duty Officer, Stand-by and Liberty. With a full complement of qualified officers, neither the Captain of the airship nor the Navigator would keep a watch, but with our paucity of officers, both the Captain and the Navigator used to keep a watch when *R.100* was at the tower.

When *R.100* arrived at Cardington it happened to be No. 1 Watch's (Squadron Leader Booth) day on. So as soon as possible after the 'secure' they were sent off to dinner, while I, with the Stand-by Watch (No. 2, Cox'n Hobbs and Engineer Charge-hand Mann) looked after the ship until they returned. There was plenty to do, as we had to fill up with gas, water, oil and petrol in preparation for a prospective flight next day.

Normally only two watches man the airship in flight, the other remaining on the ground so that the flying watches may get away quickly at the end of a flight.

I and No. 2 Watch relieved Booth and No. 1 Watch at 08.00 the following morning. My instructions were to warm up the engines in time to slip from the tower at 09.45. The cracked cylinder had been replaced by Mr Moseley, the Rolls-Royce representative, assisted by Jimmy Watson—Works Manager at Howden—and the engineers of the Duty Watch, so that we again had our full power available.

In order to be in good time, knowing the propensity of airships for not getting away punctually, I rang through at 08.45 on the engine-room telegraph 'Stand by'. This was the signal for the engineers to prepare their engine for starting, which was accomplished by means of a small auxiliary engine called a Bristol gas starter. Very soon a rattle like a machine gun was heard—this was the Bristol starter getting busy—then the propeller on the main engine was seen to struggle round in a few spasmodic jerks as the pistons were pushed down in turn by the Bristol until, with a muffled roar, it turned regularly. As soon as the Chief Engineer was satisfied that the engine was functioning satisfactorily, he would put his telegraph to 'Slow' as a signal to the officer in the control car that the engine might be run up in stages. The telegraph would be rung to 1,000 rpm and then to 1,200 rpm. As soon as the engine was warmed up sufficiently, the Chief Engineer or the Charge-hand Engineer of that particular car would ring through 'Slow' if the weather were very cold, or 'Stop' if warm. This routine was repeated for each of the six engines comprising the motive power of the airship.

A few minutes after 09.00 the Trojan van arrived with F/O Steff, Mr Savidge and the fresh food for the flight; two days' reserve rations, plus one day's emergency rations for fifty people were held on board. The rations consisted of fresh meat, vegetables, and bread, with Bovril or Oxo cubes for soup or a hot drink; all our meals during flight were cooked on board.

With the arrival of the rations things began to get busy, for with them arrived No. 3 Watch, which was the other watch to take part in the flight. No. 2 Watch was already on board, having relieved No. 1 Watch (which did the night duty) at 08.00 hours. Passengers and observers were also coming on board at intervals, which meant that water had to be released to compensate for the weight of the people and gear coming on board. At 09.30 the Captain of the ship Squadron Leader Booth, returned, accompanied by the Officer in charge of Flying, Major G. H. Scott, and the Navigator, Squadron Leader E. L. Johnston.

As Officer of the Watch, I make my report to the Captain as to engines having been run and the amount of fuel and ballast on board. He gives the order 'Flying stations' and we go to our various allotted posts. The supply services such as gas, water, petrol, electric light and telephone are disconnected and the gangway hauled up. Way down aft in the keel the lines to the garden rollers, with the exception of the aftermost pair, are hauled up into the ship and stowed in the keel. On the winch platform we receive the order 'Prepare to slip'. This is passed to F/O Luck (the officer in charge of the tower during F/O Cook's absence, sick), who gives the order 'Take strain on the wire'—a mast hand inside the tower then screws down his wheel and draws the mooring-pendant taut.

Then, 'Out stops', and the spring stops holding the ship's cone in the mast's cup are withdrawn, and the airship is left riding solely by its mooring-pendant—a short length of wire with an eye at the mast end and a stopper in the ship's cone. A report is made to the control car as to the state of the airship as shown by a device in the bows. This is calibrated in quarters of a ton light or heavy, and is operated by the minute deflection of a tube, fixed at the forward end into the bow pyramid, and its inboard end pressing onto a container of liquid connected to a glass tube in which the liquid rises or falls by the action of the bow tube. There is also an indicator giving yaw or side strain at the bow, but this did not work very well and usually showed a strain to starboard of from 3 to 9 tons both in flight and when moored. If the bow indicator

A pair of Gloster 'Grebe' aircraft attached to *R.33* at Cardington, November, 1926

R.100 over Farnborough
The ripples in her outer cover are being photographed by the small aeroplane on the left under flight conditions

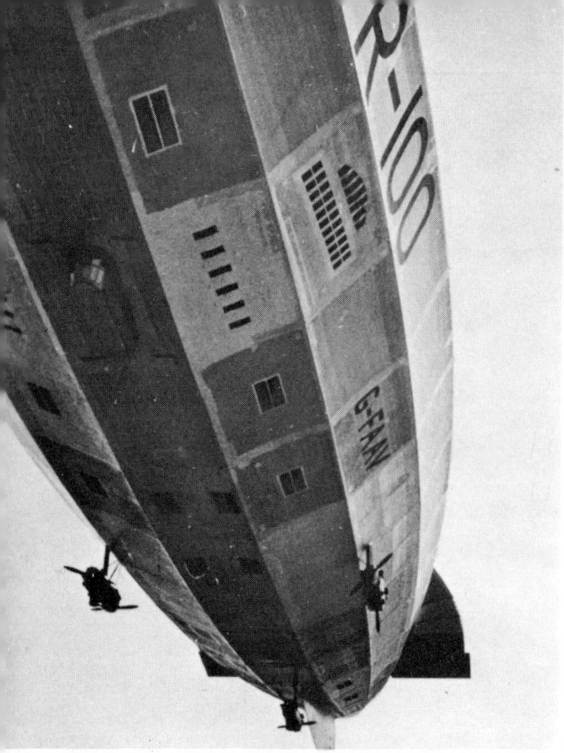

R.100 from below, showing the windows of the passenger accommodation above the control car and the ventilators at the bottom of the ship

C/H Engineer Watts being lowered over the side of an engine car at 1,500 feet

Completion of *R.100*'s first flight from Howden to Cardington, 12th December, 1929

shows very heavy, water is dropped from the bows until the indicator shows a quarter of a ton either side of zero.

A message then comes from the control car to test the lift. This is passed through the bow hatch to the Mooring Tower Officer who gives the order 'Ease up on the wire'. The wheel holding the pendant will be slackened off. If the ship is light the cone will be lifted in the cup a fraction. The Tower Officer tests this by trying to revolve the cup. If he cannot do this, he reports to the ship 'Still heavy'. If he can turn the cup he reports 'Ship lifting'. The Captain will order the remaining wheel wires to be cast off and order through voice-pipe to the winch platform 'Stand by to slip', quickly followed by 'Slip', all this being repeated to the Tower Officer, who finally orders 'Slip', and the bar, holding the hinged hook fast in the eye of the pendant, is lifted. The bow lifts slowly, drawing the cone out of the cup, the mooring-pendant with it, and the ship is free. To make sure that she will clear the top of the tower, another half ton of water is let go as she lifts clear.

As soon as the ship is well clear of the tower the engines are rung up to the required rpm and away we go, gradually gathering speed and height while the tower recedes and people below become Lilliputians.

The present trip is intended to be a speed trial. The contract speed for *R.100* is 70 mph, but the Howden X-chasers—Messrs Wallis, Norway and company—have calculated that she should attain a speed of 80 mph. Cardington are sceptical about this and want it proved. Today will see—perhaps.

CHAPTER ELEVEN

Further Flights

We slipped from the tower at 09.47 on 17th December 1929, which is about as punctual as an airship has ever been, I dare say,—only two minutes late.

The weather was ideal for the flight, being blue sky for most of the time with mist at the beginning and end. The wind was stable both in direction, which varied between north-west by west and north-west by north, and in speed which remained between 10 and 20 mph all day.

The load was made up as follows:

Crew	37 }	$3\frac{1}{2}$ tons
Passengers	8 }	
Petrol	5,650 gallons	$18\frac{1}{2}$ tons
Oil	350 gallons	$1\frac{1}{2}$ tons
Ballast		$8\frac{1}{4}$ tons
Drinking water	400 gallons	$1\frac{3}{4}$ tons
Food	700 pounds	$\frac{1}{4}$ tons
Spares	6,300 pounds	$2\frac{3}{4}$ tons
	A total of	$36\frac{1}{2}$ tons

We had been promised a trip over London, and were all looking forward like a group of schoolboys to seeing it, and to the people seeing *R.100*. We had not gone far from Bedford, however, when an engine in the after car stopped, followed in a few minutes by a report that a piece of sealing-strip fairing in the gap between the lower vertical fin and the lower rudder flap had come adrift. Temporary repairs were effected immediately without much trouble and the speed trials were continued, but it was decided, in view of the slight damage, not to attempt full speed nor to leave the vicinity of Bedford. So we spent a rather boring three hours cruising at various speeds round the gasworks.

One thing the flight did prove was the efficacy of Squadron Leader Rope's airlog. This consisted of a streamlined weight or flying head, lowered some 50 feet below the control car and carrying a spinner on its tail. The spinner was rotated by the airspeed, and at every revolution made an electrical contact controlled at will by a switch in the control car. When switched on, the number of rpm was ticked off on a speedometer. These would be timed, and the rpm read off from a calculated table would give an accurate measure of the airship's airspeed.

We enjoyed a good cold lunch in the dining-saloon, eaten in comfort but not much warmth. This was a bad start off for our electric cooking-stove and electrically heated saloon; but we found afterwards that it was due to the human factor failing, as our W/T personnel had not fully mastered the working of the switches. Fortunately it was not a particularly cold day, so we could do without it.

There is not much more to relate regarding this flight. We sent a wireless message to Cardington to say we proposed to land about four o'clock and requested that an Aldis lamp be sent to the tower head for visual signalling purposes.

We dropped our wire at 15.45 hours and were secure at 16.15 hours, completing a total of 6 hours 28 minutes since slipping, for a petrol consumption of 450 gallons.

We did not carry out all we had intended, but gained valuable information as to the airship's controllability at various speeds. This was found entirely satisfactory, the controls needing very little physical effort to operate them. The outer cover was still a worry, there being several attachments found carried away and chafing on the transverse frames which necessitated a modification of the lead of the outer cover wire attachments. As we did not reach a height at which our bags would have expanded until full—called 'pressure height'—we were unable to test our automatic gas valves, but the hand-operated valves situated in thc top of the bag functioned satisfactorily. The engines were not run above 1,400 rpm, but up to this speed they functioned without a flaw.

After landing it was found that the main wire had been damaged badly due to disconnecting it while under tension. During, or rather just after, the landing the main mooring-wire had become so badly kinked that it had to be scrapped. The cause of the kinking was that during the hauling down of the airship the wire is put under great strain which tends to stretch it and unlay the strands. This can be seen on any crane for lifting heavy loads, which will have a swivelling ball fitted just above the load. When the strain comes on the wire the ball turns with the unlaying of the wire, but the load remains stationary. The reason our wire kinked itself was that as soon as the strain was taken off the stretched or unlayed strands suddenly tried to lay themselves up again so fast that some of them ballooned and twisted themselves into a kink. This is a serious difficulty, as the cost of a new wire is no bagatelle, being in the neighbourhood of £100. We tried various remedies, but I am not sure to this day if we did finally overcome it definitely.

Although I had done a little time in *R.33* at the mooring-mast and tower, this was my first all-night session on my own.

The Officer of the Watch has several duties to perform. He must keep the airship in trim and equilibrium; he does this by watching the balancing rollers and lines attached to them, which are illuminated by searchlight from the tower. Frequent readings are also obtained of the bow indicator already described. If the roller lines are all slack, water ballast must be released until they are reasonably taut. If the ship is so light that one or more of the rollers is lifted clear of the ground, sufficient water must be taken on board to bring them down again. A steady breeze is a great help when at the tower, as use can be made of it to lift or depress the airship dynamically by the use of the elevators as in flight.

Another duty of the OOW is to keep the airship tower log-book up to date. He has to take readings of the temperature of the gas in the ship and of the air outside and enter these in the log. At intervals he must enter a record of the ballast on board and its distribution. He must also get returns of the heights of the gas-bags, usually on taking over, half-way through and towards the end of the watch. He can then judge if any bag is losing gas inordinately. The reading of the bow indicator must also be entered in the log at regular intervals. Every hour the weather conditions and barometer height must also be entered in the log-book. The barometer is usually obtained by telephone from the Meteorological Office at Cardington, but the weather itself must be observed by the OOW as actually experienced at the tower.

This night, the 17th/18th December, the airship was very easy to control. At about 10 pm we had a welcome cup of hot cocoa. By this time I had got into the woolly portion of my Sidcot suit, which Major Scott said made me look like Puss in Boots when he came round to see that everything was satisfactory at about midnight.

It was a calm, still night and very cold. The gas gradually cooled with consequent occasional releases of ballast until about 23.00 hours, when it became stable and the ship floated serenely in the searchlight with about three degrees of down elevator, to get the lift of what occasional zephyr came along. With the elevators set as above, the airship rode steadily, and we in the control car had little to do except enter up the log-book and keep an occasional eye on the rollers and their lines.

Just after midnight I was surprised to get a telephone message from Squadron Leader Johnston at the foot of the tower saying he was coming on board. When I asked him if he had come aboard to sleep he replied, 'No, to keep watch.'

'Right,' I said. 'I'm going to turn in, as there is no necessity for both of us to stay up all night with the ship riding so steadily and no trouble to control. I'll relieve you at four o'clock.' I then turned in to my bunk next to the chart room just above the control car.

I caused a little heart-burning amongst the engineers by instituting a system whereby all hands of the watch did a short spell of duty. Up till then it had been the custom for the riggers to look after the ship entirely while the complete watch of engineers turned in for the whole night. I did not think this was good enough, so split the watch in order that there was one rigger and either the OOW or the cox'n in the control car, and one engineer in the crew space above to take readings of water ballast and act as messenger if necessary. I myself usually took the watch from 20.00 hours until midnight and from 04.00 until 08.00, while the cox'n did the watch from midnight until 04.00. The others did two-hour watches in pairs—one rigger and one engineer—until 06.00, when all hands turned out to clean up the quarters and stow gear. If there was not much to clear up they were allowed to sleep on a little longer. In the end this system was adopted generally and I think all finally agreed that it was a fair method of distributing the night watches amongst the crew on duty.

The weather remained calm and cold and nothing of note occurred for the remainder of the watch. Squadron Leader Booth relieved me at 08.00 and I went off in the routine truck or light lorry which took the Duty Watch back to Shortstown.

After breakfast and a bath I went to bed, but had been asleep only a few minutes when a message arrived for me to return to the airship immediately, as it had been decided she was to be taken into the shed in order to have the entire fairing between the fin and the flap modified. So back I went to the ship at the tower, where steam was already up in the winch house, and the ship's crew on board. I reported to the Captain, and then went to my station at the winch platform in the bow. In a few minutes the gong went, and the order came through for the Officer in Charge of the Tower to test the lift of the cone in the cup. The cone was not free, so a quarter of a ton of water was released from one of the ballast-bags in the bow. This was sufficient to ease the cone, and the order was given to slip the ship from the tower. In the meantime our trail rope had been dropped and connected up to the winch wire. As soon as we were free from the head, the winch hauled us down into the hands of the waiting handling-party, who manned the ropes and cars, and hauled the airship into the shed, where she was safely berthed by 3.30 pm and the work on the modifications commenced at once.

In addition to the modification to the fairing on the fin it was found necessary to carry out other repairs and modifications as a result of the defects found during the flight. The biggest job was modifying the lead of the zigzag wires, as they were called, which held the cover in position. These were found to be chafing on the tubing of the transverse frames. The lead of all these wires had to be altered at all points where the wires crossed a transverse frame. The number of main transverse frames in the hull of *R.100* was fifteen, spaced 40 feet apart and there were sixteen sides, the cover for each side being held by thirteen of these zigzag wires. Anyone who wishes to can work out for himself the number of leads over transverse frames that had to be altered, and the length of wire that had to be re-rove. This job was carried out entirely by the riggers of *R.100*, in addition to the general maintenance of the ship, together with other smaller repairs and replacements. Our ship's engineers and riggers also carried out the modifications required on the planes. From all of which it may be gathered that, given the material, we were practically a self-contained unit capable of carrying out major repairs and modifications to both the metal and the fabric components of the airship.

I personally doubt whether any British airship has ever had such an all round efficient crew as *R.100*. We had a nucleus of very efficient and long-experienced airship-crew men and were exceptionally fortunate in being able to choose the pick of the men employed upon her construction—men who knew the construction of the ship inside out, while, last but not least, we were lucky in obtaining the services of a number of young engineers who had but recently completed their apprenticeship with the very firm who supplied the engines, Rolls-Royce.

It is invidious to make comparisons, but I do not think *R.101*'s crew possessed a similar all-round efficiency. Their nucleus was similar to *R.100*, as the ex-airship men were divided pretty equally between the two ships, but they had not the same advantage in their field of recruiting for the remainder of the crew. They were not able to recruit men from the works of the firm who built their engines. In fact, as regards the latter, I believe that until *R.101* was actually ready for flight, her crew had never started, nor taken charge of, her engines during their numerous trial runs.

All the repairs and modifications were completed by 11th January 1930, but it was not until the 16th that we were able to get out of the shed. Shortly after 9 o'clock *R.100* was taken out on to the landing-ground; here we heard the old order with which all RNAS wartime airship people were so familiar: 'Hands off; ease up the guys . . . Let go.'

At 09.20 *R.100* rose in practically a dead calm, to commence her third flight, carrying 44½ tons.

The objects of this flight were firstly, to carry out speed tests at various engine powers; secondly, to carry out turning trials at various speeds and with differing rudder angles, in order to arrive at some idea of the turning-circle of the airship. The first of these was carried out successfully, but the second was postponed on account of adverse weather conditions.

The clouds were fairly low and covered the whole sky, but at 3,000 feet we were well above them and in brilliant sunshine, with the tops of the clouds looking so like cotton wool that sometimes one had a feeling of how nice it would be to jump out and lie basking in the sun on top of them.

We cruised about by dead reckoning between Bedford and Huntingdon, carrying out speed trials. During these I was busy keeping a watchful eye on the behaviour of various components of the airship, chiefly the outer cover. When the wing cars were going full bore, I went out on to the top of the ship by way of the observation platform in the bows in order to examine the outer cover, valve hoods, planes and fins. I found on emerging from the hatch in the top of the bow that I could not close it again, as it opened inwards and there was nothing by which it could be pulled up from the outside. This was remedied later, of course. I tried to stand up and walk along the top of the ship, but after one or two attempts, gave it up, for directly I stood up the wind seemed about to lift me bodily from the walking-way, in spite of my holding tightly to the life-line which runs loosely along the top of the airship; so adopting an undignified position on my hands and knees, I crawled the whole length of the walking-way, about 200 yards long and a foot in width, until I reached the rudder fin, where I found it possible to stand up without the feeling of being pulled off. I later asked the Chief Cox'n how he and the others managed to keep upright and he said he could only do it by getting the life-line between his legs and keeping it taut behind him.

Generally speaking the cover was behaving very well; there was a distinct undulation between every frame, probably caused by the airflow over the slight protuberance of each transverse frame. In certain places, where the internal zigzag wires had been drawn too taut, little pools of water collected. The ventilator covers were all functioning properly, the suction on top of the airship holding them all slightly open, thus causing a draught up the ventilating-shaft to cause the dispersion of any gas blown off from the valves.

I re-entered the ship in the vicinity of the planes, and went up and inspected the top vertical stabilising fin from the inside. There were a few small holes in the fin cover where chafing had occurred at several suction-wire fairleads, but there was nothing to worry about, so I went down into the keel. By this time—about noon—a full-speed trial on all engines was about to commence. We had not seen the ground since about 09.30, but by dead reckoning we were over Bedford.

I spent the time during the full-speed trials inspecting the cover in the vicinity of the corridor along the bottom of the ship. There were, in places, enormous bulges which must have put a great strain on the fabric. In addition there was much more flapping and chattering of the cover on the transverse frames apparently caused by the gauze ventilating-panels in the bottom of the cover, because where there was no ventilator there was no flapping. Continuing the inspection after the full-speed trials were over—they only lasted about twenty minutes—the cover seemed to be full of small holes; some were caused by wires tied together with unwhipped ends; others by parts of the outer cover coming into contact with the petrol tanks; and yet others by the lead seal put by the AID on the lashings on the circumferential wires. Mr McWade, the Chief AID man at Cardington, who was with us on this trip, agreed that these should all be cut off. These small holes were of minor importance, but later a slit 10 inches long was discovered underneath one of the petrol tanks, caused by the cover flapping against the flange of the tank. This was soon repaired by one of the riggers, and the flange padded; this does show the necessity for unceasing vigilance and inspection on the part of the crew and others during trials. Had this not been discovered when it was, it might have meant the whole length of the panel splitting, as had occurred during the shed trials.

During most of the afternoon we cruised about the East Midlands. I remember on one occasion we sighted the ground through a break in the clouds, and saw two rivers running parallel with each other. There was much speculation and map reading as to the location of this spot, some saying it was near Sandy, Bedfordshire. If it was, we were about fifty miles out in our dead reckoning. This was quite possible, as the wind had increased considerably since the morning, and during the afternoon blew at between 30 and 40 mph at 1,500 to 2,000 feet.

From half-past one when we were over Bourne, Cambridgeshire, until about half-past four, except for that glimpse of the ground mentioned, we were flying blind. At 16.35 we received a position signal from Croydon placing us two miles north-north-east of Sleaford, Lincolnshire. It was getting dark now and as Cardington reported conditions unsuitable for mooring, we went on flying more or less heading into the wind, which was blowing at nearly 40 mph from the south-south-east. At about 5.15 pm one of the after car engines stopped. We waited in the control car for a message from the engineer in charge, but none came; a messenger was sent along to find the cause of the stoppage. The engineer said he had received a signal on the klaxon of one long blast—which meant stop engine—and it appeared that someone had inadvertently leaned against the klaxon push-knob and sounded the signal. To avoid this happening in future, little metal rings were later fitted round each of the knobs.

Not many minutes after this another engine stopped; this time it was the forward engine in the starboard wing car, which had developed a leak in its cylinder water jacket. This was repaired temporarily by means of chewing gum, and the engine restarted. Considering that the engines had been in RAF service since 1925, it says a great deal for their manufacture that we had so little trouble with them.

As night drew on the clouds lifted, and at about 6 pm, when it was already dark, we were at a height of 2,500 feet and could see a large cluster of lights on our port bow. Johnston, our Chief Navigator, after a little juggling with pencil, ruler and dividers on the map, decided the lights were Spalding in Lincolnshire. Major Scott, who was in overall charge of the test, decided that we should go and make sure, so our course was altered and we passed over the lights. It was so dark that we were still not sure what town it was, but then someone down below flashed up to us with a hand torch:

...	.--.	.-	.-..	-..	..	-.	--.
S	P	A	L	D	I	N	G

Afterwards he must have had an argument with some friends as to whether we had been able to read his message, for Squadron Leader Booth received a letter a few days later asking if we had done so. It was most useful in confirming Johnston's dead reckoning and, incidentally, showed the accuracy with which he kept track of our position.

Not long afterwards we received a wireless message from Cardington to say that conditions were suitable for landing, so we headed southward at 60 mph airspeed, making good over the ground a speed of 20 mph. As we were flying almost directly into the wind, it did not require a great mental effort to arrive at its strength of 40 mph.

We reached Cardington at 20.30 hours where the tower was a blaze of light. It was a fine sight with the red–white–red lights at intervals vertically on the tower itself and floodlights lighting up the landing-area, while the pencil of a searchlight pierced the gloom from the platform at the mast-head.

After ballasting up, which took us some little time, we came up into the wind to make a mooring. As a mistaken aid, the searchlight was shone at the control car and so blinded the cox'n that we had to request that it be shone only on the group by the 'T' on the landing-area. This they did at 22.05 and at 22.40 we received the 'Secure' from the Tower Officer—13 hours 20 minutes since leaving the ground in the morning.

As usual after each trial flight a thorough inspection of all components was carried out, defects repaired and modifications put in hand. About 8 per cent of the zigzag wires were found to be chafed or broken, most of those damaged being in the bottom portion of the airship where the outer cover in the vicinity of the ventilators and engine cars tended to flap. This movement of the cover caused the zigzag wires to render or saw on the circumferential wires. It was therefore decided to eliminate this sawing movement by putting a seizing round the zigzag wire where it passed over a circumferential wire. Only certain panels were treated in this way to see how it worked.

The bottom part of the outer cover was in a bad state even at this stage. On carrying out a thorough inspection of it between the lowest girders—the two H's—numerous small holes of about the diameter of a lead pencil were found. These were of no immediate consequence, but small holes have a nasty habit of becoming large ones, so they all had to be patched. The electric heating had not proved satisfactory and the cooking hot-plates had to be taken out and sent to the works for repair. The cylinder of the starboard forward engine which became defective during this flight had to be replaced. Finally the airship had to be refuelled, topped up with gas and ballast, and generally prepared for flight.

It was my turn for Duty Officer on the 19th January 1930. All the repairs and preparations for flight referred to above had been completed the previous night, and at 07.00 on the morning of 20th January Squadron Leader Booth relieved me, so that I might rush home for bath and breakfast. I was back in the airship by 08.30, by which time the engines were being run up.

As mentioned before, the outer cover of *R.100* was not her best point. At any speed it showed large bulges and undulations, and at certain positions it did not remain taut, but tended to flap, which must eventually have caused damage to itself. The authorities at Cardington were quite rightly not happy about these deformations, and the next flight was for the specific purpose of obtaining information as to the behaviour of the cover during high speed, and especially to see how the various modifications in the system of supporting the cover were improving its performance. It was therefore arranged that cinematographic pictures should be taken of the outer cover with *R.100* flying at full speed, the pictures to be taken from an aeroplane.

With this object in view the airship commenced its fourth flight by slipping from the mooring tower at Cardington on 20th January at 09.10 hours, carrying sixty persons and a total of 42·7 tons. On leaving, the pressure height was 2,000 feet; mean purity of gas 96 per cent; barometer 1016·1 mbs; temperature 39°F; weather conditions: wind light, sky overcast, visibility fair, air steady.

We quickly reached a height of 2,000 feet and set course for London. At 09.40 we had rather an alarming experience, for the elevator controls became jammed, fortunately for only a matter of about ten seconds. The airship was slowed down and an examination of the control leads and gear-boxes carried out. No defect, however, was found, and I do not believe the reason for the sticking was ever really established.

Soon after ten o'clock we were over London, which, as usual, was shrouded in its pall of smoke and mist. We made our way via Croydon and Brooklands to Farnborough, Hampshire, where the speed runs were commenced at 11.00 hours. An aeroplane from the RAF squadron attached to the Royal Aircraft Establishment was flown back and forth close alongside us and filmed the cover as it did so. At times it did not seem to be more than 50 feet away. I did not have much time to spend watching its evolutions, though, as I was busy inspecting the cover and fins from the inside during these runs.

There were numerous small holes in the rudder fins where bottle-screws and fairleads for wire bracings were in contact with the fin cover. The holes were the result of the flapping of the cover under the influence of the slipstream from the propellers of the after car. There were also numerous cases of the tapes coming adrift from the outer cover, in some cases causing small rents. The port and starboard fins had similar undulations to the rest of the outer cover. No damage was caused by this so long as it remained taut, but it put an unequal strain on the cord supports lashing it to the hull circumferential wires and the fin suction wires; in fact, quite a number of the cords were found to be broken. Generally speaking, though, there was no grave defect and nothing that could not be overcome by padding and patching.

Soon after noon the filming was completed and we cruised about the country at a reduced speed, making our way to Oxford among other places, which was Squadron Leader Booth's home town; soon after 14.00 hours we passed over Bedford, in the vicinity of which we remained, as the wind had increased to 25 mph. At 15.50 our main mooring-wiring was coupled to that from the tower and half an hour later the ship's conc was secure in the cup. The flight had lasted just over seven hours for an expenditure of 885 gallons of petrol.

On board during this flight we had the pleasure of the company of the ship's Chief Designer, Mr Barnes Wallis.

During the landing operations of this flight a frightening incident occurred; the main wire was being paid out and had reached to within 50 feet of its limit when there was a terrific clatter and banging as the wire took charge, owing to the breaking of the back-haul wire which secured the cable to the drum. The wire flew off the drum through the fairlead, where its progress was checked for an instant by the bobbins, the loose end whipped about the platform area in a hair-raising manner, with all of us standing helpless; had it hit anyone it would certainly have killed him. It then raced out through the aperture in the bow and whipped about most alarmingly on the tubes forming the apex of the nose. The wire jumped the sheave or pulley, over which it rides down into the cone, bent the sides of the sheave, and came to rest between the sheave and the side plates. Considering what might have happened, the damage done was surprisingly small—the main wire itself was crippled, some of the bow tubes were dented, and the sheave was bent. The wire was repaired the same evening and the manufacture of a new sheave immediately put in hand at the RAW. This was completed and fitted into the airship by 22nd January 1930.

The outer cover was still behaving unsatisfactorily, especially in the vicinity of the engine cars. It was decided not to run the wing car engines at full speed in future until further modifications were carried out with a view to giving greater support to the cover in their neighbourhood. As on previous flights, the electrical system left much to be desired. The insulation of one of the switches to the cooking-stove was found to be completely burnt out.

Just about now two members of the crew, Riggers Brown and Petch, resigned; they were fishermen from Goole and their resignations were not because they disliked airship flying, or thought it too dangerous, but simply because they were homesick. I forecasted that before six months were up they would apply to be taken back, and sure enough they did.

We had no difficulty in filling the vacancies. One of the new men, Cutts by name, I remembered as the man who had given me a shock during the construction of *R.100* at Howden the previous year. I was watching the riggers tightening up the outer cover on top of the airship, and saw this man run—run, mind you, not walk gingerly as I should have done—along a transverse girder from A to B Longitudinal. The longitudinal girders of the ship are lettered from A at the top round each side to H at the bottom; the transverse girder between the two A's at the top is horizontal, but that from A to B slopes downwards. To continue my story—as Cutts neared B Girder his foot caught in something and he tripped. My heart missed a beat and I shut my eyes momentarily for fear of seeing him go slithering head first down the cover to the ground, over 130 feet below. He managed to recover his balance, however, treating the incident as a good joke. Later he became one of the star members of *R.100*'s football team, besides being a good and willing member of the crew.

During the week following the recent flight the airship was visited by a large party of senior RAF officers (nearly a hundred of them), all clumping about the ship in heavy boots. The remainder of the time was spent in inspection and repair of the outer cover and wiring, fitting covers over the ventilators in the bottom of the ship, and generally preparing for the endurance trial. At every opportunity compass bearings were taken of heavenly bodies in order to establish the deviations of the compass. It is not possible to swing a large airship for compass adjustment in the same way as an aeroplane. Therefore we took bearings of the sun, moon or prominent stars when the airship at the tower swung round with the wind on to various headings.

Whilst the airship was moored, the possibility of a line squall, accompanied by hail or snow, was anticipated by her captain, for precautionary orders were issued that in the event of heavy gusts of wind with sudden change of direction occurring, two of the rollers were to be disconnected, and if snow were forecast or commenced to fall, the airship was to be manned by two watches, all engines warmed up, and officers recalled. However, nothing of the kind eventuated, and it was not until 26th January 1930 that orders were given for *R.100* to be ready to leave the tower at 09.00 the following day.

The objects of this, the airship's fifth flight, were as follows:

1. Endurance test.
2. Controllability, stability, and turning tests.
3. W/T trials.
4. Testing instruments, voice pipe and internal communications.
5. Testing heating and cooking installations.
6. Testing ventilation and sanitary arrangements.
7. Testing gas valves.
8. Testing mooring-gear.

For the take-off, the bow indicator at the moment of slipping showed half a ton light and three tons pull to starboard, while just after slipping the vertical indicator registered zero and the lateral, one and a half tons to starboard—showing that the lateral indicator was still not functioning correctly. Carried on this flight were fifty-six persons and forty-four tons of disposable weight.

Major Scott's intention when we left was to fly down to Spain and then to the Azores. However, we were to be disappointed in this, as the first wireless message we received was from the Air Ministry restricting the flight to a line from Ushant to the Fastnet and not go within the three-mile limit of any foreign country or Eire. This meant we could not fly further south than the Channel Islands.

We set off in a west-south-west direction at a height varying between 1,200 and 2,000 feet, but saw very little of the ground, because the clouds were so low. We did catch a glimpse of Bath and at noon estimated our position to be over Bristol, and at 12.20 crossed the foreshore of the Bristol Channel. The sky became clearer in the early part of the afternoon. We were off Minehead on the Somerset coast at 12.45, whence a course was set for Lundy Island, which was reached at 13.50.

Most of this time we had been running on three engines of the wing cars at 1,600 rpm for stretches of about four hours on each engine. This gave us an airspeed of 45 knots. During the first dog watch (16.00 to 18.00 hours), however, the wind was increasing so much that it became necessary to start up another engine in order to obtain a little more speed. The airship was behaving splendidly and we had no difficulty in controlling her in spite of some bumpy conditions and strong winds during the afternoon.

From Lundy we made for the North Devon coast, then crossed over to the south coast, which we followed up to Plymouth, where we arrived at 14.15 on 27th January. Cruising slowly on up the coast, we passed Bolt Head at 16.00 and at 16.10 set course from Start Point to the Channel Islands, after which I went and had a welcome cup of tea.

Just before I went off duty a report was received from the rigger on keel patrol that No. 10 Gas-Bag had developed a leak. It turned out to be a 10-inch tear in the crutch at the bottom of the bag where it was shaped to fit over the corridor. It had been caused by the bag chafing on an electric-lead clip on top of the corridor. The tear was, of course, repaired immediately in the same manner as mending a punctured tyre, except that the bag tear would be drawn together by needle and thread before sticking the patch on.

We were in and out of cloud crossing the Channel and before we reached Alderney at 18.00 hours it had become quite dark. Through a break in the cloud we saw the Alderney light and at 18.23 were abeam of Cape de la Hague, whence we set course for the Sussex coast, reaching Eastbourne at 21.30, the twinkling lights of which were a welcome sight after battling against half a gale of wind in pitch darkness and thick cloud for three hours.

We were checking our navigation in the darkness and cloud by W/T bearings from Croydon, getting our position about every half-hour. The method by which this was done was as follows: we would send a wireless signal which would be picked up by three widely separated ground stations—Croydon, Lympne and Pulham—by means of a direction-finding apparatus; these three stations would obtain the direction of the incoming wireless wave; the two sub-stations, Lympne and Pulham, would then wireless the bearings they had obtained to the control station, Croydon, which would then plot the three bearings on a map and obtain the airship's position at the point where the bearings intersected. The position would then be wirelessed back to the ship. It takes much longer to describe than the time necessary to carry out the operation. If I remember rightly, we only received one position which was hopelessly inaccurate during the whole series of our trials. This one gave our position as near Guildford, when we were, in fact, somewhere over the sea off the south-west of England. In thanking Croydon for the position, we wirelessed back, 'Sea very rough over Guildford!'

At 21.51 on 27th January, Croydon reported us four miles south-west of Hastings; half an hour later our position was given as eleven and a half miles south-east of Dover, while at 00.09 on the 28th we were reported as being twenty-nine miles north-east of Deal. The wind was still from the north-north-east, blowing at about 30 knots. At times we had a patch of clear sky, but most of the night we were flying through cloud which enveloped us like a dark, damp blanket and made it necessary for the steering cox'n to steer entirely by compass, not too easy an accomplishment; dexterity in doing this is only achieved after much experience, and even then it was a great strain on the cox'n as he could not take his eyes from his compass for an instant.

Squadron Leader Booth relieved me at midnight on 27th January and I turned in and slept soundly, whilst the airship plugged away into the wind, making good about 30 knots in a north-east by north direction which took us up the North Sea. We were in cloud all the time, flying by instruments only and navigating by dead reckoning, assisted by an occasional position by direction-finding wireless bearings. One of these gave our position at 02.02 on 28th January as lat. 51°37′N, long. 2°34′E, which put us about fifty miles south-east of Great Yarmouth.

I came on duty again at 04.00. It was somewhat cold, though not quite freezing, the lowest temperature recorded during the night being 34°F. Round about 5 am the wind, which had up till then been blowing from the north-east, backed to north-north-west, and we experienced some very bumpy conditions for a period of about half an hour. As the temperature dropped four degrees it would seem that the trough line to the north of a centre of low pressure must have been passed about that time.

All this watch we were flying at 2,000 feet in strato-cumulus cloud, the base of which was at 1,500 feet, occasionally we would come down below the cloud to enable Squadron Leader Johnston to check our drift and obtain an idea of the wind. This was done by dropping a calcium flare into the sea and a back bearing taken on it as it burst into flame on contact with the water. This procedure was then repeated on a different course. The drifts obtained could be plotted on paper with the course and airspeed, and the wind obtained by what is known to navigators as the 'Double drift method'. With the Hughes periscopic drift-sight it could be found on the instrument itself. After using this instrument once, everyone gave up using the bearing-plate as a check for drift, though it was still very useful for obtaining visual bearings of objects.

During the night, whilst in the cloud, we had recourse to the method of finding our track by means of three successive W/T bearings at short intervals of time from a single W/T station, Pulham in this instance. The three bearings are laid off from a point to represent the W/T station, and through this point a perpendicular is drawn to the middle bearing. On this perpendicular the time interval between bearings is marked off to any convenient scale; from these points perpendiculars are dropped to cut the first and third bearings respectively; the line joining the points of intersection is then parallel to the track, and if you have any idea at all of your ground speed you can also obtain your actual position at the time of the third bearing.

This can be clarified by the following example: Pulham signals '06.00 your bearing was 108° true.'

'06.05 your bearing was 090° true.'

'06.10 your bearing was 075° true.'

These bearings are laid off as explained above and as shown on the following diagram:

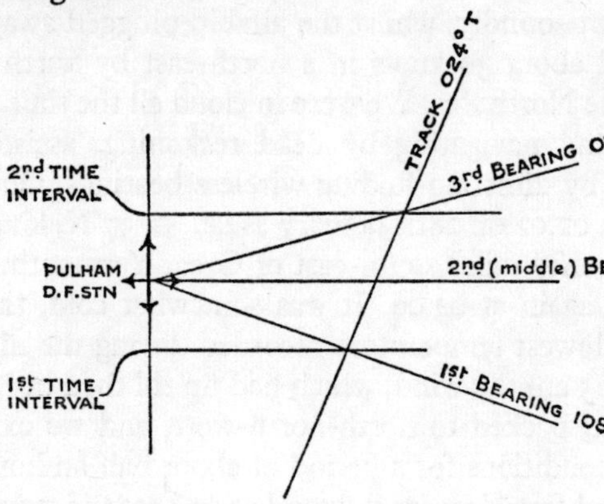

At 07.00 on 28th January we altered course to make good a track towards the south-west, the wind still being from north-north-west at about 20 knots. It was now quite light and at 08.00 we found that the base of the cloud had lifted to 2,000 feet, so we came down to 1,500 feet, where we were well clear of the cloud, and ten minutes later sighted a lightship which was very familiar to me, if to no one else on board. It had three masts and a black ball at the top of each—my old friend the Newarp light-vessel which lies about ten miles north-east of Yarmouth. It was as if we had suddenly come over my own garden, I had flown over it so many times in the war.

My watch being finished, I went and had a wash and shave in lovely hot water; then to breakfast, which consisted of fried eggs and bacon, toast, marmalade and piping hot coffee. This was something like air travel! I remember having fried some potatoes on the exhaust pipe in the after car of *R.33*, and I also managed to boil some water in that ship, but the dining-saloon in *R.100* was real luxury, with comfortable chairs, white linen and shining cutlery; the food nicely cooked by our chef, Meegan, and served by a steward, Savidge, who knew his job.

We followed the coast of Norfolk and Suffolk and turned in over the land at Felixstowe, whence we set course for London. This we reached at 10.00 and followed the Thames as far as Tower Bridge, of which we had no sooner caught a glimpse than we found ourselves enveloped in cold, damp, strato-cumulus cloud. From that moment until nearly eight hours later we only once saw an object on the earth again when we passed over the Shambles light-vessel at 13.52. We went up through the clouds and above 3,000 feet found ourselves in clear air and beautiful sunshine. Whilst in the cloud, ice formed on the ship, but this ceased as soon as we emerged into the sunshine above the cloud.

During the morning we had had some trouble with our exhaust-pipe extensions, the supporting studs of which had fractured. The first to go was on the forward engine of the starboard wing car. Watts, one of the charge-hand engineers, said he could fix it up temporarily if he could be slung outside the engine car on a boatswain's chair. Chief Cox'n Greenstreet and Cox'n Hobbs thereupon rigged up a chair or sling from one of the main girders above the car and lowered Watts down over the side; from that position at a height of over 3,000 feet, dangling in mid-air over what looked like a nice soft downy cushion of fleecy cloud, he carried out the repair. The temperature was well below freezing-point at this height and, what with this and a biting wind due to the speed of the airship, I do not know how he managed to manipulate his tools or use his fingers at all. I know I felt pretty chilly out on top of the engine car watching him do the job and taking a snapshot of him at it.

We had further trouble with exhaust-pipe extensions; one in particular might have endangered the airship, as it broke away and went through the propeller of the after car. Fortunately except for damaging the propeller, no other harm was done, but in order to avoid further risk of this nature most of the flight after this was carried out on the three forward engines, which at 1,600 rpm gave us an airspeed of 45 knots. The engine-cooling systems did not function too grandly either, as many times during the flight a good deal of water was lost by siphoning through the vent pipe.

During the afternoon we cruised over the Channel, making our way slowly towards the west. Occasionally we came down to see if the base of the cloud was low enough to fly beneath it, and it was during one of these descents that we found ourselves over the Shambles light-vessel. We had to come down to 800 feet to get clear of the cloud, so Major Scott thought it best to keep above the cloud, which was still composed of super-cooled moisture, as we found each time we entered it. The ice did not form as ice immediately; on entering the cloud the moisture would first run in streams along the cover and in a short time these streams were sheets of clear ice. If we went above the cloud, no more ice formed, while if we went below it the ice melted. By five o'clock in the afternoon the cloud base had risen so that we were well clear at a height of 1,500 feet. By this time it was almost dark, but we saw below us the numerous lights of the Brixham fishing-fleet, and at 19.00 we were off Plymouth.

We then headed for the Eddystone lighthouse, which we made the centre of our turning-trials. I was off duty, having my supper, while these were going on, as I had done the second dog watch (6 to 8 pm), and was not due on again until midnight. After supper I turned in and had a good three hours' sleep during which time *R.100* was proceeding up Channel again past Start Point, Sidmouth and Lyme Regis. At midnight when I came on again we were off Portland Bill.

The wind had decreased to about 15 mph, but the weather had not improved, as it was still overcast and we had some rain. We meandered over the Isle of Wight, Portsmouth and Southampton. At 03.15 on 29th January 1930 we ran into an occluded front with its usual heavy rain. The ship got very wet, especially in the corridor at the bottom and up in the bows. By 04.30 the front had passed and the weather began to clear. I was snug in bed again by this time when we were making our way to the westward once more, the wind having backed to the west and increased to 34 mph. We reached our old friend the Eddystone at 6 am, followed the coast of Cornwall past the Lizard and crossed the coast near Mullion, which must have brought back memories to Squadron Leader Booth, who was Commanding Officer there during the war. We passed over Truro with its bluey-green copper-covered cathedral roof shining in the morning sunlight, and so to Newquay, Bideford and Minehead, off which we carried out a further series of turning-trials.

Most of the time during the flight the wireless experts from the Royal Aircraft Establishment, Farnborough, Messrs Wells and Cox-Walker, had been carrying out trials of our wireless installations. I am afraid I cannot give any particulars of the results of these, as that department did not come within my orbit.

Over the land we had a striking picture of what the meteorological forecast terms 'fog locally', for all the valleys and low-lying areas were filled with soft-looking white fog, while the hill-tops were bathed in sunshine. We proceeded on up the Bristol Channel as far as Bristol, where we again encountered clouds. We went up through them and out into sunshine and clear weather at a height of 4,500 feet, at which height we remained for our journey back to Cardington. A Wireless Telegraphic Direction Finding—WTDF—position near noon put us at Malmesbury, which was right on our required track, so we maintained our course and arrived over Bedford at 14.00, having ballasted up on the way home by going above our pressure height and blowing off gas.

We dropped our mooring-wire at 14.50, but it was not until 16.30 that we were finally secured to the tower head. The delay was caused by the starboard yaw guy becoming fouled amongst the girder work of the mooring-tower.

After being secured F/O Steff with Cox'n Moncrieff, Charge-hand Engineer Watts and the remainder of the Third Watch took over the airship and remained with her that night. They were relieved at 08.00 hours next morning by myself, Cox'n Long, Charge-hand Engineer Stupple and No. 1 Watch. We had only a short stay at the Tower, for at 11.30 the ship was hauled down and taken into the shed. This really completed our series of trials except for the overseas flight, and other flights deemed necessary by the Airworthiness Authorities for the purpose of testing items that had proved unsatisfactory.

The defects revealed by this flight were mainly in connection with the engines. Mention has already been made of the breaking of exhaust-pipe extension supporting studs. A number of these were lost overboard during the flight, and it is thought that the rear propeller in the after engine car was damaged by one of these studs falling into it. This constituted a real danger, hence our running on the three forward engines only, for the latter part of the flight.

Damaged gear-boxes were also a serious problem, whilst the danger of ice formation was brought home to us by the discovery that the forward propellers of the wing cars had been slightly damaged by it, probably by pieces dropping off the outer cover and into the airscrew. I think this was our worst flight for ice formation. During an inspection of the bow and top of the ship early in the afternoon of the 28th January, I found the bow hatch frozen up and had to use considerable force to open it. A rag in the main mooring-wire hawse pipe was frozen as stiff as a board, while there was ice on all outside wires and tubes and on the outer cover wherever moisture had formed into rivulets.

The heating and cooking arrangements functioned quite satisfactorily, but there was no excess of heat in the saloon, even with the radiators and cooker on at the same time.

The duration of the flight was 2 days, 6 hours, 52 minutes; the distance covered was 1,780 nautical miles. This was actually to be our last trip for some time, as there were many alterations and improvements to be made preparatory to the flight to Canada, the most important of these being modifications to the outer cover attachments, and also the re-doping of the top of the ship in an effort to make it more watertight. This latter was done at the insistence of Squadron Leader Booth.

As the flying trials were virtually over, the Airship Guarantee Company were eager to hand over the airship and obtain the balance of the money due to them. Reports on the functioning of the various parts of the ship were therefore called for.

The outer cover leaked badly, and this meant that the gas-bags became soaked if the airship flew or was moored in rain. This was a potential danger, as the gas-bags were not designed to withstand wetting. So far, however, there had not been any excessive deterioration in their gas-holding properties, as the gas purity had been maintained without excessive consumption, at an average of 97 per cent throughout the ship. In addition to leaking badly, there was still excessive flapping of the outer cover, especially in the panels near the propellers. This was eventually overcome by fitting auxiliary girders in panels where the flapping was very bad, thus lessening the unsupported area of the cover in each of the panels so treated.

The passenger accommodation was designed for a hundred persons, but as there was no likelihood of the ship being able to carry such a number across the Atlantic this would be reduced considerably for the Canadian flight.

The engines had not proved altogether satisfactory, but it must be borne in mind that they were not new; they had simply been reconditioned after considerable service in RAF machines.

The W/T installation functioned satisfactorily, and experiments were carried out by the RAE experts Wells and Cox-Walker—mentioned earlier—with an instrument to obtain pictures by wireless, the idea being to have weather maps transmitted by this means and be produced ready drawn. This instrument was known as a 'Fultograph'.

The controllability and stability of the ship were excellent, and although according to the calculators at RAW we were supposed to be very tail heavy, we never noticed it in flight and the cox'ns always found her very easy to handle, both on the elevators and on the rudders. The ease of handling on the elevators was greatly assisted by Wallis's ingenious automatic clutch and free-wheel gear. This saved the Height Cox'ns an enormous amount of work, as instead of having to turn the wheel round and round it could be worked like a pump handle, and to centralise the elevators again quickly the wheel had only to be put just over top dead centre, when the clutch would be released and the elevators centralised themselves automatically. The large size of the wheels, too, was another factor in making the work of the cox'ns lighter.

A resume of *R.100*'s attributes, achievements and shortcomings to date is interesting:

Gas capacity	5,156,000 cubic feet
Unladen weight	105 tons (15 tons heavier than contract weight)
Disposable lift	54 tons (average gas purity of 97 per cent)
Maximum speed	80 mph (10 mph faster than contract)
Cruising speed	65 mph
Number of flights	5 (to 30th January 1930)
Hours flown	87·5 (to 30th January 1930)
Longest flight	54·9 hours
Shortest flight	5·6 hours
Time moored to tower	305 hours
Highest wind while moored	40 mph

The ensuing weeks were fully occupied in carrying out various modifications necessary to the outer cover and engines. The only exciting happening during this period occurred in March. The Duty Cox'n, Hobbs, informed me that No. 7 Bag had 'split from top to bottom'. This sounded ominous, but fortunately it was not quite as bad as that. Having first ascertained that there was no immediate danger to the ship, I told him to stand by while I dashed off to Bedford and collected a couple more riggers of the Duty Watch—Armstrong and Patterson.

Old Barber, the night watchman, had managed to keep the ship afloat during the night by letting go ballast. While achieving this object, it did not put gas back into the bag, which had unfortunately become nipped in the radial wiring near the axial girder—something, we had been informed at Howden, that could not occur. When, owing to the contraction of the gas due to the lower night temperature, the lower level of the gas in the bag rose above the level of where the bag was nipped, this end of the bag was prevented from taking up its natural curve inwards towards the centre. Thus an excessive strain was put upon the bag at that point. The result was that the bag gave way and although it did not turn out to be quite so bad as Hobbs had at first indicated, it was quite bad enough; we found an enormous hole in the forward end of the bag measuring 20 feet by 2 feet. Hobbs and the riggers cobbled this together as best they could, while Mann, the Charge-hand Engineer of the Duty Watch, pumped some petrol from the tanks.

This taught us a lesson not to allow the level of the gas to get above 'E' girder at any time, and more especially during the night.

The tear was too large to repair satisfactorily in position; moreover, such an enormous hole at or below the lower level of the gas meant that large quantities of air would have been sucked into the bag with a resulting decrease in purity of the gas in the bag. Squadron Leader Booth therefore gave orders for No. 7 Bag to be deflated. It was not, however, taken out of the ship, as the colossal patch measuring 26 feet by 5 feet was affixed with the bag on temporary staging inside the hull.

This seemed to be an unlucky bag, for during the inflation on 28th March, Cox'n Hobbs, who was, with Cox'n Long, myself and half a dozen riggers, positioning the bag at the top of the ship, very nearly fell through the top of the bag; he was doing something which necessitated his lying on his back on the top of the bag and, as he levered himself up on his elbow, his arm went through the bag. Fortunately the netting localised the split, which only measured a little over a foot. However, it was a reminder to us that the skin-lined single-ply bags were not so robust as the two-ply rubber fabric ones we had been used to in *R.33*.

Most of the modifications and repairs were completed by the middle of April, but it was not until the 24th of that month that the weather was suitable and *R.100* was taken out of the shed and hooked on to the mooring-tower. Unfortunately during the manoeuvre of taking her out of the shed, and just as the ship was within a few feet of being clear, a side gust hit her and the landing-party could not hold her against it. The starboard elevator flap was bumped against the shed door; another 5 feet and she would have been clear. The ship was not put back into the shed immediately, as it was thought it might be possible to carry out the repair at the tower. On inspection, however, it was found that the damage was more serious than anticipated, and after three days and nights at the tower, we once more returned her to the shed.

In spite of this mishap it was still hoped that *R.100* would leave for Canada early in May 1930. In order that there should be a party to take over the ship immediately on our arrival, it was necessary to detail one watch to go out ahead by steamer. It speaks volumes for the confidence that the crew had in their ship that, when it came to choosing who was to go by steamer and who by *R.100*, the whole crew plumped to go in *R.100*. To give every man an equal chance of going in the airship, Squadron Leader Booth organised a lottery, and the following were the unfortunates who came out of the hat as having to travel by sea: *Riggers*: Armstrong; Burgess; Kershaw; and Patterson. *Engineers*: Simmonds; Burke; Watson; Hall; Wilson; and Addinell.

The repairs to the elevator delayed their departure, and it was not until 16th May 1930 that the advance party left in the charge of Lieutenant-Commander Atherstone—First Officer of *R.101*.

As it eventually turned out, this party had a right royal time of it in Canada, because we were still further delayed in a subsequent flight by the tip of our tail breaking off, so that we did not get away finally on the Atlantic flight until the end of July. During the interval the advance party had little or nothing to do—and all day in which to do it. They had free passes all over Canadian Airways, including those to the USA, and they also had an open invitation to Dow's Brewery, where they were regaled with that firm's famous 'Old Stock Ale', wonderful stuff of pre-war strength. I can vouch for the excellence of it, because I sampled it myself later on when we did eventually get to Montreal. The day before the advance party left a photograph was taken of the entire crew—I believe this was the only photograph of *R.100*'s whole complement.

CHAPTER TWELVE

Final Preparations for the Atlantic

All the modifications and repairs to *R.100* were completed early in May and we were only awaiting favourable weather for taking her out to test the outer cover and engine modifications.

From now on the handling-party was provisionally ordered daily for 03.00 hours and as regularly cancelled each evening by a searchlight being shone into the sky from the tower from 9.30 to 10.30 pm. On the evening of the 20th May no searchlight appeared, so it was early to bed that night, as the crew's work did not merely consist in jumping on board a minute or so before the ship was taken out. The business of running up the engines, taking the lift and trim, getting stores on board and the numerous odds and ends preparatory to a flight, all had to be done before the handling party appeared, even if the airship was only being taken from the shed to the mooring-tower.

We turned to a few minutes after 2 am on 21st May and at three o'clock the landing-party assembled, were 'told off' to their positions, soon after which we heard the welcome order: 'Ease up on the guys—hands off!'—to make sure the ship was near enough to equilibrium to be lifted.

Then came 'Hold on', followed by 'Lift up on the car, walk ship ahead'—and we slowly wended our way into the open.

This time there was no mishap and in less than three minutes we were clear and on our way to the tower, there to await the scheduled time of departure, 19.00 hours.

This flight marked the occasion of Squadron Leader Booth's assuming sole control of the ship, as Major Scott did not accompany us. Punctually at 7 pm on the evening of 21st May 1930 the order to slip was given. Dropping nearly two tons of water, our cone left the cup on the tower and we floated clear, rising quickly to 1,500 feet with a total personnel on board of sixty-five, in the 48·4 tons of disposable weight.

The main object of this flight, the sixth in the series of trials, was to test the outer-cover modifications and try out the engines thoroughly. In addition, there were various other items to be re-tried or tested:

1. Re-trial of:
   (*a*) Modifications to outer cover.
   (*b*) Exhaust pipe extensions.

(*c*) Radiators.
(*d*) Fuel and water tanks.
(*e*) Repairs to No. 7 Bag.

2. Tests of:
(*a*) Fuel consumption at various speeds.
(*b*) W/T trials on long wave with Malta and Egypt.
(*c*) W/T trials of short-wave equipment.
(*d*) W/T DF installation.
(*e*) W/T visual installation (Fultograph).
(*f*) Navigational bombs and flares.

This was a pretty large programme and it took us the best part of a day to carry it out.

After leaving Bedford we set a course for London, over which we arrived about an hour later. We circled over the 'Great Smoke' for half an hour. It was amusing to hear the remarks of passengers picking out places of interest—'Look, there's Piccadilly' when we were over Elephant and Castle. About the best landmark in London was the Caledonian Market at Islington, since demolished; it covered an enormous area, and was quite unmistakable with a large octagonal building in the centre and the stalls and pens radiating from it in all directions. From this point we set our course for the mouth of the Thames. It was a beautiful evening, the sun having just set in a blaze of golden glory.

It was not long before we were over Southend, from where we set a course for the Gunfleet Sands which lie off Clacton. After carrying out various tests over the Gunfleet, we set off up the North Sea into wind, which, however, was not very strong, being less than 20 mph, from the north-east at a height of 1,500 feet.

At midnight on 21st May we passed Southwold with its red light abeam to port, and I took over the watch. We cruised gently northward on our three after engines, running at 1,400 rpm, which gave us an air-speed of 50 mph. The weather was not quite so good as earlier, as the sky became clouded over completely.

There is not much of interest to relate during this middle watch. We carried out our routine work of reading the gas and air temperatures; maintaining course and height, and checking the drift occasionally by means of dropping calcium flares into the sea, and from them taking back bearings with the Hughes Periscopic Drift Sight or the bearing-plate. We proceeded as far north as Flamboro' Head and then turned south again. All this was over familiar ground, or rather, sea, as the southern part from Southwold to Skegness was included in our Pulham patrol and north of that was part of our Howden patrol.

A few minutes after altering course off Flamborough, I was relieved by Squadron Leader Booth and Lieutenant-Commander Watt, who was formerly captain of *R.26*, and an old shipmate of mine at Pulham during the war. Watt, like myself, had come home from New Zealand at the call of airships. He was designated as Officer in Charge at Karachi. After handing over I went up to the galley and found a large saucepanful of hot cocoa on the stove. I dipped myself a steaming mugful and with it warmed and filled my inside. This reminds me of French's marionettes, one of which was a 'Hot potato man' singing:

All hot, all hot, all very, very hot,
All very, very H-O-T.
You fill your belly and warm your inside,
All for the price of a d d d
All for the price of a D

Then I turned in and slept as one can only sleep in an airship—like a top. To those who suffer from insomnia, I would say, 'Take an airship trip and you'll be cured.'

During the morning watch the weather had still further deteriorated and heavy rain had been experienced. The cloud also became lower, until its base was down to 1,000 feet and still covering the whole sky. We did not attempt to fly below it, but kept at 2,000 feet, in the cloud, of course, flying by our instruments only. This is the beauty of airship flying—cloud flying is just as easy as clear weather flying.

Whilst I was off watch we flew south as far as Orfordness and then north again as far as the Humber, where we turned in over the land towards Hull, which was hidden by low cloud, but which by dead reckoning we considered we passed at 10.15 am on 22nd May 1930. As I was not on watch again until noon, I thought I would improve the shining hour by having a look round, so I went up on to the top of the ship by way of the bow observation position. Unable to master the technique of walking upright along the top of the ship when she was going at any speed, I adopted my ignominious crawl. To make it even less enjoyable, when over half-way along, the rain began to pelt down. It was as quick to go on as to turn back, so on I went, experiencing what a cat must feel when caught in a thunderstorm whilst walking along a very high, long brick wall. I entered the inside of the ship near the rudder and, feeling I could not get much wetter, I crawled out to the port auxiliary altitude control position. This was situated in the centre of the stabilising fin close to the leading-edge of the elevator. Its purpose was to be a means of working the elevator flap in the event of the controls in the control car not functioning properly. There was another similar auxiliary control for the starboard elevator and one each for the top and bottom rudders, as I have already mentioned, all independent of each other.

I am afraid it would have been a work of art conning the airship by these auxiliary controls, although there was a speaking-tube to each position. Whoever was conning the ship would have to give his orders by this means. The cox'n who was at the auxiliary control would be seated in a little well in the fin—which was half full of water when I was out there on this occasion—and would be facing aft. However, I suppose the auxiliary control complied with the specifications, which did not apparently lay down that they should be practical, otherwise they would never have been passed by Tommy Rowntree, Sandy Bushfield or Commander Cox, the three lynx-eyed AID representatives at Howden during the ship's construction. These auxiliary controls are more fully described later.

I was over the top somewhere between ten and eleven o'clock on the morning of the 22nd May and saw nothing wrong either on top of the ship or further aft at the tail; I was looking at the latter as I sat at the auxiliary control position.

Except for some showers, in one of which I was unfortunate to get caught, the weather was better during the forenoon than it had been earlier. Anyhow, we could see the country a little, which was a change, as most of our trial flights seemed, so far, to have been carried out either in cloud, or else above them with rarely a glimpse of the earth below. In turn we passed Leeds and Manchester *en route* for Liverpool, where we were welcomed by much hooting of steamers' sirens. We could have gauged our distance or height above some of them by taking the time from the puff of steam to the sound of the hooter. We were over Liverpool on the 22nd May at noon, and after circling the city and docks we set course for Bedford. Soon after leaving Liverpool, Sir Denistoun Burney asked Squadron Leader Booth to run all engines at full speed for ten minutes—Sir Denistoun was on board as one of the representatives of the constructing company. Booth demurred at first, not considering such a test necessary, as we had already carried out our full-speed trials. However, Burney insisted, saying he wished to see how the cover modifications stood up to it. So we opened up to full speed and reached 80 mph —with the results recounted later.

I was on watch again from noon until 4 pm. The greatest bugbear for the officer of the watch was the continual asking by the passengers of 'Where are we now.' I remember someone asking me this question on the way down from Liverpool and telling him we were over Crewe when we were over Stoke. I think his opinion of my map reading was rather low after that. However, I have no doubt he was revived a few minutes later by the wonderful aroma of malt wafted up to us as we passed over Burton-on-Trent. Thus we proceeded uneventfully and blissfully ignorant until we reached Cardington; here F/O Cook, the Officer in Charge of the Mooring-Tower informed us by radio that the tip of our tail was hanging down. This news cut short any further trials and we landed as soon as we were able in the very difficult weather conditions prevailing—heavy thunder showers and squalls—which provided a very stern test for Squadron Leader Booth's first solo landing.

As we came slowly up to the tower a heavy shower struck us. This made us heavy, so Squadron Leader Booth let go some ballast and put us in equilibrium again. We had just let out our main mooring-wire and it was trailing nicely over the ground as we slowly approached the coupling-party, when the rain stopped and the sun came out, superheated our gas and we became light, lifting the mooring-wire off the ground before it could be coupled. Squadron Leader Booth gave the order to go astern, but no sooner had we got way on astern than our tail began to go down in ominous fashion. At first we thought our broken tail must have damaged the aftermost bag and it had become deflated—in fact Squadron Leader Booth sent one of the cox'ns aft to investigate. However, it was not many seconds before Booth twigged what was actually the matter—the airflow; as we went astern it was pressing down on the fins—and he quickly gave the order 'Go ahead', which done, as soon as we got way on again, we righted immediately. The Captain then slowed down and ballasted up, went round again trailing our mooring-wire beneath us, and made a perfect landing. Our main wire was coupled at 16.50, the port and starboard yaw guys at 17.02 and 17.04 respectively, and the ship's cone housed securely in the tower cup at 17.50, a very sound performance, which gave us added confidence in our skipper.

For the flight just described we had called on the services of some of the crew of *R.101* to take the places of the members of our own crew who formed the advance party in Canada. The results of the trials were generally satisfactory, though the outer cover attachment by means of taping still gave trouble, there being one 5 foot tear along a T tape in one of the lower panels. It was usually in the lower panels that these tapes caused trouble, because there the tapes collected moisture which caused rotting of the fabric. There was also much flapping in the region of the engine cars, to obviate which it was decided to divide the panels into four by means of light girders fore and aft, and athwartships, so lessening the unsupported area in these parts of the ship.

As far as the engines were concerned, the Chief Engineer, Mr W. Angus, reported no serious defects; the modifications to the exhaust pipes were satisfactory, as also were the radiators, water and fuel tanks, which had all been under re-trial. A few minor defects occurred such as two broken oil pipes; dirty plugs; two thermometers and two valve springs broken. Most of these items were put right during flight.

Consumption tests showed that at 1,600 rpm each engine consumed on an average a shade under 30 gallons per hour, while with both engines in each car running simultaneously at this speed the combined consumption was 50 gallons per hour. This consumption included the running of one AC six-cylinder engine for electrical supply during the whole period of the trials covering some thirteen hours. Gas-bag No. 7, which had an enormous hole torn in it whilst in the shed, still appeared to be losing more gas than its neighbours, but not enough to be considered serious. As regards the other tests I cannot say much, as I did not see any of the reports, but I believe the long-wave W/T tests were quite satisfactory, while the short-wave, DF and Fultograph—visual wireless transmission—installations were not. As for the navigation bombs, I do not remember them being tested at all, though they may have been when I was off watch.

Of course, the damage to our tail meant a further postponement of our transatlantic effort. This delay was further increased by the weather preventing the airship being taken into the shed until four days after our landing.

The main structure of the ship was not damaged, the part that broke away being really a light framework for fairing off the tail to a point, there being no gas-bag in that portion at all. I remember Wing Commander Colmore coming down to the shed and bemoaning the time necessary to make and fit a new tail. I suggested to him that there was no need to fit a new pointed tail at all, but to fair off the existing end with a curve. This would ensure no more tail dropping and make a stronger and lighter finish besides taking comparatively little time to make and fit. This was in fact what was done, the new part being designed, made and fitted in less than a month. Norway was not enthusiastic about the rounded tail, saying it spoiled the look of the ship to give it a blunt instead of a pointed end.

The refitting of our tail did not mean that we left immediately for Canada, as it had not been finally decided which ship should carry out the Display flight. Ultimately the Air Ministry decided this was to be done by *R.101*, so work on her was given priority. Her engines were much heavier than originally estimated and to obtain more lift it was decided to let out her gas-bag wiring. This work was eventually completed and she was taken out of the shed in the early morning of the 23rd June 1930.

Soon after she had been safely buttoned on to the tower, Mr Stupple—one of our engineers—and I were standing outside No. 2 Shed watching her, when suddenly her whole cover, especially along the top, started rippling from bow to stern with a kind of backwash of ripples from the stern, superimposed for about a third of her length.

'No cover can stand that sort of treatment for long', I said, with which Stupple agreed.

Sure enough, a few minutes later an enormous rent, some 90 feet in length, appeared along the top of the ship, followed next day by another split of about 40 feet. This, of course, meant further delay, but Mr Gerrish, the Shed Manager and his men, with Chief Cox'n 'Sky' Hunt and *R.101*'s crew, managed to patch her up in time for the Display. She took the air on 27th June 1930 for the Dress Rehearsal. For this flight Squadron Leader Booth took Atherstone's place as First Officer. I watched the final stages of that flight from my home at Sandy and was surprised at the extraordinary amount of pitching in which she indulged. I mentioned this to Squadron Leader Booth; he did not seem to think the pitching was exceptional, but said he thought her very unstable on the elevators, although quite good on her rudders, which confirmed my own impression when I first flew in her on 1st November 1929.

For the Pageant or Display flight next day I was detailed to fly in 'Grabby' Atherstone's place. We slipped from the tower at 08.25 BST on 28th June and made straight for London. It was rather bumpy over the land, the weather becoming hot, with much cumulus type of cloud forming. After flying over London we followed the Thames to Southend; then out over the Thames Estuary to well beyond the Tongue light-vessel. Conditions over the sea were delightful, the contrast with flying over the land being very pleasant, the ship riding beautifully. I began to think that her unhandiness on the elevators might after all have been due to weather conditions. She certainly flew straight and level in the stable conditions over the sea and was easily handled both in regard to steering and on the elevators. We had a cold lunch whilst still over the sea; by the time we had finished we were back over Southend Pier again.

In the Display programme we were due to fly over Hendon at ten minutes to four, so we still had plenty of time. We cruised slowly up river and ran through a cold front, which gave us a good bump up and then down, of the order of about 500 feet—quite a mild one which the elevator cox'n met very well, and the ship did not get thrown to much of an angle as very often happens. A long high cloud of cumulus type appeared ahead of us, looking white and fleecy in the sunshine. As we nosed into it, the bow of the airship came under the influence of the strong upward current, the whole ship being carried bodily upwards. In a few seconds the gust reached the tail and up it went, so that the airship was being carried upward with her nose down at an angle of about 10 degrees. An experienced man on the elevators can very often negative the angle to which the ship is thrown; after the bow has received its bump up and he has made the initial correction he must put the elevators amidships or even anticipate the tail bump by putting the elevators up a little; this is known as 'meeting her' and was done on this occasion. The ship rode through the front in good style. We then proceeded to Hendon without further event and punctually at 15.50 she was dipped in salute as she flew past King George V and Queen Mary.

Having done their piece satisfactorily everyone trooped off to tea, leaving me on watch in the control car, with Cox'n Oughton on the elevators; I forget who was steering. We passed through two or three heavy rain squalls and were being bumped about a bit. This was to be expected in the type of weather through which we were passing.

After a time, however, soon after passing Luton, which we had made a point of flying over in honour of F/O Steff, whose home is there, I began to get worried about the behaviour of the airship. She would go into a short sharp dive, and then the cox'n would get her nose up and we would make a long slow climb back to our flying height.

Directly the cox'n levelled his elevators in order to maintain his height, down would go the nose again and the procedure would be repeated.

After this had occurred several times, I remarked to Oughton that the ship seemed to be a little heavy.

'It is as much as I can do to hold her up, sir,' he replied, the while his cheery round face was simply streaming with perspiration. 'Sweating blood,' remarked Mr Gerrish afterwards.

This rather alarmed me, so I at once turned on the valve to release water ballast. After letting go what I judged to be about a ton, I asked Oughton if there was any improvement and he said she was much easier; this relieved me a good deal. It must be remembered that I was not in my own ship and although it was not my first trip in *R.101*, I could not say I was fully acquainted with her idiosyncrasies. Moreover, I was totally unused to flying in a 'heavy' ship. After flying for some ten hours in *R.100* we would have been quite light, and much more likely to have required to valve gas than water. In fact, I think this was the first time I ever really had the wind up in an airship, and I was heartily thankful when Irwin came down and relieved me at 18.00 hours.

I told him I thought the ship was heavy and as we could see the sheds of Cardington at the time I suggested making a landing straight away; as the evening was drawing in, with the consequent cooling down of the gas to make us still heavier, we would lose our false lift due to the superheating of the gas. However, he would not hear of it, saying the ship's behaviour was entirely due to bumps; when I informed him that I had let some ballast go, he added that he would have preferred to have kept the ballast for landing. The bumping about may certainly have been due to instability in the atmosphere, but this cannot account for the way the ship behaved in recovering. In my opinion she was definitely heavy, and I am inclined to think, in the light of later events, that had I not let go ballast when I did, the accident which finished her career at Beauvais a few months later, could quite possibly have happened that afternoon.

Never was I more relieved in mind than when I handed over to Captain Irwin and went up to the saloon to enjoy a well-earned cup of tea, during which time the airship carried on northward for an hour or so. We eventually made our landing to the tower at Cardington at 20.50 hours, using something like *ten tons of oil and ballast* in order to get into equilibrium before landing. This surely should have warned the powers that be at Cardington that something was radically wrong. I am afraid, however, that the ship was so much the apple of their eye that they thought nothing could be wrong with her, in spite of this heaviness at the end of each flight—which was a regular experience, judging by the amount of ballast and oil that was dropped on each occasion.

I do not think any steps would have been taken after this flight to investigate the cause of her excessive heaviness had I not made a complaint to my Captain, Squadron Leader Booth. I told him that unless I was definitely *ordered* to do so, I would not fly in *R.101* again. As it happened, this was the last flight I made in her, as Atherstone, much to my relief, was recalled from Canada. As a result of my complaint a search was made for leaks in the gas-bags. About forty small holes were discovered, due to chafing of the bags on longitudinal girders, but I doubt very much whether these could have been entirely responsible for her excessive heaviness.

The fact that *R.100* did no flying all these weeks since 22nd May did not mean that the crew were idle. In fact, they were, if anything, more occupied than normally when not flying, because all the shed riggers and fabric workers were engaged on *R.101* to get her ready for the flight just described, so that any work required on *R.100* had necessarily to be carried out by the ship's crew in so far as it applied to actual work on the airship itself.

One of the items of work carried out by the crew over and above the normal maintenance, was the fitting of rigoles on the top of the airship. This improvement was the suggestion of Chief Cox'n T. E. Greenstreet and consisted of ridges of stiff fabric stuck to the outer cover on top of the ship near the vertical fins. Their purpose was to act as collecting channels for the catchment of water, which was led into pipes and so down into the ballast bags in the corridor at the bottom of the keel. As it proved an undoubted success with *R.100*, it was later fitted to *R.101*—and I believe was also tried out on the *Graf Zeppelin.*

By the 2nd July 1930 *R.100* was once again ready to take the air, but a period of bad weather set in; it was not until the 25th of that month that we all, with the landing-party, assembled in the shed at the chilly hour of 2 am to take the ship out. A strong cross-wind sprang up, however, and it was decided to postpone her outgoing once again. As it was then too late, or early, to go home, I turned in on board until 7.30 am when I went up to the Meteorological Forecasting room and was informed that there appeared to be every chance of the weather improving later in the morning. So I went home to breakfast and returned at 9.30 am, to find the handling-party already in the shed. Soon after ten o'clock the ship was taken and walked over to the tower, where it was hooked on without incident.

The remainder of the day was spend on normal routine together with the final preparations for our last trial before the long-looked-forward-to flight to Canada. The objects of this trial—the airship's seventh flight—were to test the outer cover once again; to carry out extensive trials of different W/T installations and equipment; and finally to test the efficacy of the rainwater catchment system, that is the rigoles.

At 8 pm on the 25th July 1930, *R.100* was slipped from the tower at Cardington carrying fifty-five personnel included in a disposable weight of 39·7 tons. This figure indicates that we could have taken another 10 tons of load on board, bringing our total disposable lift to the region of 50 tons.

The flight itself was not particularly interesting. We made our usual tour round England, Wales and the Channel Islands. We first went up to Derby, where we circled round the Rolls-Royce works, then turned south-west to the Bristol Channel, at which point I was relieved by F/O Steff, and turned in to enjoy a well-earned sleep. The ship proceeded to Lundy Island and South Wales in low cloud and rain with the wind increasing to about 40 mph. Course was then altered to south-east and neither land nor sea was seen again until we emerged from the cloud over Yarmouth Pier, Isle of Wight. Course was then set for the Channel Islands, which we found bathed in warm sunshine which was reflected in blinding manner from the numerous glasshouses with which the whole island of Guernsey seemed to be covered.

We returned by way of the Needles and the Solent, and then crossed inland and made for London, which we reached about tea-time. We spent about three-quarters of an hour over the Metropolis and then set course from the unmistakable Islington landmark, the Cattle Market, for Cardington, where the ship was finally secured at 20.18 after 24 hours 18 minutes in the air.

Most of the flight was underneath or in heavy cloud, with rain falling a good part of the time. We experienced one incident which shook us out of our boredom and that was when we passed through a cold front near St Albans. We were bumped up 600 feet in about a minute, but very shortly after this we emerged from the cloud into bright sunshine. This was, I think, about the only eventful occurrence throughout the whole flight.

.100 stationary over the St. awrence River while repairs are rried out

he tail of *R.100* showing the black pair patch to her port plane ver the Atlantic

he top of the ship showing the alking way and ventilator hoods

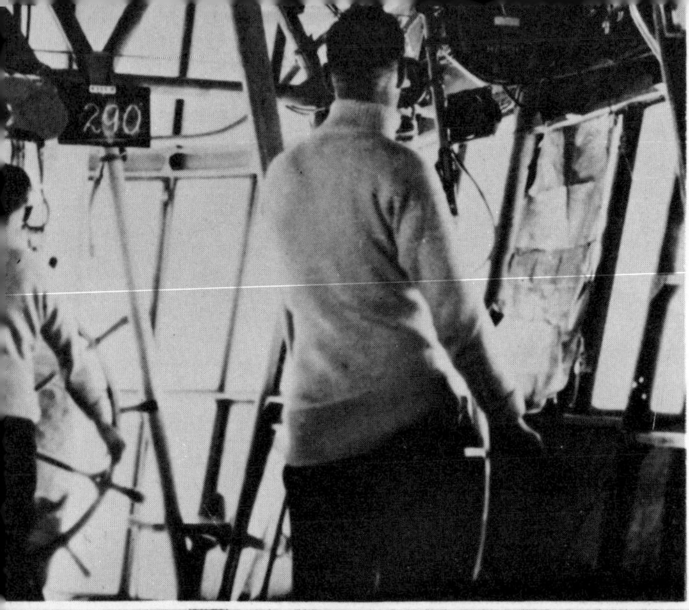

The control car during the Atlanti
flight. *On the left*, the steering cox'
and, on the right, Assistant cox'n
Long on the elevators. The figure
290 is the course being steered

Crew of R.100 *on flight Cardington–Montreal, 29th July–1st August 1930*

Back row

G. E. Long (Cox'n), L. A. Moncrieff (Cox'n), F. Williams (Rigger), H. Millward, (E), F. Hodnett (Asst. Steward), E. T. Stupple (C/h E), R. Ball (E), G. Watts (C/h E), N. Mann (C/h E), G. G. Cutts (R), T. Nobbs (Cox'n), A. Disley (W/T), G. K. Atkins (W/T), D. Lelliott (E).

Mid-row

G. R. Scott (R), L. A. Hunt (E), A. Savidge (C/h Steward), W. Angus (C/h E), Captain G. F. Meager (1st Offr.), Sq. Ldr. R. S. Booth (Captain), Major G. H. Scott (Dir. Flying), Sq. Ldr. E. L. Johnston (Navigator), F/O M. H. Staff (2nd Offr.), Captain M. A. Giblett (Met. Offr.), F/Sgt. T. E. Greenstreet (C/h Cox'n), S. T. Keeley (W/T), J. Jowett (E).

Front row

A. F. Wiseman (R), F. Gaye (E), C. Flatters (R), J. F. Meegan (Chef), H. Cumley (E), G. H. Rumsby (R), J. M. Sturgeon (E), H. W. Clark (E).

Whilst over the Channel I managed to get one or two sights of the sun with a bubble sextant, those about noon being useful in confirming our latitude, as we had then been over the sea for about a couple of hours. At other times of the flight, of course, we were watching the behaviour of the outer cover, especially where we had stiffened it up in the neighbourhood of the engine cars. I am afraid it still could not be classed as watertight, but there was much less flapping near the engines.

The DF wireless installation was tried at frequent intervals and appeared to give fairly satisfactory results, but Squadron Leader Johnston was not entirely satisfied as to its accuracy. The Fultograph was also disappointing in the airship, though quite good results had been obtained in the control room at Cardington; this was the instrument which we had been hoping would give us teleprinted weather maps. Wireless photography had not at that time developed sufficiently to warrant us carrying weighty equipment which could not be guaranteed to function, so the efforts of Wells and Cox-Walker—'Tich' as he was affectionately called—the experimental officers from the RAE, Farnborough, went for nothing in so far as our Atlantic flight was concerned.

Major Scott, who was in charge of the trials, was quite satisfied with the airship's all-round performance; so instead of being put into the shed she was kept at the mooring-tower, and preparations were made for the long-anticipated flight to Canada and back. This was to be the culmination of the series of trials before *R.100* was taken over by the Air Ministry. Her preliminary trials had proved more or less satisfactory—her speed was greater than that contracted, but her lift was less. The hull was exceptionally strong and we had no fear of the engines letting us down; what gave us real cause for anxiety was the fabric work on the airship—the outer cover and the gas-bags. A year previously Squadron Leader Booth had reported on the bad condition of the outer cover, and how, through its not being watertight, the gas-bags would be adversely affected. They were already three years old and had been stored in the airship at Howden under anything but ideal conditions. In fact, Squadron Leader Booth stated that he did not consider the airship was then in a fit state to carry out regular long overseas flights unless a new outer cover were provided. The usual squabble arose between the contractors and the Air Ministry, who both refused to incur the additional expense. Eventually a compromise was agreed upon; the top half of the cover was to be doped, while certain portions were to be given better support, and an improved system used for attaching the lower panels. As usual with compromises, this one was only partially successful. The new attachments and supports functioned excellently, but the cover still leaked very badly, especially at the main frames, so much so, that whenever we flew through heavy rain a perfect cascade of water would fall between the bags. Herr Strobl, who was mainly responsible for the manufacture of the bags, had informed Booth that half a dozen good soakings would be enough to ruin the gas-bags.

As the previous trial had been carried out chiefly to test the outer cover, the 27th July was spent carrying out an inspection of the new supports in the vicinity of the engine cars, and also of the new system of attachment in the lower panels. Both these improvements appeared to be satisfactory, so everything was now on the 'top line' for the long trek to Canada.

The 28th July was a very busy day for everyone. Wing Commander Colmore, Director of Airship Development; Major Scott, Assistant Director for Flying; Squadron Leader Booth, Captain of *R.100*; and Captain Giblett, Superintendant of the Airship Meteorological Division, had been in frequent conference at the forecasting room examining and discussing the charts and weather probabilities with the forecasting staff at Cardington—Messrs Kaye and Durst.

Squadron Leader Johnston—Chief Navigator—had been busy getting all his charts and navigation gear on board, and, assisted by Chief Wireless Operator Keeley, taking out the Fultograph and DF installations which had not worked well enough during the trials to justify taking them on the trip.

F/O Steff—Second Officer—and Mr Savidge—Chief Steward—were engaged in getting the necessary victuals on board. The stores officials, Messrs Charlton and Finch, gave us everything we asked for—sometimes more. I remember sending along for a couple of Royal Sovereign pencils and a soft rubber and was agreeably surprised to receive a dozen pencils and half a dozen erasers. This had rather an amusing sequel during the voyage, for every time I produced a pencil Johnnie would make a grab at it and say it was his. When he had collected about half a dozen and still saw me with one, he tumbled to the joke.

Chief Cox'n F/Sergt Greenstreet and the Cox'n of the Watch, Moncrieff, had been engaged with the riggers in gassing and taking in ballast, while the Chief Engineer, Mr Angus, and Charge-hand Engineer Mann were engaged with the engineers in refuelling and generally preparing the engines for flight. Gassing and refuelling were carried on up to midnight, by which time the gas-bags were 95 per cent full, while we had on board 34·5 tons of petrol (10,440 gallons), 1·5 tons of oil and 5·5 tons of water ballast.

We carried a crew of thirty-seven and seven other officials and observers. Each officer and official was allowed 30 pounds weight of baggage, and the crew 15 pounds each. These weights included the container. My own baggage weighed only 24 pounds and was contained in a small linen kit-bag. The weights allowed excluded clothing being worn and also flying-clothing, which consisted of the lining of a 'Sidcot' suit, a sweater, a leather cap and short woolly lined boots. Except at night, we rarely wore any other clothes than a sweater under our blue reefer suits. When the cold warranted it we donned the woolly lining of a 'Sidcot' suit, which is a wonderfully warm garment—though I got ragged for looking like an enormous Teddy Bear or pantomime Puss-in-Boots.

Most of the supernumeraries came on board early in the evening of 28th July and spent the first part of the night comfortably in bed. Some of them slept right through and did not even see us leave the tower, but woke up next morning to find us well on our way.

I had been on duty all day, superintending gassing, ballasting and fuelling, and at midnight I was relieved by Squadron Leader Booth, who told me to go and get a couple of hours' sleep, which I did gladly. It had been a long, tiring day. At 2 am on 29th July I relieved Booth in the control car. He gave me instructions to warm up the engines straight away, and to have the balancing-wheel wires got on board, except the after ones, which were not cast off until a few minutes before we left the tower. He went to the foot of the tower to spend the last few minutes with his wife.

We were due to slip from the tower at 02.30, and all the officers and crew not on duty or asleep were at the foot of the tower taking farewell of their wives and friends. I could see my little Austin car down below and hoped someonc would come along to relieve me for a few minutes, so that I could get down to wish my wife and baby boy good-bye.

Time went on; the engines were all running and being warmed up and the wheel wires hauled on board—still no one appeared. At about five and twenty minutes past two they all trooped on board in a bunch, so with a quick 'D'you mind if I pop below for a couple of minutes' to Booth, down I went as quickly as the lift could take me. Mrs Booth met me at the bottom of the lift and said, 'Come on, Meag, your wife is wondering what has become of you.'

I hurried through the crowd to our car, and there was little Griffith—named after his grandfather, Griffith Brewer—not yet eighteen months old, all wrapped up in woollies, standing up on the back seat with a surprised look on his dear little sleepy face, as if to say, 'What's all this fuss and bother about, and why have I been wakened up and dragged out of my nice warm cot at this unearthly hour of the night?'

After our good-byes my wife dashed away in the car whilst I made for the lift. It must be awful to be a woman whose duty it is to look on and wait in suspense and anxiety until their husbands or loved ones return; all they get out of it is some of the reflected glory of their menfolk's achievements.

As far as feeling any anxiety as to the outcome of the flight, no thought of failure ever entered my head, nor for that matter anyone else's on board, except perhaps Colmore, who disliked flying at any time; all the more credit to him, therefore, for coming on such a trip as this. All the regular members of the crew naturally considered their ship the best; a goodly number of them had been engaged in her construction. For myself I was glad I was in *R.100* for this trip, since as a result of my last flight in *R.101* I considered she was too unstable in pitch and too heavy and sluggish for my liking.

When I again reached the top of the tower the entrance gangway was just about to be hauled up into the airship. I wished Wing Commander Cave-Brown-Cave and Squadron Leader Nixon, who were on the platform, a hurried good-bye, and climbed on board. Booth met me at the entrance with 'Come on, Meag, you nearly missed the bus!' We went down to the control car, where we found that the remaining ballasting-wheels had been cast off, and the airship was floating as a free weather vane, being held only by the cone in the cup on the top of the tower.

The meteorological conditions just before leaving were as follows: Barometric pressure: 1,006.6 mbs, with a falling tendency. Temperature: 56.4°F, with a slight inversion. Wind: south-west, 20 mph, rather gusty. Weather: fine and clear. Cloud: small amount, 2/10ths of sky covered with alto-stratus.

The latest weather map showed a depression centred over the north of Ireland. The wind circulates in a counter-clockwise direction around a centre of low pressure in the Northern Hemisphere; this being so, with a depression centred over Northern Ireland the wind to the south of the centre would be from the south-west or west, whilst to the north it would blow from the east or north-east at a height of about 1,500 feet, where the wind blows approximately parallel to the isobars—lines of equal pressure. A careful study of the pressure distribution along a route is therefore a vital part of pre-flight preparation on the part of an air pilot and air navigator. This particular pressure distribution was the main factor in deciding our route to lie in a north-westerly direction at the start of our journey, instead of steering due west directly we left Cardington. Had we steered west we should have run into a south-westerly gale off the south of Ireland. When we were safely moored to the tower at St Hubert, Montreal, a week later, we had a visit from an officer of a merchant vessel which was off the south-west of Ireland when we left Cardington; he said he was amazed when he heard over the wireless that we had set off, as his ship was at the time bucking into a south-westerly gale, and he thought we should never make the trip, as the wind was blowing between 40 and 50 knots.

CHAPTER THIRTEEN

The Flight to Canada

At 2.48 am GMT on 29th July 1930 the order to slip is given and WE ARE AWAY.

As soon as the ship is well clear of the tower, the engines are opened up and away we go, amid cheers and tootings of motor horns, with a wide sweep round, and set our course to the north-westward. There is no time to watch sights below or wave farewells—which would not be seen anyway. All the riggers are spaced along the corridor getting the gas-bags crutched properly over the corridor. If this is not done just before the bags are up to pressure, there is a danger of excessive strain being placed on one section of the bag if it should get misplaced. F/O Steff is in charge of crutching the bags aft of the passenger accommodation, whilst I look after the forward part. Owing to the airship starting off very nearly full of gas, the average fullness of the bags being 97 per cent, there is no difficulty in getting the bags crutched snugly over the corridor, for they had been well positioned during gassing up before leaving. The bags are up to pressure at a height of 1,000 feet.

Having inspected the positioning of the bags right along the corridor, I report everything OK to the Captain, who then gives instructions to send the crew to Watchkeeping Flying Stations. I pass this on to F/O Steff, F/Sgt Greenstreet and Mr Angus, and then myself turn in, as I am due to take the morning watch at 04.00.

Booth, although Captain of the airship, is acting as a watchkeeper and is keeping the first watch immediately after the ship leaves Cardington. Of course, this should not be—the Captain of a ship should not have to keep a watch. In fact, I believe ours are the only large airships where this practice is carried out. The *Graf Zeppelin* carried three airship pilot watchkeepers and three navigator watchkeepers in addition to the Captain, while on the US Airship *Akron*, neither the Captain nor the Chief Executive Officer kept a watch; the *Akron* also carried three flying watchkeepers and three navigating watchkeepers. In my opinion, three pilot navigator watchkeepers are necessary for long flights. The pilot navigator watchkeepers should be competent to carry out the navigation of the airship during their watch, with the Captain (also a First-Class Navigator) supervising. For this particular flight we carried a separate

Meteorological Officer, Captain Giblett, M.Sc. He was also carried in *R.101* on her flight to India, and tragically lost his life two months later when she crashed at Beauvais soon after leaving.

We commence the flight to Canada running the three forward engines in each car at 1,400 rpm and the after engines of the two wing cars at 'slow'—1,000 rpm. The latter are only kept running so as to get properly warmed up and are very soon stopped. With the three forward engines running at 1,400 rpm we achieve an airspeed of 47 knots (54 mph). At the height at which we are flying, about 1,000 feet, the wind is blowing at 30 knots from the south-west and we make good over the ground only 36 knots, our direction being nearly north-west.

I am due to come on watch at 04.00, but as I was on duty all day yesterday, Booth, like the white man he is, has split the watch with me, which means that I do not have to relieve him until 06.00, thus giving me an extra two hours sleep. There is nothing like airship flying for making one sleep, and I am no sooner in my sleeping-bag than I am asleep. I scarcely seem to have closed my eyes than I am awakened and told it is a quarter to six. I quickly slip on my clothes and 'Teddy Bear' suit and relieve Booth in the control car.

While I have been asleep we have passed over the Midlands close to Wellingborough, Northampton and Rugby with its small forest of tall W/T masts each topped with a red light.

Weather reports and forecasts are received by wireless at regular intervals. The W/T ops under Keeley are certainly kept busy; if they are not sending a message they are either receiving one from Rugby on long-wave, or from Cardington on short-wave. Keeley, by the way, was one of the crew on board *R.33* when she broke away from the mooring-mast at Pulham in 1925. In addition to their wireless duties, the W/T personnel are also responsible for the electrical installation, Operator Disley being detailed for this specific duty.

It is sad to have to relate that two of our operators on this flight, Keeley and Atkins, were lost with Captain Giblett in *R.101* a couple of months later; our other operator, Disley, was one of the six survivors from that dreadful disaster.

Every six hours a report is sent from the airship to Cardington giving the position, course and speed made good since the previous report, finishing with any remarks of interest. Every message is prefixed with a code word which indicates the number of engines at cruising speed and if any are temporarily or permanently out of order. Either Mr Eldridge, Clerk to the Captain, or Captain Giblett keep the Watchkeeping Officers up to making out the report punctually; I know that I for one often forget all about it until Giblett comes down to the control car and in his quiet way whispers in my ear: '18.00 hour report!'—or whatever time is due—and pushes the form in front of me with the 'met' information already on it. Otherwise Eldridge would come along and ask for the report so that he might take it to the DAD for the insertion of his remarks.

When I relieve Squadron Leader Booth at 06.00 we are passing over the old Roman-Saxon city of Chester. The great port of Liverpool in a haze of smoke is somewhat to starboard of our course, so we alter course a little in order to pass directly over the city. This we do a few minutes later amid the shrieking of steamers' sirens and train whistles. We can see the steam coming from the whistle and some seconds later hear the actual sound. Two buildings in Liverpool which impress themselves on my mind are the white City Hall and the red sandstone Cathedral, in course of construction, which seems to cover an enormous area.

Two minutes after passing over Liverpool we take our leave of English soil, crossing the foreshore at Formby Point, on which I take a back bearing when we are well out over the sea, to see if we are making a correct course for the Isle of Man. At 07.00 we pass the Morecambe Bay light-vessel lying about three miles away to starboard. Before we sight the Isle of Man we run into a rain cloud which blots out view of everything. Emerging from the cloud we see the Sugar Loaf Mountain in the Isle of Man dead ahead, so we alter course to run parallel to the coast. A few minutes after eight o'clock we pass over the Point of Ayre at the northern end of the island. Johnston and Steff relieve me and I go to the saloon wash-place, where Steward Hodnett brings me a can of piping hot water with which I wash and shave, and then sit down to a lovely hot breakfast of fried eggs and bacon, followed by hot buttered toast, marmalade and freshly made coffee which is served by Mr Savidge, our Chief Steward, looking very spick and span in a white coat and dark blue trousers. He is in his element and much happier than on one of the western ocean liners—the *Majestic*, in fact—which he left to join us in spite of the fact that he must have dropped about £400 a year—such is the thrall of airship flying.

We pass the Mull of Galloway in cloudy weather, but still maintain our course towards the north-west, as the wind is still from the west, indicating that we have not yet passed to the north side of the depression. At 09.30 we passed the Belfast mail-boat and a few minutes later were over the group of rocks called 'The Maidens'. We carry on past Rathlin Island, where it starts to rain and gives us an opportunity of trying out Greenstreet's rigoles. We continue north-west until at 11.00 hours we reach the Head of Islay at the southern end of the Isle of Islay. Here we find ourselves at last in the north left-hand portion of the depression. The wind now being north-easterly, not very strong, but a help none the less. We alter course to the west and stop the after engine of the after car, so we are now running on the three forward engines of each car at 1,400 rpm, which gives us an airspeed of 45 knots. As the wind is helping us to the tune of about 15 knots, we are bowling along at about 60 knots or nearly 70 mph.

After breakfast, although officially off duty, I make a tour along the corridor to inspect the positioning of the bags. I found some of our passengers or observers busy pumping fuel from the corridor tanks up to the service tanks above the engine cars. This was a never-ending job, being done in two-hourly spells by our willing supernumeraries.

After my tour of the corridor I go over the top of the ship, as usual ignominiously crawling along the foot-wide catwalk to inspect the outer cover and valve hoods. It is a long crawl that has no end and on reaching the cruciform girder which acts as a rudder and fin post, I climb along it out to the auxiliary control positions on each of the horizontal stabilising fins. The operator has a little well let into the trailing-edge of the fins and can work the elevator flap by means of a small hand wheel; there are four auxiliary control positions, one for each elevator and one each for top and bottom rudder. If there was an emergency, instructions would have to be conveyed by means of voice-pipes from an auxiliary control position underneath the corridor at Frame 15, where a compass, altimeter and statoscope are fitted. It is difficult to say how the engines would be controlled, unless by verbal instructions along the corridor. Why we had no intercom telephones is beyond me: let us hope we shall never have occasion to use these auxiliary controls, as I consider they would be quite impractical!

Whilst I was out on the starboard fin the airship passed through a very heavy shower of rain followed by a hailstorm. With the speed of the ship, the hail fairly cut my face, so I quickly went inboard and closed the flap, but not before I had become soaked with rain and could see that the little well was half full of hail. Until I arrived back in the control car in my streaming clothes no one there had realised the heaviness of the shower, nor were they aware that we had passed through or beneath a thunderstorm—hail is always an accompaniment of a thunderstorm or at any rate always falls from a thunder-cloud—cumulo-nimbus. I quickly changed and Meegan the cook dried my wet things in the galley.

The fact of our having passed through a hailstorm bore out in a striking manner the accuracy of the first weather forecast which warned us to expect local thunder as far as long. 10°W, for although we experienced no actual thunder or lightning, hail is invariably associated with it.

We are in wireless communication with the DF station at Malin Head at the north-west corner of Ireland, from whom we receive at intervals our true bearing from the W/T station there—I have earlier described how these bearings can be used to ascertain our track, position and wind.

At noon GMT (which we have been keeping until now) the ship's clock is put back one hour, as we have now entered Zone plus one, which means that local time is one hour behind Greenwich time. We shall thus have two eleven o'clocks and two noons today and this would mean that, if the usual watchkeeping times were adhered to, the OOW and the Duty Watch would have to do an extra hour's duty. This is obviated, however, by the forenoon watch being relieved at 'First noon', while the afternoon watch is relieved at 15.30 instead of at 16.00 hours, so that the afternoon watch and the first dog watch split the extra hour between them.

The last part of the British Isles we see is Tory Island off the north-west of Ireland, which we pass at 11.25 GMT, when it lies some five miles away on our port side. We expect to see nothing more except sea, sky, cloud, ships or icebergs until we sight Belle Isle between the northern end of Newfoundland and Labrador, a distance of about 1,700 nautical miles away. So we feel now that we have actually started to cross the Atlantic in earnest on this the twenty-sixth non-stop crossing of the North Atlantic—by all types of aircraft—and the eleventh airship crossing.

Just before lunch I went up to the observation position in the bow on top of the ship and took an ex-meridian altitude of the sun. I took four good sights in quick succession, the ship being nice and steady. The average of these four sights was used for working out our latitude by observation, which came out as lat. 55°22′N. Johnston also took a series of sights about the same time and obtained an observed latitude of lat. 55°24′N, so our sights coincided very well. Johnston used a Mark VII RAE Booth bubble sextant, and I used an earlier model, Mark V. Our dead reckoning position was at the same time lat. 55°24′N, long. 07°50′W.

For lunch that day we had chops, peas and potatoes followed by some tinned fruit and a cup of coffee. Soup was also on the menu, but as it was tomato soup, which I can't abide, I did without. So far the electric cooker is functioning well.

The day seemed interminable, as the clock was continually being put back, due to our travelling westwards. The passengers while away the time playing cards or sleeping the first day out, as most of them had been up all night.

During each watch the Officer on Duty would don a pair of surgeon's rubber gloves and expose a Petrie dish. These are small circular tins, about three inches in diameter and a quarter inch deep, filled with gelatine. The idea of these frequent exposures in the open air through the window is to see what, if any, bacteria are floating about in the air over the Atlantic. They are named after Professor Petrie of Bristol University, who has asked for the experiments to be carried out. (I do not believe that any positive results were obtained).

Whoever is doing the navigating—Booth, Johnston or myself in our respective watches—in addition to conning the ship and taking an astronomical sight when opportunity offers, at approximately two-hourly periods, if the surface is visible, drops a small box filled with aluminium dust ; on hitting the sea the box bursts, and the dust spreads over the water, giving a perfect mark on which to check our drift and ascertain our wind speed and direction as well as our ground speed. Our airspeed is measured by the air log invented by Squadron Leader F. M. Rope and described earlier.*

The dust bombs are our day markers—during the night we use calcium flares which, on striking the water, burst into flame. Another method of checking our ground speed during daylight, with the sun shining and no cloud below us, is by timing the passage of our shadow over a well-defined point—at sea, a white horse is the usual mark.

Round about tea-time on the 29th mild excitement is caused by our sighting a whale spouting away on our port side. Most of the time we are cruising along on four engines, giving us an airspeed of 52 knots—or nearly 60 mph. At times we give three engines a rest, running only one engine in each car.

The wireless log shows we are frequently getting bearings from ships. As we have no directional apparatus on board, the procedure is for a ship to pick up our signal and plot its direction. It then signals back its own position and our bearing. The navigator then plots the steamship's position on our chart, and lays off our bearing from it. This, of course, only gives us a 'position line' on which we lie at some unknown point. If we can get another ship to take our bearing at more or less the same time, simultaneously if possible, our position is where the two bearings cross, called the 'cut'. A single bearing is still of use, however, for when we receive another, we can adjust the first by the distance we have gone along our track and thus obtain a cut. The first bearing we received was from the *Winchester Exporter* at 22.30 hours GMT (Zone plus 2) on 29th July; an hour later we received simultaneous bearings from the *Montclare* and the *Caledonia*, which gave a good cut. We can say with confidence that our position at midnight GMT, or 10 pm local time, was lat 53°05′N, long. 21°00′W, about 800 miles on our way, for a consumption of 2,200 gallons of petrol.

* Rope, in my opinion, had the best mathematical brain amongst the staff at Cardington. He was not with us on the Atlantic flight. His death amongst those on *R.101* when she crashed at Beauvais was a sad loss which I personally felt tremendously, as we had been together at Capel-le-Ferne Airship Station in 1916, where he had been particularly kind to me, then a young inexperienced airship pilot; we also served together in 1918 at Ciampino, whither we had been sent by the Air Ministry to take over *SR.1*.

We cannot yet put the date as the 30th July 1930, as the clock has again been put back an hour. In another hour, however, we shall be able to do so. I relieve Johnston for the middle watch which means I shall now be pilot and navigator until relieved by Squadron Leader Booth at 4 am.

To avoid confusion of times I must try to remember to give both GMT, in which the navigational log is kept, and the equivalent local time at ship, LST, in which the flying-log is kept, a note being made in it each time the clock is put back an hour (going west) which means we have made good another 15 degrees of longitude. Zones to the west of Greenwich are called plus zones because you add the zone to the local time to get GMT; and vice versa for zones east of Greenwich.

Very soon after I come on watch we see the lights of a steamer ahead and a little later pass over her. She is the Cunarder *Ausonia* which sailed from Southampton five days ago.

At 4 am local ship time I am punctually relieved by Squadron Leader Booth, and proceed to the galley, where there is a saucepan of hot cocoa simmering. I help myself to a mug of it and then turn in and sleep like a log until eight o'clock. Usual ablutions with steaming hot water, and breakfast on cereals and fresh milk, bacon, eggs, coffee, toast and marmalade.

Whilst I have been asleep the wind has backed right round almost to south; and is increasing as we come under the influence of a depression which has moved up from the West Indies since yesterday. We edge a little to the northward and soon have the wind abaft our beam from 155 degrees. Though this is not a direct tail wind, it is helping us considerably, as it is blowing at 30 knots, and we are making good 70 knots at 9 am (noon GMT), 30th July 1930. We can, however, see nothing, as we are flying in cloud. A little before this we received a set of three simultaneous bearings from *Megantic*, *Arabic* and *Manchester Shipper*, which gave us an accurate position of 54°20′N, 37°50′W. This was at 7.55 am local time (10.55 hours GMT).

We should long ago have been in communication with Louisburg, but did not achieve contact with them until about 8.45 am, (11.45 GMT) 30th July. In fact, we were completely out of touch with land stations on either side of the Atlantic for some 600 miles and over a period of nine hours.

Two of the engines which have been running continuously so far are now stopped for examination. They are in perfect condition and only require a change of sparking-plugs and the replacement of a rocker-arm bush on one of them.

During the forenoon I made an inspection along the keel and discovered a couple of tears about a foot long in the outer cover just aft of the passenger accommodation. A rigger soon drew the edges together with needle and thread and doped a fabric patch over them. The sky has cleared, so just before lunch I went up to the observation position in the bow and took a series of sun sights. These did not take long to work out, as the sun was nearly on the meridian.

Eldridge had organised a sweepstake on the day's run—from noon to noon. He himself is the lucky winner with a run of 1,095 nautical miles.

At 8 pm local time (midnight GMT, as we are in Z plus 4), I take over the first watch (8 pm until midnight). Our position, with 1,700 gallons of fuel left, was lat. 52°15′N, long. 54°00′W, some 3,286 miles on our way.

At about a quarter to nine there is tremendous excitement amongst those in the control car, for we can see a light flashing ahead slightly on our port bow or, in the parlance of the log, 'one point on the port bow'. As there are thirty-two points in the compass (360 degrees), one point equals $11\frac{1}{4}$ degrees so the light is this amount to the left of dead ahead. It is identified from our Light List to be from the lighthouse on Cape Bauld, which is situated on the northernmost tip of Newfoundland; within half an hour, at 9.15 local time on 30th (01.15 GMT on 31st July), we pass over Belle Isle, an island lying between the north point of Newfoundland and the southern tip of Labrador. Our time for crossing from shore to shore, from the last point in Ireland to the coast of Newfoundland, is 37 hours 39 minutes or 46 hours, 27 minutes since casting off at Cardington.

There is dense fog in the Strait of Belle Isle, but the weather clears as the Gulf of St Lawrence opens out ahead, though below us there is a bank of cloud, through breaks in which we occasionally see ships plugging along.

Wing Commander Colmore hopes we shall make our destination by tomorrow morning, Thursday, and with this in view we open up all six engines, as we have plenty of fuel. However, old Giblett, our Met Officer, rather damps our ardour by reporting that we may expect head-winds for the remainder of the journey and, in fact, the wind has already veered to south-west at about 25 knots, which reduces our ground speed to some 35 knots.

At midnight local time F/O Steff takes over from me. It is a beautiful starlit night above us, though we could not see the water below on account of low cloud, and I thought it a good opportunity to get some star sights with the bubble sextant. This is, in my opinion, by far the best means of obtaining a 'fix', provided of course, the stars or planets are visible. I have often wondered why more use is not made of this method in ships at sea.

If the Pole Star is visible it is a simple matter to obtain one's latitude, as its altitude is the latitude of the place. As the Pole Star—or Polaris, to give it its correct name—does not lie exactly over the Pole, but cirmculocutes it at a small distance, a small correction has to be made; this is tabulated in the Nautical Almanac, so it presents no difficulty. Having obtained my latitude in this way, I then took altitudes of the stars Altair and Vega, whose direction or bearing were a wide angle apart—about 45 degrees—and so gave a very good cut for a fix, which gave our position as lat. 50°40'N, long. 58°13'W. at 05.02 GMT on 31st July 1930. I then had my usual mug of cocoa and turned in.

My cabin on this outward journey is up on the starboard promenade deck above the saloon. My bed is a single duralumin bunk bolted to the bulkhead; it has a piece of canvas stretched across the frame, tauter than a hammock. I prefer a kapok sleeping-bag to a mattress; inside the bag is a linen slip; outside I cover myself with a blanket. Once inside the bag one is a living example of 'as snug as a bug in a rug'.

By dawn on 31st July we were well into the Gulf of St Lawrence, flying between the north coast of Anticosti Island and the Canadian shore. We were still running on all six engines at cruising speed, which gave us an airspeed of 65 knots, making good 40 knots. The landscape on either side was most uninspiring, as it was almost entirely forest interspersed with numerous lakes. There seemed to be as many trees lying on the ground as standing.

At 8 am LST we are past the western end of Anticosti and thus enter the River St Lawrence. As the wind seemed to be of less velocity nearer the south bank of the river, we steer over to it; our ground speed at once increases by about 6 knots. The shimmer of the sunlight on the breeze-rippled water is an unforgettable sight.

We pass over the *Empress of Scotland* and a little later over the *Duchess of Bedford*, both ships looking perfectly beautiful with their white paint gleaming in the sunshine. A Canadian flying-boat from Rimouski keeps us company for a time, being replaced by others a little later. A few minutes before noon we pass Father Point, made famous as the spot off which Dr Crippen was apprehended in 1909 when flying from justice, this being the first time that wireless telegraphy had been used to effect the arrest of an escaping criminal.

Two of our largest bags, Nos. 7 and 8, each of over 500,000 cubic feet capacity, giving a lift of some 15 tons, have been causing some anxiety by showing signs of leaking, so a party of riggers headed by Cox'n Hobbs climbs along the radial wires between the bags. They find about half a dozen 3-inch slits along the central radial wire.

One can usually tell that gas is escaping by the peculiar smell, although textbooks tell us hydrogen has no smell. Its effects are insidious and unnoticeable until you suddenly lose consciousness and your grip. The Tower Officer at Cardington, F/O George Cook, lost consciousness in this way when searching for leaks between bags in *R.9*. He fell from the middle of the ship and was badly injured. The usual way we tested the effects of gas on ourselves when searching for leaks, or otherwise climbing about the interior of the ship above the gas level, was to sing, talk or whistle a tune to oneself; if one was becoming affected by gas the voice became high-pitched or parrot-like, or the whistle became very shrill.

The receipt of a wireless message from the Montreal police asking for our ETA, so that they could make arrangements for traffic control, makes us realise that we are at last drawing towards the end of our journey. We are not there yet by any means, and much is to happen before eventually we do arrive. When we are about fifty miles from Quebec our skipper, much against his better judgement and inclination, is prevailed upon to open up the engines to 70 knots; the time is 13.25 LST and we are over Green Island. The object is to land before dark today, the 31st July. It turns out a proper case of more haste less speed, for with the sun shining in practically a clear blue sky we are struck by a gust broadside on and given the most terrific roll I have ever experienced in an airship. The time is 14.40 hours local time—19.40 GMT—and we are passing the mouth of the Saguenay which flows into the St Lawrence from the mountains to the northward; we have just experienced what is known to meteorologists as a 'white squall', the cause of which is the cooler air from the mountains flowing down the slopes and along the river valley which acts as a funnel. Unlike a black or storm squall, a white squall cannot be seen approaching; this one hits us without our being aware of its presence until we are actually struck by it.

In the parlance of the sea, the 'ship is thrown almost on her beam ends'. I had always previously boasted that an airship never rolls, but this is one with a vengeance!*

At the moment of the first impact I was washing my hands and had to hang on to the rail to steady myself. I immediately went down into the keel just forward of the saloon and there met Mr Norway; for a few seconds we watched the passenger accommodation sling wires to see if we could detect any movement. The passenger accommodation was not an integral part of the ship, but was slung by wire cables to the framework of the hull. We could not discern any movements, so I proceeded to the control car to see if any damage had been reported. The engine-room telegraph bells from the starboard and after cars were ringing for assistance—strange to say, in the light of what had actually happened, there was no call from the port wing car.

* Afterwards Mr Norway thought its amplitude was of the order of 10 degrees; I think it was more than double that, for our Chief Engineer, Mr W. Angus, told me that he was in the keel at the time and he could see the sky through the ventilators in the lower panels of the ship!

The engines were slowed down immediately, and Major Scott asked me to go along and investigate. In company with Squadron Leader Archie Wann and Mr Norway I hurried aft along the corridor. In the bottom fin could be seen two tears of about 3 feet in length. This was not very serious, though if left the fin would soon be whipped by the airstream into ribbons. I detailed Cox'n Moncrieff and Rigger Wiseman to repair the damage and left Wann superintending. I then made my way up a transverse girder to the starboard fin, where I found there was more extensive, though not alarming, damage—unless, of course, it was left. Here the outboard edge of the fin was split longitudinally for some 10 or 12 feet.

Whilst I went down to fetch help for repairs, Mr Norway, who had accompanied me out to the fin, climbed out to the damaged part and did his best to prevent further damage by holding the torn pieces together as best he could, a difficult job with the fabric flapping in the airstream and doing its best to tear itself to ribbons.

I collected Hobbs and Williams, who, armed with fabric, needles, thread and dope, soon got to work on repairing the damage.

Although no report of any damage had been received from the port wing car, I thought it would be as well to check up on both the port and the top fins. I asked Norway to go and check on the port fin while I climbed up the cruciform girder and inspected the top fin. This did not take long, as, being inside the fin, I could see at a glance that no daylight was showing anywhere through the fabric forming the fin.

For my own satisfaction I thought I had better have a 'look see' at the port fin myself, so made my way along the horizontal arm of the cruciform girder to the port fin—and what a sight met my eyes: the fabric forming the underside of the fin just abaft the leading-edge was literally in ribbons, and there was an enormous hole gaping in the underside of the fin, large enough to drive a double-decker bus through—and this was no exaggeration, believe me.*

I spent no time gazing at it, but hurried as fast as I could down to the corridor. Here I met Mr Norway and he started to describe the damage to me. I am afraid I cut him short—he stuttered terribly—and told him I knew all about it and must report immediately to the Captain; I thought we might be able to repair it.

'You'll never repair that hole,' Norway said. Anyway, I hurried to the near-by speaking-tube, rang the gong and was answered by Squadron Leader Booth himself. I told him the extent of the damage and added that I thought we could make a repair if he would send along Chief Cox'n Greenstreet and as many riggers as he could spare. I told him my

* The size of the new panels inserted when *R.100* was at St Hubert tower measured 15 by 12 feet.

idea for repair was to run lines of cord across the opening and on these to stretch canvas or fabric over the hole. The canvas I had in mind was that which covered the cruciform girders to prevent chafing. Booth agreed and must have passed on the idea to Greenstreet, for a few minutes later the latter came along the corridor laden with an enormous roll of cotton fabric.

'Where the devil did you get that from?' I asked him.

He admitted somewhat sheepishly that instead of discarding the corridor covering when instructed to take it out to lighten ship for the long flight to Canada, he had stowed it away in his locker thinking it might 'come in useful'—and so it did. Having the fabric all ready to hand enabled us to get on with the repair job without being delayed by taking down the covering over the cruciform.

We soon had a gang of riggers at work tying down the loose ends and stretching cod-line across the opening. These riggers were augmented by the men from the other fins as soon as they had completed repairs. Ultimately we had all the riggers in the ship on the job with the exception of Cox'n Long, who was at the steering or elevator.

Whilst carrying out the repairs the engines had, of course, been slowed right down to a speed sufficient to countervail the wind, giving us steerage way, but preventing us being blown backwards. The wind was still practically dead ahead and blowing about 20 knots. I remember seeing through the damaged fin a long narrow sandy island over which we remained stationary practically the whole time the repairs were being done. Being up on the fin, I had no means of checking our position with reference to the map, but there is an entry in the log against the time of 21.10 GMT $Z+4$ (4.10 pm local time): '*Over Grosse Island north of Quebec*', and an hour later '*Completed temporary repairs to fin*'.

It is difficult to describe the conditions or difficulties under which the fin repairs were carried out. It must be remembered that there were no girders in the neighbourhood of the damage where the riggers could get a foot- or hand-hold, except at the outer edge of the fin or inboard at one of the main longitudinal girders. In between these two was a series of wires to which the fin fabric was laced. It was along these wires the riggers had to work. Fortunately the thickness of the fin at the hole was such that with their feet on the lower wire they could steady themselves with a hand on the upper wire. But it was, in the language of the RAF, 'dicey work'. I had the utmost difficulty in getting the men to put a rope round their waist with the other end made fast to the structure. They were working in these conditions with nothing between them and the river 1,500 feet below, but they took it as all in the day's work. One or two incidents stick in my mind. Cox'n Hobbs had joined us after finishing the repair on the starboard fin. He was just about to do the tightrope

Arriving in Montreal, 1st August 1930, the gangway not yet connected

Landing at Cardington from Canada.
Lord Thompson, Air Minister, in trilby, congratulating Sq. Ldr. Johnston, the navigator. On Lord Thompson's left: Sq. Ldr. Booth, Captain; Capt. Meager, First Officer; and F/Sgt. Greenstreet, Chief Cox'n

R.100's main corrido
looking towards the
passenger accommod
tion from the bow

One of *R.100*'s wing
cars with the engines
removed

R.100 being disman
the gasbags still in pl

act with no net when I noticed he had no safety rope on. I insisted he put one on, and the look of disgust on his face made me think I had committed lese-majesty. An amusing incident occurred when Squadron Leader Booth came up to 'D' Girder, from which I was superintending the work, to see how the job was progressing. While standing on the girder beside me, he noticed one of the riggers, Flatters by name, resting for a moment right out at the outboard edge of the fin where there was a small fringe of the fabric left on the girder, in which he was sitting hammock-fashion with his legs dangling over the edge. His weight made a large bulge in the fabric. Booth, seeing this, turned to me and said: 'Whose bottom is that? If he's not careful, he'll make another hole there!'

About two hours after receiving the first damage reports, it was considered safe to open up the engines to half speed which gave us about 50 knots airspeed and we bid farewell to the sandy island over which we had hovered so long.

All thought or hope of landing today is now out of the question, so we do not try to force the pace, but creep along against the wind, making good about 25 knots. At about tea-time we are over Quebec, but as I am making an inspection over the top of the ship at the time, I do not get a sight of the city. I do get a sight of Quebec Bridge, however, which spans the St Lawrence a little higher up the river. It is still daylight, but getting dark, as the sun is hidden by a heavy bank of cumulo-nimbus or thunder cloud, for which we are directly heading. I go back to the control car, having come on for the second dog watch at 18.00 hours local time. There is an entry in the flying-log '*18.05 Quebec Bridge 146 st. miles to go, at 27 mph = 5h. 25m = 23.30 hrs, ETA.*' In other words, at our present speed we hope to arrive at Montreal at about midnight local time. However, I am counting the chicks before they're hatched, for when about half-way between Quebec and Montreal, just before reaching a township called Three Rivers, we run slap bang into a line squall thunderstorm. The rain and hail beat a proper tattoo against the windows of the control car. In the control car with me is Squadron Leader Johnston, who is navigating, all the others are up in the dining-saloon, where I had hoped to be in ten minutes.

We hit the storm—or rather the storm hits us—at 7.40 pm local time on 1st August 1930. We first feel the gust under our bow which puts the nose up; then, as the squall moves aft, it gets under our tail and tilts the ship with her nose down at an angle of 25 degrees or more. At this angle we are whisked upwards from 1,200 to 3,000 feet in about one minute. I had just made a note that we 'are steadying' at this height, when another and more violent upward gust strikes us and we shoot up to about 5,000 feet. Unfortunately I cannot make any more notes, as all lights except the dim ones over the instruments have been switched off. The reason for this is that during the second and more violent gust one of the men in the crew quarters immediately over the wireless cabin, had been thrown off balance, fallen and knocked over a drum of red dope, sliding along the deck in it, on his posterior. (He has a wonderful red patch on the seat of his trousers for the rest of the time we are in Canada.) When I see the red liquid falling into the wireless cabin just behind me, I think at first that someone up above has had an accident. However, the strong pungent smell of dope soon disabuses me of this idea—and as dope is highly inflammable, Major Scott orders the lights to be switched off to prevent risk of fire. This of course, plunges everything into pitch darkness, as we are in the middle of dense cloud and the sun has by now gone down.

Norway calculates that the vertical speed of the second gust was something of the order of 50 mph; he thinks our angle down by the nose must have been something like 35 degrees, whilst Giblett reckons we were rising at the rate of 4,000 feet per minute; anyway, the liquid in the pitch indicator disappeared from view and its limits are 20 degrees either way.

At the time of the first gust under the tail I was hurled against a stanchion which saved me being pitched against the glass around the front of the car. I then went over to the chart table and made the few notes I mentioned earlier. Up in the dining-saloon the Chief Steward, Mr Savidge, was collecting soup from Meegan, the chef. In their own words 'the ship gave a sudden lurch and nearly stood on its nose'. The soup spilled all over Mr Savidge, whilst everything movable in the galley and saloon—pots and pans, vegetables, bread, cakes, meat, knives, forks, spoons and crockery went hurtling down the gangway into the forward corridor—much of this is found next day almost up in the bows.

I am due to be relieved at 8 pm, but this is not to be, for after our previous experience it is necessary to inspect the fins, especially as, being dark, no damage can be seen from the engine cars. So along aft I go, to the port fin first this time, where I find that our repair has stood up to the buffeting very well—no doubt because of its slackness. Not the starboard fin, however; this has sustained further damage with two long tears of about 20 feet each in its underside. There is nothing for it—repairs must be put in hand immediately or we shall have another repair à la port fin. This means I shall lose my supper—in any case it has all disappeared up the corridor—having already missed my tea.

The job is not so easy as the previous one on the same fin, as the work has to be done by the light of hand torches. However, it does not entail much tightrope walking and with the help of some volunteers from the engineers the repairs are completed satisfactorily by about midnight ship's time, by which time we can see the huge electric cross erected on Mount Royal at Montreal as a beacon for ships navigating at night on the St Lawrence, for it can be seen for many miles.

We reach the city of Montreal at 01.10 DST—Montreal Daylight Saving Time—on 1st August 1930. It is indeed an enchanting sight—a fairyland city of a million lights, broken mid-way by the dark shadow of the river; and dominating all is the huge electric cross on Mount Royal.

There are still thunderstorms about, but they are very local and we cruise about, dodging them until it is nearly daylight, when we make our way slowly in the direction of St Hubert Airport, a dozen miles away. Dawn has not broken when we reach the Airport and the vari-coloured lights on the mooring-tower and aerodrome present a very attractive sight.

In ballasting up before landing we have to valve very little gas, as we have collected nearly five tons of rainwater from our 'recovery plant' on top of the ship. In the heavy rain during the line squall we collected a third of a ton in about ten minutes.

The correction we had to make to our altimeter reading owing to difference in barometric pressure since it was set at Cardington was plus 208 feet.

Finally just as dawn is breaking we steer straight for the mooring-tower head to wind. At about the boundary of the aerodrome—St Hubert is one of the few airports which caters for both airships and aeroplanes—our main wire is paid out, whilst our after engines are put into reverse. As soon as our wire touches the ground it is collected by a party of three from the tower crew who couple it to the Thomas block on the tower wire laid out on the landing-ground in preparation. Normal procedure for hauling in proceeds and 'Ship secure' is called by Lieutenant Commander Pressey, RCN, the Tower Officer, at 5.37 am Montreal time (DST) which is Eastern Standard Time plus one hour (09.37 GMT) on 1st August 1930. It is lucky we landed so early as the roads leading to the airport, even at this early hour are crammed with cars of every description. What it is going to be like later can be imagined only too easily!

Immediately the gangway is lowered on to the tower top, Pressey is on board to congratulate us. He is so overcome with emotion and relief that the tears are streaming down his cheeks: 'Don't mind me, chaps; I can't help crying, I'm so pleased to see you.'

Pressey is a great fellow, so unassuming and willing to do all he can to help. He has the most strikingly beautiful wife, too, with a lovely, rather pale complexion offset by a mass of flaming red hair—natural colour, too!

We have completed the 3,364 nautical miles from Cardington in 78 hours 49 minutes, consuming 8,935 gallons (29½ tons) of fuel. On landing we have 1,505 gallons left.

CHAPTER FOURTEEN

Toronto and Return to England

In spite of the earliness of the hour, there were about 10,000 people at the Airport to welcome us; people from all over Canada had come to see us.

As soon as we had made all our connections, and had ballast wheels slung, most of us went below where there was a great array of Press people. For the first time I realised what a 'battery of photographers' means.

To cope with anticipated traffic and crowd difficulties, the Canadian Defence authorities, at the request of the Montreal Police, mobilised the Royal Canadian Dragoons. They were encamped in tents near the entrance to the Airport and we officers were made honorary members of their Mess, which I for one appreciated very much, as it meant we could get our meals hot in their marquee instead of having them cold in the ship—we did not run the ship's cooker whilst at the tower. Another great honour paid to us was to have a posse of Royal Canadian Mounted Police, with a captain at their head, to regulate the hundreds who actually came on board. Some were stationed at the base of the tower and regulated entry to the lift, whilst others were at the top of the tower controlling actual entry into the ship. This had to be done pretty carefully so as not to upset the equilibrium. The Mounties are certainly a fine body of men and looked very picturesque and smart in their scarlet tunics, blue breeches with broad yellow stripe, highly polished riding-boots and gaiters, with a broad-brimmed slouch hat with yellow and red tassels. The captain's uniform of dark blue looked quite drab beside that of the men.

After breakfast in the RCD Mess, where our host was Major Baty, we were officially welcomed by the Mayor of Montreal, Mr Houde, and the City Council. This was literally a wash-out, for just as we had gathered on a platform in the open with rows of chairs in front, there was a proper cloud-burst and the crowd stampeded. Fortunately it did not last long, but they were rather loath to come back to sit on wet chairs.

To attempt to recount or describe all the various social activities during our stay in Canada, would require a book to itself, so I will confine my narrative mostly to happenings connected with the airship and my own activities. The main preoccupation after the initial welcomes was to put in hand the repairs to the port fin. The company which built *R.100*—The Airship Guarantee Company—was a subsidiary of the firm of Vickers. The Chairman, Sir Dennistoun Burney, and their Chief Engineer, Mr Nevile Shute Norway, soon got in touch with the Canadian Vickers Company, and with the aid of drawings made by one of our ship's engineers, Len Hall, who had been in the drawing office during the airship's construction at Howden, they soon had the fabric department of Canadian Vickers's factory at Montreal working on preparing the panels for the enormous patch.

It was my day off on Saturday, 2nd August, so I went into Montreal and looked up some friends of my schooldays. The city was *en fête* for our arrival. Practically every shop had prominently displayed '*Welcome to* R.100', and songs and poems were made and recorded in French and English:

Viens-tu avec moi mon père,
On vait aller à Saint Hubert
Va donc atteler ta jument;
On vait aller voir l'R Cent.
Mais regarde moi donc, petit noir
Tu as mis ta chemise en alouvert;
Il y a un trou de dans
Qui est aussi grand que l'R Cent.

There were several more verses.

We carried on normal watchkeeping, which meant that we had one night on the airship and two off it, which we spent at the 'Mount Royal' Hotel, whose management had very hospitably given each officer a room for his own use. This was a great boon, as it allowed us to get clean away from the airship and the thousands crowding to see her.

Parties of twenty at a time were allowed on the ship and shown over the passenger accommodation. Archie Wann organised this in the first place and when the arrangement was running smoothly handed over control of it to the OC, Royal Canadian Dragoons, with the Mounties at the top and bottom of the tower. The main difficulty was to keep the party on the move so as to delay the next batch as little as possible.

Sunday, 3rd August, I had just arrived at Mount Royal when the telephone rang for me; it was Major Scott asking me to return to the ship at once, as No. 7 Bag had split at the top, due to the cord netting round the exhaust trunk having carried away, and he wanted me to examine the netting at all frames.

When I arrived there I found they had nearly finished repairing a split of about 5 feet in length along the top of the bag. The bags were kept in position and from chafing against the girders by panels of wire netting. These also transmitted the lift of the gas to the hull by means of catenary wires.

In addition to the wire netting, a large panel of cord netting was stretched across each of the transverse frames to prevent the flat ends of the gas-bags becoming nipped by the radial wires from the transverse frame to the junction at the end of each section of the central girder. This cord netting also acted as a guard to keep the end of the bag from chafing on the exhaust trunk which extended from the automatic valve at the bottom of each bag up through the inside of the ship at each transverse frame to a vent in the top of the outer cover. This was for evacuating gas blown off when the ship went above pressure height (full of gas).

These vents and trunks allowed rain to get between the bags and rot the cord netting in the vicinity of the exhaust trunks with the result that the netting frequently gave way. The frequent wettings also deteriorated the gas-bags.

The job Hobbs and I had taken on was to go all round each side of the transverse frames and repair any broken cords we found as we climbed round the frame from the bottom of the ship (130 feet diameter). This was the most exhausting job I have ever attempted as it had to be done inside the cover mostly at the top of the ship where the heat was intense as the doped cover acted like a glass-house. In the open air the temperature was about 90°F in the shade—imagine what it was like inside the ship's cover with this sun beating upon it. We each did alternate frames and continued next day with the weather still as hot. Near the exhaust trunks at the top the netting was quite rotten and needed much repairing.

I was to have gone to Toronto to attend a dinner in honour of *R.100* given by the civic authorities there, but I had to give this a miss; when I came down after sweating blood all morning I was too exhausted to hurry and change from my sweat-soaked overalls—no exaggeration—into my glad rags and catch the plane which was just about to leave. I had very nearly dehydrated myself and all I could do was to stagger to the serving-hatch and asked Savidge to make me a pint of lemon squash which I drank in a gulp, thus replacing some of the moisture lost.

I have always regretted since that I did not make the effort, as two of my oldest friends came from Toronto; John Barron, who had been my CO in Italy during the First World War was actually at the dinner and Gene Lockhart, whom I had not seen since we were at school together—he became quite a film star and at school he had made a magnificent and very funny 'Dame Hatley' in our school play *Black-Eyed Susan*.

Although I did not attend the dinner, I have a beautiful souvenir of the occasion in the shape of a silver cigarette-box which I have before me now as I write; on it is engraved:

Presented by the Corporation of the City of Toronto,
Major Bert S. Wemp Mayor
to
Capt. George F. Meagher [sic]
of the Dirigible R–100
August 6th 1930

I shall treasure it till I die.

However, I did attend a magnificent banquet at the Windsor Hotel, Montreal, given by the City Council, there being over 700 guests. There was an enormous menu which included a delicious 'Bombe Glacée R-100'.

During that night I was awakened at about 5 am by a violent thunderstorm; peal upon peal of thunder with immediate terrific jagged lightning, and hail beating a tattoo on the window. I thought of Steff who was Duty Officer that night. It must have been a pretty trying time, but he managed very well and no damage was done to the ship, though I believe one sudden change in the wind swung the ship round through 180 degrees.

The fitting of the new panels on the port stabiliser had now been completed and we were all set for what we termed the 'Local Flight'; rather a misnomer for a flight lasting twenty-six hours and covering nearly a thousand miles. The objects of this flight were to show *R.100* to various other Canadian cities and towns and, of course, included a visit to the capital, Ottawa. It was also a means of demonstrating to the personnel of all three Canadian services, as well as representatives of the Press, the undeniable comfort of travel by airship—and it enabled us to test the efficacy of the repairs to the fin covers. A secondary object was to carry out trials of the Radio Beacon at La Prairie, about six miles from St Hubert.

We slipped from the tower at St Hubert at 18.18 DST on 10th August 1930. We had now become somewhat wary of thunderstorms and as we could see one in the direction in which we were going, we gave it a wide berth. At 7 pm we finally set our course in a south-westerly direction towards the capital, passing over Hudson Heights an hour later and in a further hour were flying over a place with the good old romantic-sounding name of Plantagenet. Soon after 10 pm we reached Ottawa, and flew round and round over the city whilst a description was broadcast from the ship by one of the Press representatives on board. My most lasting impression of Ottawa was the almost ethereal beauty of the

Houses of Parliament perched on a hill and bathed in the ghostly but soft light of a brilliant full moon in a clear sky.

After about two hours we set course for Lake Ontario, passing over Smith's Falls about midnight. When passing over a small township not far from the lake, I always remember Major Baty, OC Royal Canadian Dragoons, rolling 'Gananoque', the name of the place, round his tongue in a broad Canadian accent. He recognised it at once, as he had been a cadet at the Military Academy at Kingston, and knew all the countryside round about. We passed over this latter town about half an hour later; then Peterborough, still keeping over the land, reaching Toronto at a quarter to five in the morning.

It was somewhat early to show ourselves to this fine city, so we set course for Niagara Falls, of which we had a splendid view from 2,000 feet, the weather still being fine and clear. It was a magnificent panorama and a thrilling sight to see the enormous volume of water falling over both the Canadian Horseshoe Falls and the American Falls, with Goat Island perched precariously in the middle and, as it seemed, on the very brink. Then there was the cauldron of water down below, throwing up a cloud of mist almost as high as the brink of the falls, with whirlpools skirling around as the water came to the surface and eventually flowed away through the narrow channel of the rapids a little further downstream.

By-passing the Falls is a large canal or series of locks called the Welland Canal. What impressed me was the enormous length of the barges using it, as well as quite large steamers. We then cut across to Hamilton, which brought back to mind some very pretty girls Booth and I met on board the Cunard liner *Antonia* when we were on our way to Detroit to take part in the 1927 Gordon Bennett International Balloon Race.

As the weather remained fine and clear, we made our way again to Toronto and flew over the city. We found, however, that over the land the atmosphere was becoming decidedly bumpy, as the sun was now beginning to get quite hot and was warming up the land with the resultant convection currents, indicated by fleecy-looking cumulus clouds forming.

To enjoy more stable conditions, we cruised about for a while over Lake Ontario just off the city before setting course eastwards across the lake.

Whilst crossing the lake, as there was not a great deal to see and it was not my turn for watch-keeping, I took the opportunity of climbing up over the top of Frame 14, which we had not managed to get to on Wednesday. It was again frightfully hot work—inside the cover, of course—and again I became wringing wet with perspiration, but it was worth it, as I found quite a large expanse of gas-bag netting broken on both sides of the girder. These I repaired as best I could, though it was somewhat of a lash-up and would have to be done properly as soon as we returned to a shed. In fact, most of the cord netting required renewing, as it was becoming rotten with the wettings to which it was continually being subjected.

Fairhaven was reached at midday, when we altered course to the northward and arrived over Kingston again half an hour later. We now proceeded over the Bay of a Thousand Islands, which is the outlet from Lake Ontario of the St Lawrence River. We passed Brockville a few minutes after 2 pm and Cornwall an hour later.

The main reason for flying directly over Cornwall was in connection with the radio-beacon experiments we were carrying out with the beacon station at La Prairie. This station was sending out a four-course beacon with the goniometer set to give a course on Ottawa. We had tried it on the outward journey, but the beacon signals had petered out some ten miles short of Ottawa. On the return flight the beacon was set to pass through Cornwall and our actual course checked with it at that point. The general idea of the beacon system is that the beacon sends out a signal along a beam on which the signal is a continuous note; if off the beam, the receiving station—the aircraft—will pick up a certain letter in morse which indicates on which side of the beam it lies.

We proceeded leisurely down the St Lawrence, keeping near the American bank so as to give our Canadian guests a better view of their own country instead of their having to look straight down to see what they were passing over. Some of them became rather touchy about this and asked why we were hugging the American shore, so to please them we went over to the Canadian bank.

Just before reaching Montreal we flew over a short length of broken tumbling water—La Chine Rapids—the rocks on either side of the narrow channel are practically at the surface. From above it appeared impossible for any surface craft to live in those tumbling waters, yet in 1927, Booth, Steff and I had shot those rapids in a sizeable river steamer. How the pilot threaded his way through the rocks without tearing the bottom out of the boat is beyond me.

Montreal certainly seems to be the home of thunderstorms, for we spent two hours cruising round the city dodging them. During this cruising around the reduction gear of the forward starboard engine broke up and burst the casing; pieces of the gear-box went into the propeller, which threw them up into the ship, damaging not only the propeller but the base boom of the transverse girder and main joint at No. 9 Frame. When the breakdown was first reported I went along to see what damage had been done. When I arrived at the hatchway above the starboard engine car I found Charge-hand Engineer Watts standing on top of the car examining the damaged prop. Watts was a native of Worstead, a Norfolk village where Worstead cloth originated, though I do not believe any is manufactured there now. Watts, poor chap, was unhappily killed soon afterward on his motor-bike on Christmas Eve 1930, while riding home to spend the holiday with his parents.

We had another slight mishap to an engine before we landed. The magneto of the starboard rear engine failed, which threw out the timing; the engine could not then be run in reverse and for this reason was stopped.

We finally secured at St Hubert at a quarter past eight in the evening, having been in the air for 25 hours 37 minutes and having covered a distance of 805 miles and consumed 2,650 gallons of fuel, which worked out at a third of a ton per hour.

Amongst the passengers on this flight was General McNaughton, who later commanded the Canadian Army in the Second World War; and Group Captain Stedman, who became the Chief Engineer of the RCAF.

Mr Norway devised a method of patching up the damaged main joint, this being carried out by our own engineers. There was also the damaged magneto to be changed, whilst the question of what to do about the disabled engine was the subject of a conference of VIPs—Colmore, Scott, Booth, Burney and Norway. I believe Norway had invented a kind of gantry for changing engines at the tower, but this was not available at Montreal, even if a spare engine had been available. It was finally decided to leave the engine where it was and fly back on the remaining five. The deciding factor in this decision was the prevalence of westerly winds across the Atlantic.

Ever since we landed I had been feeling pretty 'dickey', so I went and saw a doctor. He diagnosed 'Montreal throat'—another term for laryngitis, I believe. He gave me some tablets to suck which certainly did the trick, for my sore throat disappeared like magic. To improve the shining hour and keep fit I went round No. 7 Frame and netted down the exhaust trunk at the top—a note in my diary says: '*Left another suspender behind.*'

Except for getting stores aboard and rounding up the passengers, there was now nothing to stop us setting out on our homeward journey.

At 9.30 pm DST on 13th August 1930 (01.30 GMT on 14.8.30), we slipped from the tower at St Hubert. We had a tremendous send-off; there seemed to be thousands of cars all with their headlights full on and hooting wildly. The last thing I remember seeing was Commander Pressey waving like mad from the top of the tower—mouth wide open—probably shouting out a farewell message of 'Good luck'.

We circled over Montreal with its myriad lights as if loath to leave it.

Finally we set course for home, but we were many miles down the St Lawrence before we finally lost sight of Montreal's great illuminated cross.

We had on board many more passengers than on the outward flight. Most of them were representatives of various leading Canadian and English newspapers. We had one very special passenger in the person of M. Jacques Cartier, a direct descendant of the original Jacques Cartier, the French discoverer of the St Lawrence River. In 1535 he ascended the St Lawrence as far as the site of what is now the City of Montreal (I have just looked this up in the Encyclopaedia). M. Cartier was specially nominated for the flight by the Canadian Prime Minister.

Although we carried no mail nor merchandise on the outward journey, for the homeward flight we had some special mail consisting of the following: Letters from the Prime Minister of Canada to the PM of Great Britain and to the Secretary of State for Air; from the Minister of Defence to the Secretary for Air; from the High Commissioner's Office to the Secretary of State, for the Dominions; and from the Mayor of Montreal to the Lord Mayor of London. In addition we carried some special cargo consisting of a box of cut flowers for Queen Mary and King George; and a case of peaches for the Prince of Wales, a gift from the St Catherine's Flying Club, Ontario.

Two hours after leaving Montreal we were over Quebec. The weather, so far, had been kind; with the wind behind us we were making good 80 mph, running three engines only, at cruising speed of 1,600 rpm. At midnight we were over the sandy island where we had spent two hours repairing the port fin. Colmore in his official log of the return journey, names this as 'Green Island'. Whether it was Green or Grosse Isle I have no means of checking, except that there is a 'Grosse I' on the chart a little way past Coudres Island, but I can find no 'Green Island'.

We had an uneventful journey down the St Lawrence, reaching the west point of Anticosti at 6.15 am on 14th August. The wind, though still behind us, was decreasing in strength. We followed the coast of Newfoundland through the Strait of Belle Isle. Newfoundland is one great mass of small lakes and forest, a most inhospitable-looking place. At noon local time we passed Belle Isle itself (850 miles in thirteen and a half hours) and we should not then see land again until we reached Ireland.

One of our engines hereabouts blew out a sparking-plug to the consternation of the engineer on watch. The weather so far had been fine and clear though a little cirrus cloud was visible at Belle Isle. This type of cloud is often the first indication of a depression. Soon after passing Belle Isle we saw several large icebergs, due no doubt to the icefloes in higher latitudes breaking up in the warmer weather at this time of year.

When we were about 500 miles out on the Atlantic an indication of a depression coming up from the south-west was given by the sky becoming covered with cirro-stratus cloud. Before long we were bucking into a strong north-east wind which reduced our ground speed considerably, though we had opened up another engine. The oncoming of this depression was unexpected, for when over the Gulf of St Lawrence we had received a favourable report from Cardington that winds would be westerly all the way across.

I well remember, however, Giblett our Met Officer getting very hot under the collar with Johnny Johnston—who besides being Chief Navigator was also in charge of the W/T Section—for allowing Press messages to crowd out a weather report which he, Giblett, said would have given him an indication of this depression. We were soon in the thick of it, with heavy rain which had an unfortunate sequel, as the rain came through the outer cover and down the exhaust trunks. Some of it penetrated into the cooking-apparatus in the galley and threw it out of action, which meant no more hot food or heating, and the temperature dropped to 45°F. One good effect of the rain, however, was that we collected no less than seven tons of water ballast.

In order to minimise the adverse effect of the strong north-east wind, we altered course to south-east, so as to get the wind abeam and ourselves heading towards the southern part of the depression, where we could expect favourable winds, as may be better understood from the following rough sketch:

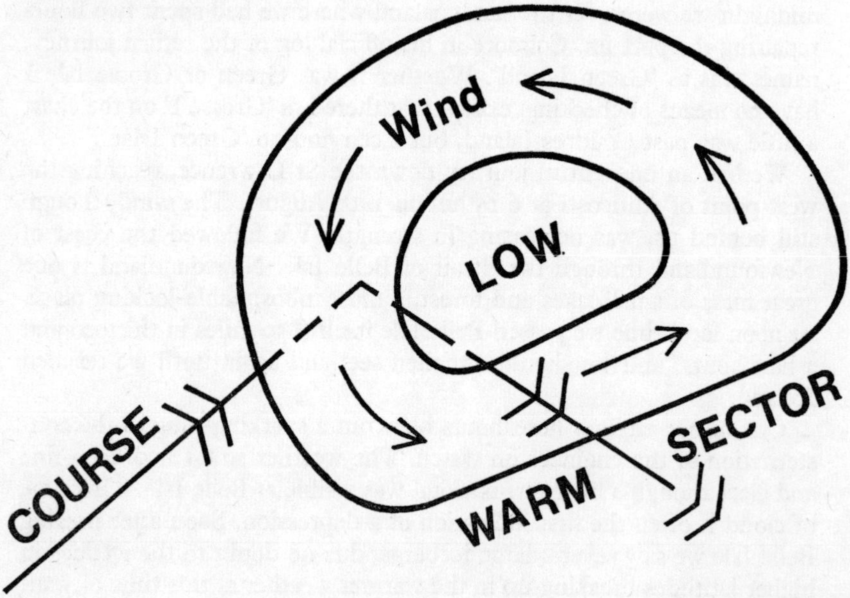

The wind gradually backed, and after coming into noticeably warmer air, I took a drift and found the wind was due west at 40 knots. This indicated that we were in the warm sector in the southern part of the depression.

At 10 am local time, 15th August, 1930, we were approximately half-way across the Atlantic, our position being lat. 52°40′N, long. 33°10′W, our course was 115 degrees—about east-south-east—making good 40 knots.

I think we must have been somewhat north of the steamer track, for we did not get nearly as much help from liners as on the outward flight. As for seeing any shipping, it was not until well over half-way across that we sighted the SS *Beaverbrae*, the only ship we actually set eyes upon between Belle Isle and Ireland. Unfortunately I have no note of the time nor the position at which we passed over her, though I managed to get a photograph of her.

Just before lunch I went up to the observation position in the bow and took a series of sun sights to check our latitude. When I worked them out and found my sights gave a latitude sixty miles north of our dead reckoning latitude, I was disgusted with myself for having, as I thought, made a mess of my sights, so I kept the result to myself. However, Johnston, having seen me come down from the observation platform, asked me what result I had obtained. I said I had taken a 'bum' set of sights, as I had an intercept of sixty miles. 'Let me see them', he said. So I passed him my sight book; he checked over the working and found it correct. 'My intercept was seventy-nine miles, so your sights confirm mine,' he said, 'allowing for difference in time and the run between.'

In short, we were off our desired track by a considerable amount due to a change in the wind of which we were in ignorance through being unable to take a drift—there was cloud below us.

Mr Eldridge had again organised a sweepstake on the day's run from noon to noon. This time Mr Norway was the lucky winner with a distance of 1,250 nautical miles. Passengers staked in dollars on the return flight, to lighten themselves of Canadian money.

At some time during the day I made a point of visiting the engine cars; for the wing cars there is a walking-way from the keel corridor out to the side of the ship, where a vertical ladder is attached. This is normally closed into a streamlined shape; it can be opened from bottom or top by winding a miniature winch. In the inside walls of the ladder are built steps like those sometimes seen on a dock wall, down which one climbs shielded from the wind by the ladder. The engine cars are perhaps the warmest place in the whole ship, though they are all rather cramped, especially the wing cars—in addition to the two Rolls-Royce engines for driving the ship each wing car has an AC 12 horse-power motor-car engine for driving the generators for our lighting, heating and cooking arrangements. There is also a small Bristol gas starter engine in each car with which the main engines are started up. With two engineers on duty, there is not much room to move about, though there is room between engine and car walls for the engineers to attend to either side of each engine.

During the homeward flight there was no wireless gap where we were out of touch with both sides of the Atlantic, as on the outward journey. For 600 miles after leaving Montreal—from 01.30 hours to 10.40 GMT on 14th August 1930—we remained in touch with St Hubert Airport. We then turned over to Louisburg until we reached position 52°20'N, 35°00'W at 11.25 GMT, 15th August, 1,300 miles from that station, when communication was opened up with Portishead, Somerset, at a distance of 1,400 miles. At 03.15 GMT, 16th August, we were in direct touch with Cardington, distant 365 miles, and, of course, remained so until we landed.

With the large number of Press people on board, the W/T schedules had to be strictly adhered to; if they were not, it might mean our missing important messages—as did happen when a met report was missed earlier. It must be remembered that only one operator was on duty at a time, so it was only 'single-line' traffic; he could not receive messages whilst sending and vice versa.

Each Press correspondent was allowed to send messages of up to a hundred words four times each day. Their 'copy' was dropped into a post bag which the Duty W/T Op collected at certain set times. If the Press man missed the post, his message had to wait until the next collection. Of course, official messages and weather reports took priority. I pitied the harassed operators trying to fit it all in.

At 1 pm local time of 15th August it was decided to lay a course for the north of Ireland, as the wind was from the southward—actually south-west. By steering the new course we should have the wind on our starboard quarter helping us. At 4 pm local time we found the wind had veered to south-west by west, so it was decided to make our landfall after all at the Fastnets. We were now steering practically due east from a position in lat. 52°45'N, long. 24°20'W, about two-thirds of the way across from Belle Isle.

Although not directly behind us, the wind was still on our starboard quarter and we were bowling along splendidly making 65 knots on four engines at cruising speed. Most of the flight over the sea we had been flying at 1,000 feet, but at about midnight local time, we increased our height somewhat, hoping the wind would conform to the rule we learned in meteorology that in the Northern Hemisphere it veers and increases with height. Our speed, anyway, increased to 70 knots.

At midnight I left the Captain on watch and turned-in without undressing in the Duty Officer's cabin, which was just above the control car. My own cabin up on the passenger deck had been allocated to Fergus Grant, the representative of the *Times Gazette* of Montreal and the *New York Times*. He wrote a very lively account of the flight and sent me a copy.

I had been asleep about a couple of hours when I was awakened by pressure in my ear-drums. Those who have done any ballooning will have experienced this on changing altitude fairly quickly—one usually overcomes it by swallowing, thus equalising the pressure inside and outside the ear. I knew at once that something out of the ordinary had happened; I jumped out of my sleeping-bag still in my 'Teddy Bear' suit, and went below to find out the reason. Booth was at the elevator himself. 'The silly young mutt nearly had us in the ditch,' he told me. He had taken the elevator himself, as the young chap who had been on it had brought the ship down to about 500 feet, had Booth not grabbed the wheel from him we should probably have headed straight into the Atlantic. The lad was quite a youngster and our latest recruit amongst the riggers. I believe it was his first trick at the elevators, which being the case, the Cox'n should really have stood by him. Anyway, Booth soon brought the ship up to 1,500 feet again on an even keel. All's well that ends well and I returned to bed. It just shows, however, that the OOW cannot relax vigilance for one moment.

An hour before the above happening, at 02.45 GMT—1.45 am local time—on the 16th our navigator had made our desired landfall at the Fastnet Rock, south-west of Cape Clear, which is the south-western point of Ireland. We headed across the Irish Channel for Lundy Island off the north coast of Cornwall, which we reached at 06.45 GMT (Zone zero). We then proceeded up the Bristol Channel past Barry and Cardiff, crossing the foreshore of England at Avonmouth with its numerous oil tanks. We were over Bristol at 8.15 am on Saturday, 16th August 1930, being escorted by two aeroplanes from Filton aerodrome close to Bristol.

We then set course straight for home at Cardington, *en route* passing over the old-world towns of Cirencester and Bicester. We flew over the shires of Gloucester, Oxford and Bedford, the English countryside looking very beautiful with its kaleidoscope of fields and woods and trim hedges. At a quarter to ten that morning the enormous sheds at Cardington were sighted dead ahead. Before dropping our wire, however, we veered off a couple of miles in order to salute the town of Bedford; then back to Cardington, where our arrival was something of an anticlimax after our tumultuous welcome in Montreal.

We lowered our main wire at 10.35 am, 16th August 1930. As soon as this was coupled, the yaw guys were lowered and at 11.06 the officer in charge of the mooring tower, F/O George Cook, reported 'Secure'.

And so ended our flight to Canada and back, thus completing the series of trials.

In order that the crew should get away promptly, whilst the main wire was being hauled in, the riggers lowered away the balancing-wires for attaching to the heavy rollers on the ground; these act as counter-weights when the ship is moored. They are a great help to the OOW in keeping the ship in equilibrium. If the wires are hanging in bights it is a sign that the ship is heavy. If a roller is being lifted off the ground it indicates that the ship is much too light.

By the time the ship's gangway was lowered on to the tower top, quite a crowd had gathered at the foot of the tower, mostly friends and relations of those on board or connected with the Royal Airship Works at Cardington; amongst them was Lord Thompson, our Air Minister.

A watch formed of members of the crew of *R.101* under the charge of 'Grabby' Atherstone came on board and relieved *R.100*'s crew—our spare watch were returning by sea—and we all trooped off to our various homes.

The bare details of the homeward flight from Canada were as follows:

Left St Hubert, Montreal	01.30 GMT 14.8.30
Secured Cardington, Bedford	11.06 GMT 16.8.30
Duration	57 hours 36 minutes
Distance flown	2,955 nautical miles
Personnel on board	56
Fuel consumed	6,315 imperial gallons
Fuel remaining on landing	3,270 imperial gallons
Average consumption	109·6 gallons hour

Early next morning, Sunday, 17th August 1930, a landing-party was assembled and took *R.100* into the shed—from which she never again emerged as a whole.

A programme was laid down for us to fly again to Canada later on in 1931 after *R.101*'s return from India. Unfortunately the crash of *R.101* at Beauvais, with heavy loss of life, supervened. After the Official Enquiry following the disaster, this question of continuing airship development was raised in Parliament. Booth and I attended the debate in the House when, on the Motion of the Prime Minister, it was decided to carry on the development of airships. My recollection of his speech in support was that, if we gave up airship development now, it would be showing the white feather and a betrayal of those who had sacrificed their lives in the crash.

And then, within the year, with the call for further economies in government spending and with one stroke of the pen, the whole airship programme was axed and *R.100* was sold for scrap.

Appendix I

SOME STATISTICS OF *R.100*

Constructed by the Airship Guarantee Company at Howden, East Yorkshire.

Managing Director	Sir Dennistoun Burney
Designed by	Barnes Neville Wallis, F.R.S.
Asst. Designer	J. E. Temple
Chief Calculator and Chief Engineer	N. S. Norway
Hydrogen Plant	Major P. L. Teed
Works Manager	J. Watson
Engine Installation	S. Palmer
Chief Draughtsman	W. Horrocks
Total capacity	5,156,000 cubic feet
Length	709 feet
Max. diameter	133 feet (136½ feet including control car)
Fineness ratio (length to diameter)	5½ to 1
No. of gas bags	15
Largest bag	No. 7; 551, 890 cubic feet
Total fin area	11,400 square feet
Fin length	125 feet, extending from 12 to 15 frame.
Total lift	156 long tons (under standard conditions and gas purity of 95 per cent)
Total weight	105 tons
Disposable lift	51 tons

Engines: 6 Rolls-Royce 'Condor' IIIB of 660 h.p. in tandem in three cars; rear engines reversible. Started up by Bristol gas starter, one to each car.

Electric Power: Supplied by two AC 6-cylinder engines in the wing cars to run 15 k.w. generators for lighting, heating of passenger quarters, cooking and WT.

Girders: These were made up of helically wound strips of duralumin rivetted to form a tube. The tubes were braced together to form a triangle. The joint between longitudinal and transverse girders was a simple but ingenious interlocking V/Y arrangement, the V taking the transverse and the Y the longitudinal girders.

Outer cover: This was made of linen doped with aluminium.

Gas bags: These were made of one-ply cotton lined with gold-beaters' skin.

It will, no doubt, surprise people to know that the total number of standard parts comprising the complete airship hull was only eleven.

NAVIGATIONAL & WIRELESS EQUIPMENT CARRIED FOR THE ATLANTIC FLIGHT

Compass: 'America' type dead-beat compass, gimballed in a binnacle. (This type had been specially designed by the Sperry Company for the flying boat *America* in which Lieutenant Porte, RN had intended to fly the Atlantic in 1914, but his health gave way, and World War I intervened.)

Schilovsky-Cooke turn indicator.

Mark VII RAE 'Booth' Bubble sextant: used by Chief Navigator. A similar Mark V sextant was used by the First Officer.

Hughes Periscopic Drift Sight: a most useful instrument for taking drifts and measuring ground speed. The periscope allowed drifts to be taken in comfort from inside the control car. Previously it had been necessary to open a window and lean out into the airstream which was decidedly unpleasant in cold weather at a speed of sixty knots.

Sea markers used with the drift sight were, by day, aluminium dust bombs, and by night, calcium-phosphide flares.

Electrical air log: Invented by Squadron-Leader Rope—another most useful instrument.

Air-speed indicator: of trailing 'Pitot-head' type.

Marine chronometer (*Eight day*)*:* For maintaining GMT.

Deck Watch: For taking astronomical sights.

Goodwin's *Alpha*, *Beta*, *Gamma* tables; Inman's and Davis's tables.

Nautical Almanac and Admiralty Charts.

SIGNALS AND WT EQUIPMENT

Aldis signalling lamp worked off a 12 volt accumulator which also ran the Air Log.

Transmitters: TX.15, and T.22.

Receivers: RX. 18a for long and medium waves. RX. 36 for short wave.

Appendix II

OFFICERS AND CREW OF *R.100*

Captain Sq Ldr R. S. Booth, AFC, RAF
1st Officer Capt G. F. Meager, AFC
2nd Officer F/O M. H. Steff, RAF
Navigator Sq Ldr E. L. Johnston, RAFO
Chief Cox'n Flt Sgt T. E. Greenstreet, RAF
Chief Engineer Mr W. Y. Angus
Chief WT Op Mr S. T. Keeley
Chief Steward Mr A. H. Savidge

WATCHES

No. 1	No. 2	No. 3
Riggers	*Riggers*	*Riggers*
Asst. Cox'n G. E. Long	Asst. Cox'n T. Hobbs	Asst. Cox'n L. A. Moncrieff
C. H. Rumsby	S. C. Armstrong	R. L. Burgess
R. L. Deverell	A. F. Wiseman	F. Williams
L. Cutts	D. M. Kershaw	G. R. Scott
C. Broughton	E. R. Patterson	C. Flatters
(E. Petch)	(J. E. Brown)	
Engineers	*Engineers*	*Engineers*
Charge-hand	Charge-hand	Charge-hand
E. J. Stupple	N. Mann	G. Watts
H. Millward	J. Jowett	D. L. Simmonds
F. Gaye	H. Cumley	A. F. Burke
H. N. Clark	L. W. Hunt	C. Watson
J. M. Sturgeon	H. Addinell	L. Hall
R. Ball	D. Lelliott	H. Wilson
WT Operators	*WT Operators*	*WT Operators*
A. Disley	G. K. Atkins	W. Larkins

Saloon Staff

Chef: J. F. Meegan, and C. Nesbitt
Asst. Steward: F. Hodnett or Curran
Galley Boy: Megginson
Asst. Cooks: Bowen and Smith

Appendix III

FLIGHT PERSONNEL

FIRST FLIGHT

16th December, 1929. Total on board—57

AIRSHIP CREW

Officers

Major G. H. Scott, OBE (Officer in charge of Flying and Training)
Sq Ldr R. S. Booth, AFC, RAF (Captain)
Sq Ldr E. L. Johnston, OBE, RAFO (Navigator)
Capt G. F. Meager, AFC (First Officer)
F/O M. H. Steff, RAF (Second Officer)

Engineers

W. Y. Angus (Chief Engineer)
E. T. Stupple (Charge hand)
N. Mann (Charge hand)
G. Watts (Charge hand)
F. Gaye
H. Millward
R. Ball
H. W. Clark
J. M. Sturgeon
H. Addinnell
H. Cumley
L. W. Hunt
J. Jowett
D. Lelliott
H. Wilson
D. L. Simmonds
C. Watson
A. F. Burke, and L. Hall

Riggers

F/Sgt T. E. Greenstreet, RAF (Chief Coxswain)
T. Hobbs (Asst. Cox'n)
L. A. Moncrieff (Asst. Cox'n)
G. E. Long (Asst. Cox'n)
C. Broughton
C. H. Rumsby
J. E. Brown
R. L. Deverell
A. F. Wiseman
C. Armstrong
D. M. Kershaw
E. Petch
R. Burgess
C. Flatters
F. Williams
G. R. Scott

WT Operators

S. T. Keeley (Chief WT Op)
A. Disley (Operator & Electrician)

WT Observers from RAE Farnborough

Mr Wells
Mr Cox-Walker

Cook
C. Nesbitt

ROYAL AIRSHIP WORKS PERSONNEL

Sq Ldr R. B. B. Colmore, OBE, RAF, Director of Airship Development
Sq Ldr F. M. Rope, RAF, Design Staff, Cardington

Airship Guarantee Representatives

Sir C. D. Burney	Managing Director
Mr B. N. Wallis	Designer of R.100
Mr N. S. Norway	Chief Engineer
Major P. L. Teed	Gas Officer, Howden
Mr Hessell Tiltman	Design Staff
Mr J. Watson	Works Manager, Howden
Mr Horrocks	Chief Draughtsman
Mr Lansdowne	Calculator
Mr Clewloe	Fabric Department

Rolls-Royce Representative
Mr Moseley (Engineer)

Duration: 5 hours 37 minutes
Distance: 150 st. miles

Petrol used: 380 gallons	*Remaining:* 5,120 gallons
Ballast used: 3½ tons	*Remaining:* 4¼ tons

EIGHTH FLIGHT

CARDINGTON, BEDFORD, TO ST HUBERT MONTREAL

29th July–1st August, 1930. Total on board—44

CREW

Officers

Sq Ldr S. Booth, Captain and Navigator
Sq Ldr E. L. Johnston, Chief Navigator
Captain G. F. Meager, First Officer and Navigator
F/O M. H. Steff, Second Officer
Captain M. A. Giblett, Meteorologist
Major G. H. Scott, AD(F)

Engineers	*Riggers*
W. Y. Angus (Chief Engineer)	F/Sgt T. Greenstreet (Chief Cox'n)
E. T. Stupple (Charge hand)	L. Moncrieff (Assistant Cox'n)

N. Mann (Charge hand)
G. Watts (Charge hand)
R. Ball
H. W. Clark
J. Jowett
H. Millward
J. M. Sturgeon
H. Cumley
F. Gaye
L. Hunt
D. Lelliott

T. Hobbs (Assistant Cox'n)
G. E. Long (Assistant Cox'n)
C. Broughton
C. G. Cutts
R. L. Deverell
C. Flatters
C. H. Rumsby
F. Williams
G. R. Scott
A. F. Wiseman

WT Operators
S. T. Keeley (Chief Op)
A. Disley (Op and Electrician)
G. K. Atkins

Saloon Staff
A. H. Savidge (Chief Steward)
J. F. Meegan (Chef)
F. Hodnett and Curran (Assistant Stewards)

Others
Wing Cmdr R. B. B. Colmore, DAD
Sq Ldr A. H. Wann, RAF
Mr McWade (Ch. AID, Cardington)
Mr A. Eldridge (DAD's Secretary, and Captain's Clerk)
Sir D. Burney
N. S. Norway
Lt Cmdr Prentice, RN (Admiralty Representative)

Duration: 78 hours 49 minutes
Distance: 3,364 nautical miles
Petrol used: 8,935 gallons — *Remaining:* 1,505 gallons
Ballast used: 1 ton — *Remaining:* 10 tons (5½ tons collected)

R.100 OUTWARD FLIGHT—CARDINGTON, BEDFORD TO ST HUBERT, MONTREAL

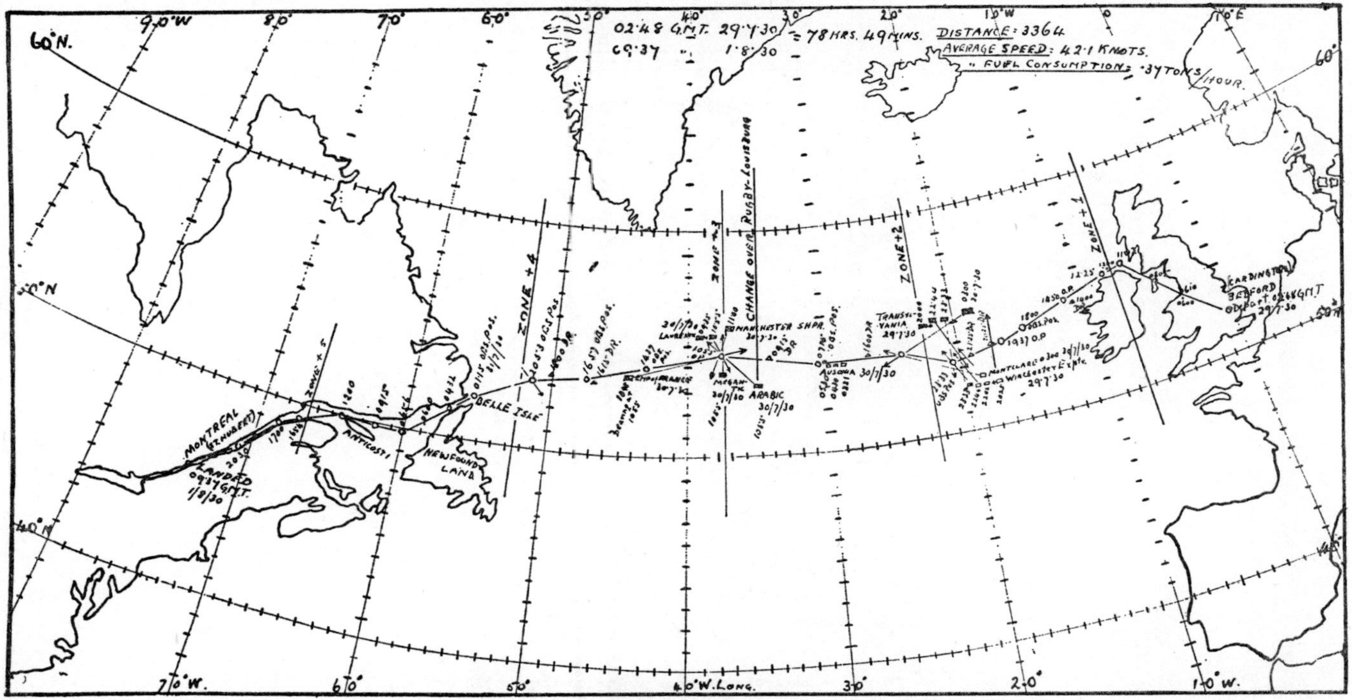

SR.1 SKETCH OF INTERNAL SUSPENSION SYSTEM. NOT TO SCALE

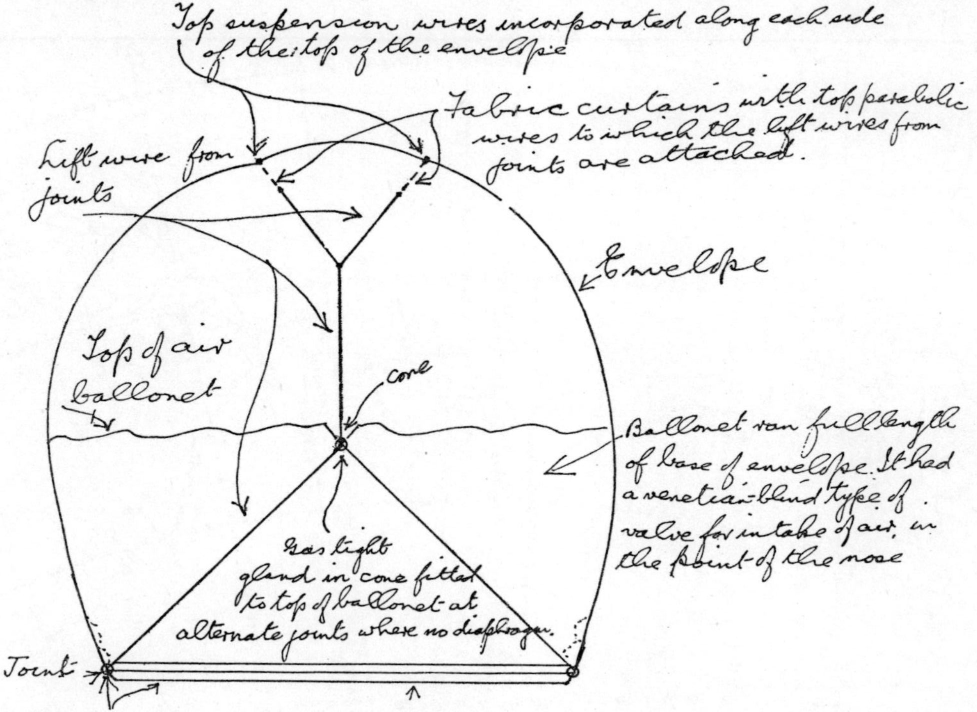

Longitudinal and transverse △ tubular steel girders were fitted along the base of the envelope. There were fifteen ball and socket joints along each side of the base. To each of these joints (which were machined out of the solid) were attached the bottom parabolic wires and the lift wires through centre of airship, dividing again to the top parabolic wires in the curtain on each side along the top.

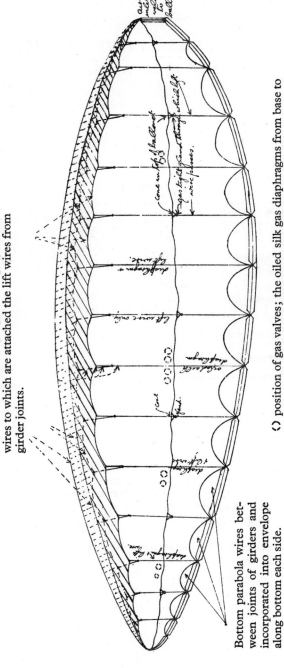

Top suspension wires incorporated into top of envelope each side; to these are hung the fabric curtains carrying the top parabola wires to which are attached the lift wires from girder joints.

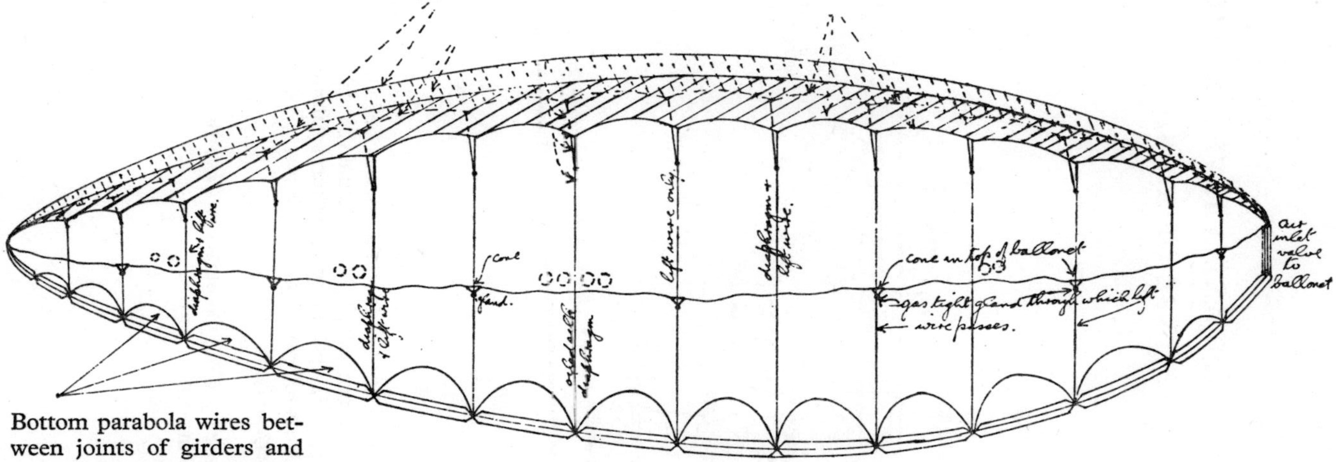

Bottom parabola wires between joints of girders and incorporated into envelope along bottom each side.

() position of gas valves; the oiled silk gas diaphragms from base to top of envelope are immediately beside each pair of valves, dividing the envelope into six gas compartments.

BLOWER PIPE AND VALVES ON SMALLEST TYPE OF AIRSHIP

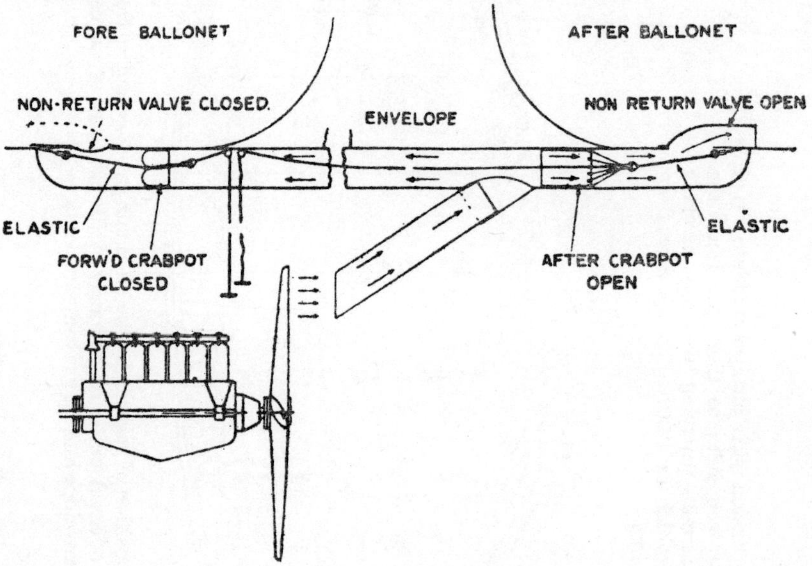

'The distribution of this air to the various ballonets necessitates the use of shut-off and non-return valves. It was found that fabric valves arranged in the form of a sleeve, which can be partially turned inside out, gave very effective results. This valve is referred to as a "crab-pot". It is very easily operated and is almost completely airtight.'

— From a lecture by Wing Commander Cave-Brown-Cave to the Royal Aeronautical Society in 1919.

Index